Mountain Rail Ad

P9-AFU-733

Durbin Rocket

Departing Elkins & Durbin Depots • Gift Shops • RailYard Restaurant

New Tygart Flyer Cheat Mountain Salamander THE POLAR EXPRESS™ Castaway Caboose

EXPERIENCE WEST VIRGINIA FROM A MOUNTAIN RAIL PERSPECTIVE!

The Durbin & Greenbrier Valley Railroad offers Mountain Rail Adventures aboard historic locomotives departing from two charming depots — Elkins and Durbin, April through December. Choose from riverside jaunts on a classic steam locomotive to a wilderness excursion over the mountains in our comfortable, climate-controlled passenger cars. Enjoy a satisfying meal on the Mountain Explorer Dinner train on special event dates. Then, end the season with THE POLAR EXPRESS™ trip, available select weekends in November and December.

1.866.760.9417
Online Reservations / Schedules / Videos
Mtn-Rail.com

WVTOURISM.COM
West Virginia
Wild and Wonderful
800-225-5982

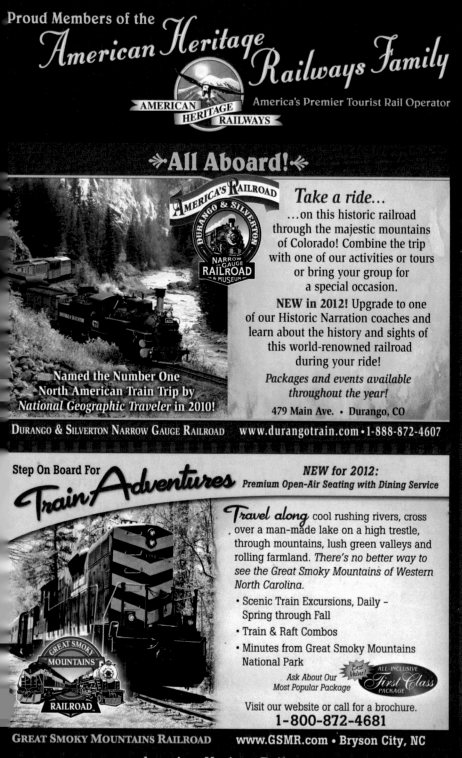

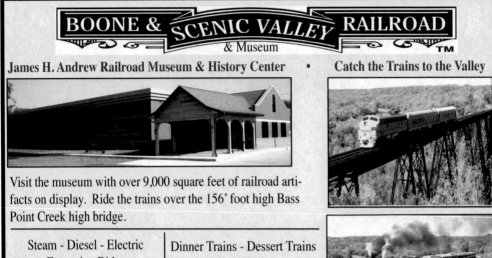

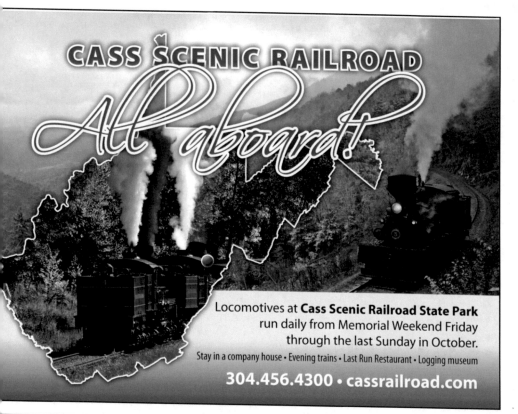

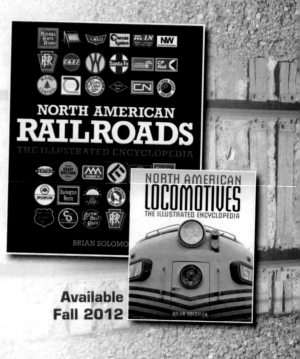

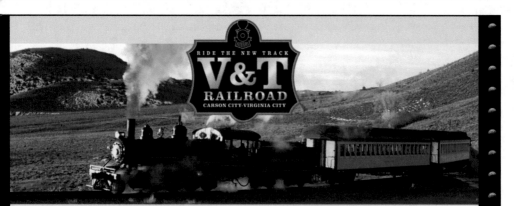

GREAT SCENIC RAILWAY JOURNEYS

Guide to North America's Tourist Railways and Museums

Published by: Wide Eye Productions®
Winston Salem, NC
2012

Great Scenic Railway Journeys: The Guide To North America's Tourist Railways and Museums is a companion book to the Emmy-award-winning Public Television Series. It is designed for travelers and rail enthusiasts. All of the information contained in this book has been compiled with help from participating railways. The use of pictures is with express permission from participating railways or directly from the series.

3rd EDITION

Cover Art by Ben Slavens and Robert C. Van Camp
Book Design by Robert C. Van Camp
Book Layout by Jessica Fox and Marvin Veto

Library of Congress Catalog Card Number:
ISBN: 978-0-9801178-0-6
Second Printing 2010
Printed in the United States of America

David and I hope that you get a chance to visit some of the railroads and museums that we have featured in this book. We would especially like to thank the Public Television members who support our series by pledging to their local Public Television stations. If you are not a member of the Public Television family, we encourage you to become a member. Your support helps us continue to produce new programs and products that help educate and entertain viewers on railroad history world-wide. To learn more about Public Television, please visit its website at www.pbs.org. For more information about the Great Scenic Railway Journeys programs and additional products, please visit our website at **www.gsrj.com**.

David Holt is the host of the Great Scenic Railway Journeys programs. Robert C. Van Camp is the creator and producer of the Great Scenic Railway Journeys programs.

For more information about David Holt, his music, and available products go to www.davidholt.com.

Table of Contents

*Featured on: Great Scenic Railway Journeys

*Featured on: Great Scenic Railway Journeys

*Featured on: Great Scenic Railway Journeys

WASHINGTON

WEST VIRGINIA

WISCONSIN

WYOMING

CANADA

*Featured on: Great Scenic Railway Journeys

Introduction

Railroading in the United States and Canada was once the premier way to travel. The elite had their own railcars, and for most the fun was in the journey. For forward-thinking industrialists, the railroad was an economical way to connect manufacturing plants to the remote natural resources that made them wealthy.

As the railroad grew, it became the number-one employer in many towns, both big and small. People today can tell the stories their grandparents told about working on the railroad. It's no wonder that a romance that began in the 1800s with those big iron horses continues today.

Since the birth of the American railroad in 1828, railroads have played a key role in both uniting and expanding America. Today the American railroad is slowly disappearing. Over sixty percent of all railroad track laid in North America has been abandoned and torn up. For every mile of track scrapped, another link to our past is lost forever.

A few railroads and railroad sites have been saved from this fate and turned into tourist railways and museums. These railroads and museums are a living link to our historical transportation past. They take us away from the fast-paced world of today and into a slower environment of beauty and moving history, and create a passion to preserve our transportation roots.

Great Scenic Railway Journeys: Guide to North America's Tourist Railways and Museums has visited many railroads over the last decade for its Emmy-award-winning series on Public television. We hope that this companion guide will get you excited about visiting the railways and museums that dot North America's canvas.

DISCLAIMER: In our research we've attempted total accuracy, but our primary source of information has to be the railroad itself. On most websites the railroads make it clear that schedules and fares can change without notice. In some cases excursions will be canceled as well. Please make every effort to confirm information before visiting any of the sites in this book.

Our thanks to all the rail volunteers and employees who helped us secure the information in this book.

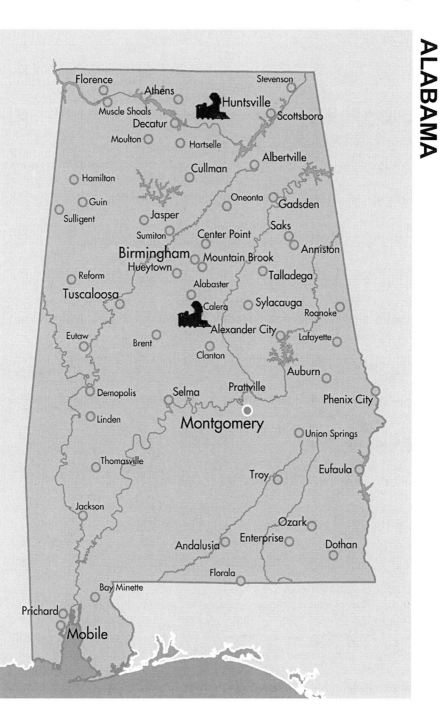

ALABAMA

HEART OF DIXIE RAILROAD MUSEUM
Calera, AL

Visitors at the Heart of Dixie Railroad Museum discover the pleasure and gentle excitement of the local passenger train when it was small-town America's link with the world. The clock is turned back over fifty years as riders experience a scenic trip through the forests of Shelby County on our historic train comprised of passenger cars built between 1910 and 1950. They are pulled by early, first-generation diesel-electric locomotives. Refreshments, railroad hats, shirts, toys, books, and collectibles may be purchased in an on-board shop inside a 1925 Southern Railway baggage car.

The Heart of Dixie Railroad Museum is the official railroad museum for the state of Alabama. The Calera and Shelby Railroad, operated by the museum, is a portion of the former Louisville & Nashville Railroad's Alabama Mineral Railroad established in 1891. Presently operating on 5 1/2 miles of track out of Calera, the C & S Railroad extends to Springs Junction.

Visitors to the museum can view railroad memorabilia in more than 100-year-old L & N and Southern depots and see 5 steam locomotives, 9 diesel-electric locomotives, over 50 cars, and many pieces of equipment in an operating railroad yard. The museum's most exciting new attraction is a ride on a fully restored steam-powered train operating on the Shelby and Southern Railroad. This 2-foot narrow gauge line takes  passengers on a curving route adjacent to Buxahatchee Creek and the museum's C & S Railroad. The exhibits serve as a living monument to railroad history and provide a fascinating look into a world now very much changed.

SCHEDULES AND FARES
The Heart of Dixie Railroad Museum is open Monday through Saturday, even when the trains are not running. The trains run from March through December. Fares vary according to the excursion but are generally below $20. Special excursions and group rates are available throughout the season. Please call ahead to schedule handicapped boarding. Please call or check website for current schedules and fares.

EQUIPMENT
Locomotives:
(2) General Motors EMD SW, 1951

No. 3, narrow gauge, 4-4-0 steam locomotive
No. 3, narrow gauge, 4-4-0 steam locomotive
No. 38 Baldwin 2-8-0 steam locomotive
No. 4046 Alco 0-6-0 steam locomotive
0-4-0 saddle tank steam locomotive
No. 1850, 1853 and 1861 Fairbanks Morse H12-44,
Diesel electric locomotives:
No. 40 Davenport 0-4-0 fireless steam locomotive
No. 37 Baldwin S-8 type, diesel-electric locomotive
No. 103 ALCO HH900 type diesel-electric locomotive
Other Cars:
(4) open-sided, bench seat, covered narrow gauge passenger cars
No. 1062 Coach, 1910
No. 2202 Budd, domed passenger car, 1948
No. 2931 Pullman Standard baggage car, 1925
No. X481 Caboose
No. 2931 Pullman Standard stainless steel coach, 1950

CONTACT
Heart Of Dixie Railroad Museum
1919 Ninth Street
Calera, AL 35040
205-668-3435 (Birmingham)
800-943-4490 (other areas)
205-668-9900
www.hodrrm.org

Photos: Heart of Dixie Railroad Museum

HISTORIC HUNTSVILLE DEPOT
Huntsville, AL

The historic Huntsville Depot, built around 1860, is one of the nation's oldest remaining railroad structures. Your tour includes a one-hour guided experience of the three-story building. You won't want to miss the Civil War exhibit, which features graffiti written by soldiers. You can also listen as Andy Barker, the robotic ticket agent, tells of Alabama's railroad history. There's even a "kid's corner," complete with try-on costumes, train puzzles, and maps.

The historic Huntsville Depot, built around 1860, is one of the nation's oldest remaining railroad structures. Your tour includes a one-hour guided experience of the three-story building. You won't want to miss the Civil War exhibit, which features graffiti written by soldiers. You can also listen as Andy Barker, the robotic ticket agent, tells of Alabama's railroad history. There's even a "kid's corner," complete with try-on costumes, train puzzles, and maps.

The depot is part of the EarlyWorks Museum Complex, which also houses Alabama Constitution Village and EarlyWorks Children's Museum. The Children's Museum is the South's largest hands-on history museum. The depot is listed on the National Register of Historic Places. It once served as the local passenger house and the corporate offices for the Eastern Division Headquarters of the Memphis and Charleston Railroad.

SCHEDULES and FARES
The museum is open Wednesday through Saturday. It is closed Thanksgiving, Christmas Day, January, and February. There are adjusted hours in early May because of the BBQ Festival. Please call or check website for current schedules and fares.

CONTACT
Historic Huntsville Depot
320 Church Street
Huntsville, AL 35801
256-564-8100   256-564-8151(fax)
info@earlyworks.com
www.earlyworks.com

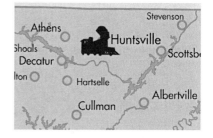

Photos: Historic Huntsville Depot

NORTH ALABAMA RAILROAD MUSEUM
Huntsville, AL

The North Alabama Railroad Museum is dedicated to preserving railroad history. Chase Depot, the smallest Union warehouse in the country, is the centerpiece. Visitors can view an informative video presentation on-board a railcar. The museum features several restored railcars, including one that was once used as a Railway Post Office; a day coach, and a Pullman sleeper. Over 20 pieces of rolling stock have been preserved, including both freight and passenger equipment and three historic locomotives.

While visiting the museum, enjoy a scenic ten-mile train ride from Chase to Normal over the Mercury & Chase railroad. This train consists of a sixty-passenger air-conditioned coach, an observation car that was once used for baggage, and a converted dining car. Travel along a portion of the Huntsville branch of the historic Nashville, Chattanooga and St. Louis Railway. Enjoy a leisurely ride through the woods and over a high hill with a breathtaking view of a babbling brook in the valley below.

SCHEDULES and FARES

The North Alabama Railroad Museum is open from April through October. Other days and times are by appointment. There is a fee for guided tours, but self-guided tours are free. Donations are welcomed. Train excursion fees are generally under $15.00. Celebrate Mother's Day and Father's Day with a ride on the Mercury & Chase. Package deals are available for special occasions. Additionally, the museum features a Senior Caravan, a Goblin Train, a Thanksgiving Express, and a Santa train. Rentals are available. Please call or check website for current schedules and fares.

EQUIPMENT
Locomotives:
11 - Under rest., 1926
484 - S-2, In service, 1949
1543 - S-4, Parts Loco, 1952
Other cars/coaches:
Hosp. car SAC diner, 1943
Ocmulgee River sleeper, 1949
Heavyweight, Clere Rf coach, 1929
2 Pullman heavyweight coaches, 1926
3 Budd stainless coaches, 1939, 1940, 1947
Villa Real sleeper, 1911

CONTACT
North Alabama Railroad Museum
694 Chase Road
Huntsville, AL 35815
256-851-NARM
256-851-6276
http://www.suncompsvc.com/narm

Photos: North Alabama Railroad Museum

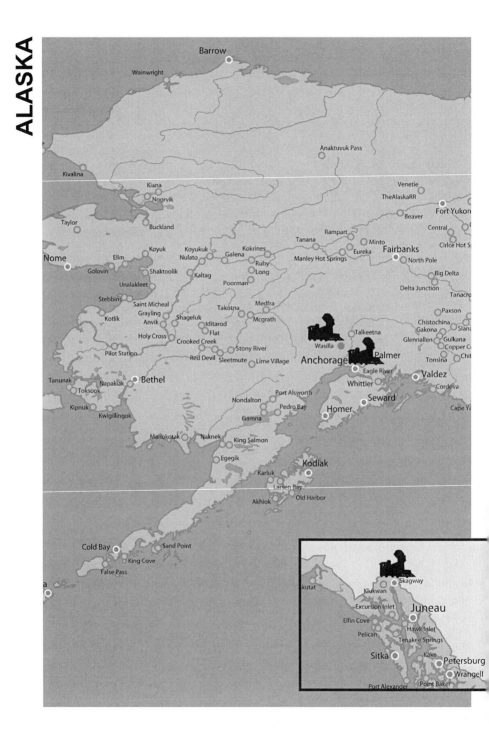

ALASKA RAILROAD
Fairbanks, AK

The Alaska Railroad route spans more than 500 miles from Seward to Denali National Park on to Fairbanks. Travelers journey through alpine forests, coastal regions, and traverse two major mountain ranges * in a land twice the size of Texas. In summer, trains run daily to and from eight major stops along the rail belt. During the winter, trains run between Anchorage and Fairbanks on weekends. Adventure packages and day trips include premium accommodations and sightseeing tours to make planning your vacation seamless.

Alaska Railroad trains feature large picture windows, friendly onboard staff, forward facing reclining seats, open-air vestibules, non-smoking cars, onboard dining for additional cost, and assigned seats. Step up to Gold Star and travel aboard double-deck luxury dome cars. Or choose Adventure Class aboard single level cars and bask in the scenery.

The Coastal Classic winds through the Kenai Mountains past massive glaciers and towering peaks, through lush green valleys and over river gorges. A top destination, Seward, has made the list of *National Geographic Adventure Magazine's* Top Ten Summer Sport Meccas. The coastal city of Seward sits at the head of Resurrection Bay, surrounded by the Kenai Fjords National Park and Chugach National Forest.

Denali Star: Denali Park is the major rail stop for the Denali Star. Famous for its wildlife and the majestic Mt. McKinley, Denali Park spans more than 6 million acres.

Glacier Discovery: The Glacier Discovery will take you to the Whittier in time for the day cruises. You may choose to ride the train all the way to Grandview or hop off the train at Spencer Glacier for a raft trip. Dressing in layers will help you prepare for Alaska's weather changes. Temperatures average around 65 degrees during the summer months.

While you visit the Alaska Railroad, the Greater Wasilla Chamber of Commerce invites you to visit our offices, which are located in the historic Wasilla Railroad Depot. Our Chamber is involved in a long-term restoration of the Depot, which is on the National Historic Register.

SCHEDULES and FARES
The Alaska Railroad runs a summer and winter schedule with fares varying according to excursion. Reservations are recommended. Please call or check

website for current schedules and fares.

EQUIPMENT
16 SD70MAC Locomotives
9 custom-built passenger coaches
3 vista dome-style coaches to its fleet

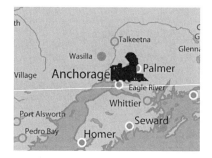

CONTACT
Alaska Railroad
411 West First Avenue
Anchorage, AK 99501
907-2645-2494
907-265-2621 TDD
800-544-0552 Outside Anchorage
www.akrr.com
reservations@akrr.com

Photos: The Alaska Railroad

MUSEUM OF ALASKA TRANSPORTATION AND INDUSTRY
Wasilla, AK

As entrepreneurs and industrialists realized the rich resources of Alaska's terrain, they also realized the need to develop the transportation and technology to reap the benefits. The Museum of Alaska Transportation and Industry (MATI) is dedicated to providing a home for the transportation and industrial remnants and to telling the stories of the people and the machines that opened Alaska to exploration and growth.

Railroads played a critical part in Alaska's history, and MATI offers an impressive collection of over 30 items of rolling stock, primarily from the Alaska Railroad. The museum also includes impressive exhibits of Alaska's rail history. And next door to the museum is the Alaska Central Railroad, a 1.5 inch-to-the-foot scale railroad operated by the Alaska Live Steamers. Scheduled operations are on the third Saturday during the

summer months, with unscheduled operations on most Saturdays during the summer. MATI also offers impressive artifacts and exhibits of other modes of transportation and industrial growth-aircraft, mineral extraction, fishing, and agriculture. Established in 1976, the museum is located on a 20-acre site in Wasilla, approximately 50 miles north of Anchorage.

SCHEDULES and FARES
The Museum of Alaska Transportation and Industry is open May through October. Tuesdays through Fridays are by appointment only. Fares are generally under $15 for adults. Group rates and guided tours are available upon request. Please call or check website for current schedules and fares.

EQUIPMENT
Alaska Railroad steam locomotive cranes No. LC-56 and No. LC-57
Alaska Railroad wooden caboose 1019
Alaska Railroad tan No. ARRX1666 built in 1916
Alaska Railroad 2-door hopper No. 6043
Department of the Interior, Bureau of Mines
mine safety car No. 5
WWII Pullman troop sleeper

CONTACT
Museum of Alaska Transportation and Industry
P.O. Box 870646
Wasilla, AK 99687
907-376-1211
907-376-3082(fax)
rmorris@alaska.net
www.alaska.net/~rmorris/mati1.htm

Photos: The Museum of Alaska Transportation and Industry

WHITE PASS & YUKON ROUTE RAILWAY
Skagway, AK

The White Pass & Yukon Route Railway is probably the most spectacular narrow gauge rail journey in North America. Vintage diesel engines depart the colorful gold rush town of Skagway, Alaska, several times a day in the summer.

Built in 1898 during the Klondike Gold Rush, this narrow gauge railroad is an International Historic Civil Engineering Landmark - a designation shared with the Panama Canal, the Eiffel Tower and the Statue of Liberty. The WP&YR railway was considered an impossible task but it was literally blasted through coastal mountains in only 26 months. The $10 million project was the product of British financing, American engineering and Canadian contracting. Tens of thousands of men and 450 tons of explosives overcame harsh and challenging climate and geography to create "the railway built of gold."

The WP&YR climbs almost 3,000 feet in just 20 miles. Passengers can experience the steep grades of up to 3.9%, cliff-hanging turns of 16 degrees, two tunnels and numerous bridges and trestles from the comfort of restored vintage passenger coaches. Panorama windows provide spectacular views of the infamous Dead Horse Gulch, where stampeders abandoned their animals in their mad quest to the north. Near the top of the White Pass, breezes beckon the

summer flowers to wave along with the American and Canadian flags. Other banners waving high include the Alaskan state flag and flags from the Yukon and British Columbia. This mountain pass is the international boundary where Canadian Mounties once checked each man's gear to make sure he could survive the harsh north.

Words fall short in describing the saw-toothed ridges and glacially carved horns of the coastal mountains through which the narrow gauge track winds.

SCHEDULES and FARES
The White Pass & Yukon Route Railway operates from May through September with fares ranging from $45 to $250 depending on the excursion. Passports may be required for some excursions. Please call or check website for current schedules and fares.

EQUIPMENT
20 diesel-electric Locomotives
2 steam locomotives
80 coaches
3 tie machines

CONTACT
White Pass & Yukon Route
P.O. Box 435
Skagway, AK 99840
800-343-7373
907-983-2217
info@whitepass.net
www.wpyr.com

Photos: Michael Anderson & John Hyde

Did You Know...

In 1604, the first British railway was built. It was called a Wagonway, and the rails were made of wood. The "Wagonway" was only 2 miles long.

It was not until 1825 that steam powered freight and passenger service started on the Stockton and Darlington Railway in England.

ARIZONA

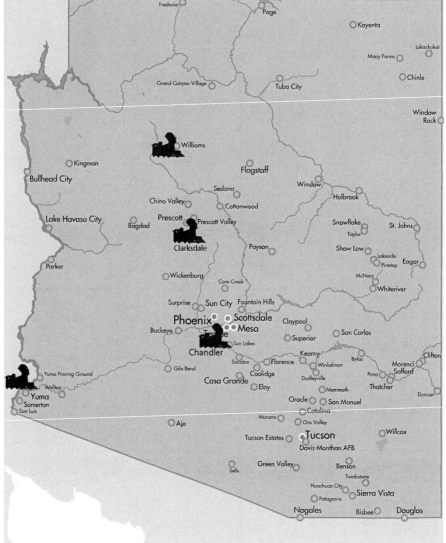

Fredonia
Page
Kayenta
Lukachukai
Many Farms
Grand Canyon Village
Tuba City
Chinle
Window Rock
Williams
Kingman
Flagstaff
Bullhead City
Sedona
Winslow
Chino Valley
Cottonwood
Holbrook
Lake Havasu City
Bagdad
Prescott
Prescott Valley
Snowflake
St. Johns
Taylor
Clarksdale
Payson
Show Low
Lakeside
Pinetop
Eagar
Parker
Wickenburg
McNary
Cave Creek
Whiteriver
Surprise
Sun City
Fountain Hills
Phoenix
Scottsdale
Claypool
Buckeye
Mesa
San Carlos
Tempe
Superior
Sun Lakes
Chandler
Kearny
Bylas
Clifton
Sacaton
Florence
Winkelman
Morenci
Yuma Proving Ground
Gila Bend
Coolidge
Pima
Safford
Casa Grande
Dudleyville
Thatcher
Wellton
Eloy
Mammoth
Duncan
Yuma
Oracle
San Manuel
Somerton
Catalina
San Luis
Marana
Oro Valley
Ajo
Tucson Estates
Tucson
Willcox
Davis-Monthan AFB
Sells
Green Valley
Benson
Tombstone
Huachuca City
Sierra Vista
Patagonia
Nogales
Bisbee
Douglas

ARIZONA RAILWAY MUSEUM
Chandler, AZ

After 20 years in the same location, the Arizona Railway Museum is being moved from Armstrong Park to Tumbleweed Park. The mission, however, will remain the same: to acquire, preserve, and restore railroad equipment and artifacts with relevance to Arizona and the Southwest. The new location allows the museum more space to achieve its goals, with room for future expansion. The six acres being used at Tumbleweed Park afford more tracks for display cars and locomotives. Also in the works, a multipurpose building to house displays and artifacts.

Select pieces of rolling stock have already been restored to operating condition. The new location will allow volunteers more room to restore even more cars.Four of the museum's passenger cars have been used for special trains such as Operation Lifesaver and Make-A-Wish. The pride of the collection, ex-Santa Fe "Vista Canyon" is Amtrak compatible and is available for charter. Other cars are available for static lease and can be configured for meetings or dinners.

SCHEDULES and FARES
The Arizona Railway Museum is open weekends from Labor Day through Memorial Day. Entry to the museum is free although donations are encouraged and graciously accepted. Guided tours are available for a fee. Please call or check website for current schedules and fares.

EQUIPMENT
Imperial Manor sleeper, 1938
Desert Valley, Ex-Southern 16, 1890
A.T.S.F. 999741 Wide vision, 1978
SP 413 Bay window, 1947
SP 4603 Bay window, 1978

CONTACT
Arizona Railway Museum
330 E. Ryan Road
Chandler, AZ 85244
480-821-1108
www.azrymuseum.org

Photos: FP45 No. 615 courtesy of Bart

GRAND CANYON RAILWAY
Williams, AZ

The historic Grand Canyon Railway still travels from the rustic Route 66 town of Williams, Arizona, to the Grand Canyon historic district with all the charm and style of the Old West and all the comforts of the modern age.

A trip aboard the railway is highlighted by a live gunfight at Williams Depot every morning. During the trip, strolling musicians serenade passengers with traditional cowboy and train songs. Best of all, the train stops about 200 yards from the edge of the South Rim of the Grand Canyon, one of the most spectacular vistas in the world.

Grand Canyon Railway offers many advantages to travelers visiting Grand Canyon National Park. Train passengers avoid a wait at the park gate, and they don't have to drive the busy two-lane highway that runs the 65 miles from Interstate 40 north to the park entrance. Passengers also get an opportunity to interact with friends and family outside of the car, and enjoy the family-oriented entertainment aboard the train. From Williams Depot, the train travels north to Grand Canyon Depot. Both depots are on the National Register of Historic Places, and Grand Canyon Depot, located in the heart of Grand Canyon National Park, is one of the few log-construction train depots still standing in the United States.

Train travel was once the primary means of getting to the Grand Canyon. The 65-mile spur line cutting north from Williams replaced the bumpy stagecoach ride. The Grand Canyon Railway carried the first passengers to the rim of the Grand Canyon on September 17, 1901.

SCHEDULES and FARES

Vintage steam engines pull the train between Memorial Day weekend and Labor Day weekend. Diesel engines do the job the rest of the year. The train makes the trip to the canyon every day except Christmas Eve and Christmas Day. Fares range from $30 to $170 depending on travel choices. Please call or check website for current schedules and fares.

EQUIPMENT
Locomotives - Steam:
No. 29, 2-8-0 type, SC-3 class, Alco, 1925
No. 4960, 2-8-2 type, 01-A class, 1923
No. 539, 2-8-2 type, 1917
Locomotives - Diesel:
No. 2134, GP-7 type, 1953
No. 6762, 6768, 6773, 6793 and B-Unit 6871, FPA-4, Alco, 1959
17 Harriman coaches, 1923
Club car
Cococino car
Kokopelli car
Café car

CONTACT
Grand Canyon Railway
233 N. Grand Canyon Boulevard
Williams, AZ 86046
800-843-8724 (reservations)
800-843-8723 (group sales)
928-773-1976 (international)
928-773-1610
www.thetrain.com

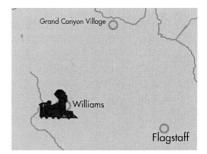

Photos Courtesy: Grand Canyon Railway

VERDE CANYON RAILROAD
Clarkdale, AZ

Verde Canyon Railroad is Arizona's longest-running nature show. The four-hour scenic ride includes views of Sinagua Indian ruins, bald and golden eagles, waterfowl, wildlife, and a 680-foot man made tunnel. The nature show is seen from panoramic windows along the wilderness route. In the spring and summer see great blue heron and black hawks; fall and winter bring brightly colored foliage and the arrival of migratory bald and golden eagles.

This historic route is between two national forests,

adjacent to a wilderness area. It follows the upper Verde River and is ideally situated above the heat of the desert and below the cold of Arizona's high country. The railroads of north central Arizona were all built to support Arizona's richest copper mine, located in Jerome. The first rail line, the Atlantic & Pacific Railroad, was completed in 1882, connecting Jerome to Ashfork.

The Verde Canyon Railroad (formerly the Verde Valley Railroad, operated by the Santa Fe, Prescott and Phoenix Railroad) was financed by Senator William A. Clark for a hefty $1.3 million. A miracle of engineering, the 38-mile line was built in just one year, from 1911 to 1912. It took 250 men using 200 mules, picks, and shovels and lots of Dupont black powder explosives to lay these rails. Today the same railroad would cost in excess of $38 million.

SCHEDULES and FARES
The Verde Canyon Railroad is a "train for all seasons" and runs year-round on a varied schedule. Fares vary according to your chosen excursion. Please call or check website for current schedules and fares.

EQUIPMENT
2 FP7
2 GP7
1 GP9
2 coach cars
7 first-class cars
6 open-air gondolas
EQUIPMENT Cont.
1 luxury caboose

CONTACT
Verde Canyon Railrad
300 North Broadway
Clarkdale, AZ 86324
800-320-0718
info@verdecanyonrr.com
www.verdecanyonrr.com

Photos: Verde Canyon Railroad

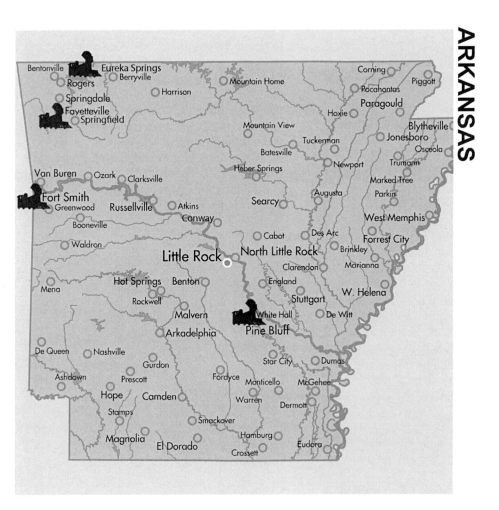

ARKANSAS

ARKANSAS AND MISSOURI RAILROAD
Springdale, AR

A trip on the Arkansas and Missouri Railroad offers you a window seat to history. Take a journey back to the golden age of travel in beautifully restored turn-of-the-century passenger cars with elegant inlaid mahogany interior. Travel over trestles that offer views for miles through a tunnel all the way to the top of the Ozark Mountains. And to make your trip more enjoyable, each excursion train is staffed to provide nostalgia for the beginning and seasoned rail traveler alike!

Enjoy a 134-mile round-trip journey from Springfield to Van Buren. You'll have a 2.5 hour stopover in historic Van Buren, a quaint town often featured in movies and television with plenty of shopping and dining choices for everyone. Or choose a shorter 70-mile round-trip jaunt from Van Buren to Winslow. There are also a variety of specialty train trips scheduled throughout the year, including "Mardi Gras of the Ozarks," "Blues and Barbecue," Halloween trains; and Christmas trains.

The Arkansas and Missouri Railroad is a proactive shortline that is committed to continually improving its wide range of commercial and passenger services. This dedication makes a trip on the railroad a must for the young and old!

SCHEDULES and FARES
The Arkansas and Missouri Railroad runs regular excursion trains from April through September with special Fall Foliage tours from October through mid-November. Other holiday theme trains and charters are also available. Prices vary according to excursion and date but are generally under $60. Please call or check website for current schedules and fares.

EQUIPMENT
6 T-6s
2 RS-1s
1 RF-32
12 C420s
1 C-630

CONTACT
Arkansas and Missouri Railroad
306 East Emma Street
Springfield, AR 72764
800-687-8600
479-751-8600
479 751-2225 (fax)
info@arkansasmissouri-rr.com
www.arkansasmissouri-rr.com

Photos: Arkansas and Missouri Railroad

ARKANSAS RAILROAD MUSEUM
Pine Bluff, AR

She weighs 368 tons and measures 100 feet from front to back. Her appetite is huge. She consumes 150 gallons of water and 15 gallons of oil per mile. She's Engine 819, Pine Bluff's legendary Queen of Steam, housed at the Arkansas Railroad Museum.

The Arkansas Railroad Museum is located in the Old Cotton Belt Shop buildings. Engine 819 was built at the Cotton Belt Route machine shop for the St. Louis Southwestern Railway in 1942. Engine 336 is also on display along with memorabilia from railroads that operated in Arkansas and East Texas. Your visit is enhanced by the many retired railroad men with firsthand knowledge of the railway.

SCHEDULES and FARES
The Arkansas Railroad Museum is open year-round, Monday through Saturday. Admission is free; donations are accepted. Special tours are available but will need to be scheduled. Please call or check website for current schedules and fares.

EQUIPMENT
7 diesel locomotives

CONTACT
Arkansas Railroad Museum
1700 Port Road
Pine Bluff, AR 71613
870-535-8819
www.pinebluffonline.com

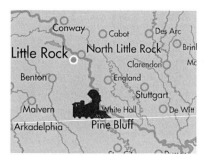

Photos: Arkansas Railroad Museum

EUREKA SPRINGS AND NORTH ARKANSAS RAILWAY
Eureka Springs, AR

Known as America's Little Switzerland, Eureka Springs is nestled snugly in the hills of the Ozark Mountains in Northwest Arkansas. What better way to enjoy this home to artists, writers, musicians, and others than a ride on the Eureka Springs.

On the Excursion Train you can chat with the conductor and crew while switching operations are explained. It's a sight, sound, and hands-on action experience of how America once traveled. The ES & NA saw its first visitors in 1883. The restored Eureka Springs depot houses a turntable, handcar, vintage locomotives, and other rolling stock. The collection of vintage equipment at ES&NA is the Ozarks' largest.

SCHEDULES and FARES
The Eureka Springs and North Arkansas Railway is open from April through October. Lunch and dinner trains are available, with fares generally under $50. Casual or semiformal attire is suggested for the dinner train. Reservations for the dinner train are recommended. Please call or check website for current schedules and fares.

EQUIPMENT
No. 1, 1906 Baldwin 2-6-0, steam, wood burning (display)
No. 201, 1906 Alco 2-6-0, steam, oil burning (used in the construction of the Panama Canal) (display)
No. 226, 1927 Baldwin 2-8-2, steam, oil burning (yet to be restored)
No. 4742, 1942 SW-1 Switcher, diesel (operational)

CONTACT
Eureka Springs and
Northern Arkansas Railway
299 North Main Street
Eureka Springs, AR 72632
479-253-9623
depot@esnarailway.com
www.esnarailway.com/

Photos: Eureka Springs and North Arkansas Railway

FORT SMITH TROLLEY MUSEUM
Fort Smith, AR

The story of public transportation in Fort Smith closely parallels the history of over 1,000 cities and towns in the USA. The mission of the Fort Smith Trolley Museum collection is preserving that history.

The Fort Smith Street Railway Company began operation in 1883 with three mule-drawn railcars, offering the area's first public transportation. As these cars progressed through the unpaved streets, the "Gee" and "Haw" from the drivers could be clearly heard. In the mid-1890s "Fort Smith & Van Buren Electric Street Railway Light & Power Company" began operating electric cars on North 5th street. By 1899, all Fort Smith Street Railway Company lines were electrified. These two companies were combined in 1903 and after reorganization became Fort Smith Light and Traction Co., predecessor to Oklahoma Gas and Electric Company.

The early cars we operated with a motorman and a conductor. By the mid-teens, with more automobiles and paved roads, small lines were losing riders. 1n 1920

Fort Smith received its first order of lightweight single man "Birney Safety Cars." The goal was to improve ridership by giving faster and more frequent service with less labor and electrical usage. This was marginally successful, and on November 15, 1933, streetcar service ended. The next day a new company began bus service that ran until the late 1960s when public transportation came to an end in Fort Smith. Recently Fort Smith has started again providing public transportation for its citizens.

In 1979 the Fort Smith Historical Society decided to publish an article on the history of local public railway transportation for its biannual offering. The result was the finding of the bodies of Fort Smith Birneys. The Fort Smith Streetcar Restoration was founded to restore the cars. In 1985 the Fort Smith Trolley Museum was founded, and in 1991 a restored Birney car was put into service. The museum's collection has all four types of streetcars operated in Fort Smith as well as a collection of the buses that followed.

SCHEDULES and FARES
The Fort Smith trolley runs year-round. The Museum is open on weekends year-round. Weekday tours are available by appointment. Please call or check website for current schedules and fares.

EQUIPMENT
7 electric streetcars
2 passenger cars
3 cabooses
3 freight cars
4 locomotives

CONTACT
Fort Smith Trolley Museum
100 South 4th Street
Fort Smith, AR 72901
479-783-0205
info@fstm.org
www.fstm.org

Photos: Fort Snith Trolley Museum

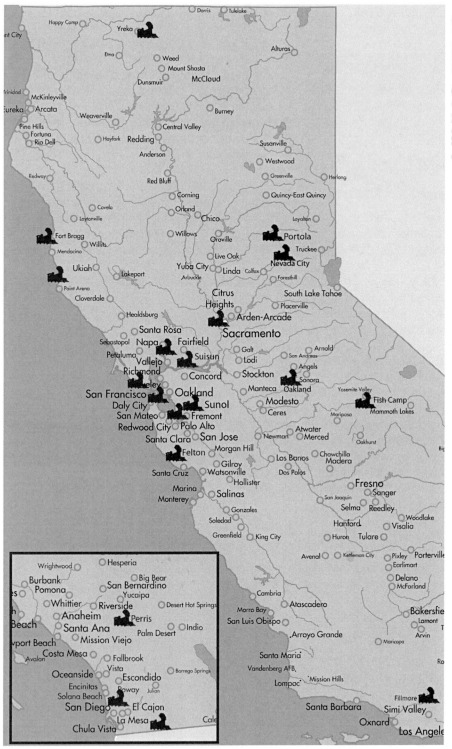

CALIFORNIA STATE RAILROAD MUSEUM
Sacramento, CA

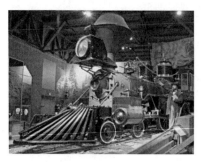

Widely regarded as North America's finest and most visited rairoad museum, the California State Railroad Museum and its Museum Store are located at the corner of 2nd and I Streets in Old Sacramento.

There is much to see and experience, and at least 1 to 2 hours are suggested to tour the Railroad Museum's many displays. Among these are a sleeping car that gently rocks through the night, a 1930s dining car filled with railroad china, and a million-pound steam locomotive with the cab open for your inspection!

Every day, guests can expect to find knowledgeable, uniformed docents throughout the museum, ready to answer questions and discuss the magic of railroading. Please note that exhibits change regularly.

SCHEDULES and FARES
The California State Railroad Museum is open daily except on Thanksgiving Day, Christmas Day, and New Year's Day. Close by is the Sacramento Southern Railroad that operates steam-powered weekend excursion trains from April to September, with special holiday "theme trains" operating on selected weekends from October to December. Please check its listing.
Admission is generally under $10. Please call or check website for current schedules and fares.

EQUIPMENT
On Display:
20 locomotives and cars, ranging from the first locomotive of the Trans-Continental Railroad to streamlined locomotives and passenger cars.

CONTACT
California State Railroad Museum
111 "I" Street
Sacramento, CA 95814
916-323-9280 (Front Desk)
916-445-7387 (Business Office)
www.californiastaterailroadmuseum.org

Photos: California State Railroad Museum

FILLMORE AND WESTERN RAILROAD
Fillmore, CA

The Fillmore and Western Railroad was named after J. A. Fillmore, the general superintendent of the Southern Pacific's Pacific Division. Fillmore is the self-proclaimed "Last, Best, Small Town in Southern California." Take a ride on the Fillmore and Western and decide for yourself.

Short Line Enterprises, founded in 1967, spent the first five years of its existence buying, selling, and trading mostly 19th-century locomotives, passenger cars, and freight cars from the property departments of major movie studios. This activity, combined with Short Line's experience in buying, selling, and evaluating railroad equipment led to the company's emergence as one of the foremost appraisers in America of rolling stock and other related railroad items. It also focused the company on its long-term path of providing movie trains for the film industry.

After moving its operations several times to be more conveniently located to the movie industry, Short Line was moved to Fillmore in the 1990s--the perfect site for a home for Hollywood's "movie trains" and the catalyst Fillmore needed for the revival of its 1930s-era Central Business District. In 1996 Short Line

Enterprises became the film division of the Fillmore and Western Railway Company. Operations expanded from movie work and limited passenger trips to regularly scheduled weekend passenger excursions and Southern California's only Murder Mystery Dinner Train.

SCHEDULES and FARES

The Fillmore and Western Railroad is open every weekend of the year. Reservations are strongly suggested for special theme trains, including Murder Mystery, 4th of July trains, Halloween, Christmas trains, and RailFest. Adult fares are generally under $25. Please call or check website for current schedules and fares.

EQUIPMENT

1914 2-8-0 Baldwin steam locomotive
1891 0-4-0 Porter
No. 1 Sespe
1949 F7 engines Nos. 100 and 101
GP30s and Alcos
Extensive freight and passenger cars

CONTACT

Fillmore and Western Railroad
351 Santa Clara Avenue
Fillmore, CA 93016
800-773-8724
805-524-2546
805-524-1838 (fax)
info@fwry.com
www.fwry.com

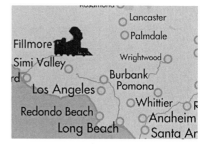

Photos: Fillmore & Western Railroad

GOLDEN GATE RAILROAD MUSEUM
San Francisco, CA

The Golden State Railroad Museum (GGRM) is a nonprofit organization dedicated to the preservation of steam and passenger railroad equipment, and the interpretation of railroad history in the San Francisco Bay Area.

The GGRM is maintaining its website so that visitors can keep up with progress.

SCHEDULES and FARES
Please call or check GGRM's website for special excursions and passenger rates on its popular steam locomotive 2472.

EQUIPMENT
Southern Pacific #2472, Southern Pacific #141 "Oakland," Southern Pacific #2979, Union Pacific @#5901, Southern Pacific #1487, Southern Pacific #6378 and #6380, Southern Pacific #293, Southern Pacific #2097, 2143 & 2156, and Southern Pacific #5131.

CONTACT
Golden State Railroad Museum, Inc.
1755 East Bayshore Road, Suite 19A
Redwood City, CA 94063
650-365-2472
2472info@ggrm.org
www.ggrm.org

Photos: Golden Gate Railroad Museum

NAPA VALLEY WINE TRAIN
Napa, CA

Riding the Napa Valley Wine Train is like stepping back in time and experiencing history for yourself. Passengers relax on a three hour round trip through the Napa Valley, where they dine on fresh gourmet food and enjoy the view of the breathtaking vineyards. The antique train cars date as far back as 1915 and have been restored to the opulence of the age of luxury train travel. The Wine Train also hosts a variety of special events like winery tours, Vintners Lunches and Wine Education Dinners.

The train itself has two engines, three kitchens, four Pullman lounge cars, two dining cars, an open air car and an elegant 1952 Vista Dome car. The 'Chef de Cuisine,' or Kitchen car, allows guests to watch as their meals are created right on board. Another unique car, the glass topped Vista Dome, is only one of ten made by Pullman Standard in the 1950's.

The Napa Valley Railroad, built in 1864, was mainly used by the Southern Pacific Railroad to haul freight until 1984 when stopped running through the valley. In 1987, Vincent DeDomenico, one of the inventor's of 'Rice-a-Roni,' purchased the Napa Valley Railroad with the intention of creating a unique, high-quality dining experience that would preserve the transportation corridor. The Napa Valley Wine Train still runs today on it's 25 miles of track between Napa and St. Helena.

SCHEDULES AND FARES
The Napa Valley Wine Train runs year-round. Prices ranges from $49.50 to $184 per person. Please call or check the website for current details.

EQUIPMENT
First and only CNG (Compressed Natural Gas) converted locomotive
FPA-4 Diesel Locomotive
Circa 1950's glass-topped car, featuring high-backed chairs and elevated seating. Lavishly restored 1915 vintage Pullman carriages with swivel lounge chairs, love seats, rich polished woods and etched glass
Dining cars with all accouterments Silverado railcar, featuring open-air American frontier theme.

CONTACT
Napa Valley Wine Train
1275 McKinstry Street
Napa, CA
800-427-4124
707-253-2111
707-253-9264 (fax)
www.winetrain.com

NEVADA COUNTY TRACTION COMPANY LLC
Nevada City, CA

The Nevada County Traction Company is operated by the Nevada County Historical Society on the grounds of the Northern Queen Inn. In 1988 the society was in need of a location to display its historic train relics. The Ramey family provided land in an attempt to lend a hand in preserving a piece of Nevada County history.

Workers began building the narrow gauge railroad in 1874. The line was originally 22 miles long, beginning in Colfax and destined for Nevada City. Engine No. 5 was featured in over 200 movies and TV programs and was returned to Nevada County from Universal Studios in 1985.

NCTC offers a 90-minute excursion. The first half hour is spent on the train to History Hill, where you will get out for a guided tour through the Chinese Cemetery (1860 to 1932). The Northern Queen Inn restored this area in 1997. Then you will take the half-hour train ride back. This excursion is partly narrated.

Daily excursion cars are open-top, so you can view the trees, and with four excursion cars up to 100 riders can be seated. Enjoy riding through 15 acres of tall pines, cedars, sugar pine, and many more wonderful trees. The train will roll on 60-pound and 35-pound rail; this train ride is almost 3 miles round trip.

Bathrooms and drinking water are available by the depot and next to the Chinese Cemetery trail head.

SCHEDULES and FARES
All rides require six or more paying riders with scheduled departures from the depot. Fares are generally under $15. Please call or check website for current schedules and fares.

EQUIPMENT
No. 5 Engine Lima wood burner, 1910
Plymouth diesel locomotive, 1961

CONTACT
Nevada County Traction Company LLC
402 Railroad Avenue
Nevada City, CA 95959
800-226-3090
530-265-0896
530-265-0869 (fax)
depotpeople@nccn.net
www.northernqueeninn.com

Photos: Nevada County Traction CO, Tim O'Brien

NILES CANYON RAILWAY
Sunol, CA

Located 20 miles north of San Jose, California, in the town of Sunol, the Niles Canyon Railway offers train rides to the public on the route of the original transcontinental railroad. This portion of the right-of-way was completed in 1869 and is being rebuilt by volunteers. They are truly a National Historic Treasure.

Even though it is very close to the metropolitan San Francisco Bay Area, the railroad is located in the scenic and historic Niles Canyon. You can board in both Sunol and the Niles District of Freemont for the

13-mile round trip that lasts about an hour, ten minutes. Sites of historical interest include the places where Charlie Chaplin and Bronco Billy made silent films, and the beehive kilns that made brick for the rebuilding of San Francisco after the 1906 earthquake. Also, Farwell Bridge is one of two remaining pin-connected Pratt truss bridges in the United States.

SCHEDULES and FARES
The Niles Canyon Railway operates on Sundays from January through October. Trains depart from Niles or Sunol. Donations are requested. Please call or check website for current schedules and fares.

EQUIPMENT
10 steam locomotives
10 internal combustion locomotives
2 rail motor cars
12 diesel engines
7 passenger cars
They also have several cabooses, with some open to charters

CONTACT
Niles Canyon Railway
37001 Mission Boulevard
Freemont, CA 94539
925-862-9063
pla_ncry@ncry.org
www.ncry.org

Photos: Niles Canyon Railway

ORANGE EMPIRE RAILWAY MUSEUM
Perris,CA

The Orange Empire Railway Museum offers visitors a chance to ride on the classic trolleys, passenger trains, and other equipment of Southern California's railroad past.

On a typical weekend two trolleys are running on the half-mile dual-gauge Loop Line, and another train is operating on the 1.5-mile standard gauge main line. A Pacific Electric interurban car also operates on the main line on selected weekends. The train is usually an electrical or diesel-powered freight train (with multiple cabooses), or consists of passenger train cars. You can experience riding in one of the early Los Angeles streetcars and a more modern PCC on the loop line, and ride in either a caboose (the cupolas are very popular with the kids) or an open gondola on the freight train. The cars and locomotives are selected on a rotating basis from our historic collection.

Workers at the Orange Empire Railway Museum are dedicated to educating visitors. They invite you to see the documents and artifacts on display.

SCHEDULES and FARES
The museum railway operates every weekend and on most major holidays and also on weekdays for charters and other special events. The museum grounds are open every day with the exception of Thanksgiving and Christmas, when the museum is closed. Train tickets are good for an entire day. Fares are generally under $15. Please call or check website for current schedules and fares.

EQUIPMENT
The Orange Empire Railway Museum boasts of an extensive collection of locomotives, trolleys, and passenger cars reminiscent of Southern California's railway history.

CONTACT
Orange Empire Railway Museum
2201 South A Street
St. Perris, CA 92570
951-657-2605
951-943-3020
oerm@juno.com
www.oerm.org

Photos: John Smatlak

PACIFIC SOUTHWEST RAILWAY MUSEUM AT CAMPO
Campo, CA

The Pacific Southwest Railway Museum at Campo offers a number of opportunities for the public to experience historic railroading, from regularly scheduled weekend train rides to monthly Mexican rail excursions. Additionally, various special holiday events are offered, including the North Pole Express. The Golden State locomotive is the standard weekend excursion train running out of the Campo facility. The ride is a 12-to-16-mile round-trip journey into the history of railroading in the Pacific Southwest. It takes about 90 minutes.

Another excursion takes you to Tecate, Mexico, for a one-day rail adventure. You can also visit La Mesa Depot. It has been restored by the museum to its 1915 condition. Reservations are required for the Tecate excursion.

SCHEDULES and FARES
The Campo Depot is open every weekend except Christmas and New Year. Fares vary according to the excursion. Please call or check website for current schedules and fares.

EQUIPMENT
80 pieces of rail equipment available for inspection

CONTACT
Campo Depot
31123-1/2 Highway 94
Campo, CA 91906
or
4695 Nebo Drive
La Mesa, CA 91941
619-478-9937 (weekends)
619-465-7776 (weekdays)
http://psrm.org

Photos: Josh Breslow

RAILTOWN 1897 STATE HISTORIC PARK
Jamestown, CA

Located in the heart of California's Gold Country, Railtown 1897 State Historic Park is one of only two preserved steam-era shortline railroad roundhouse complexes left in the United States. The Historic Jamestown Shops and Roundhouse are an intact and still-functioning steam locomotive repair and maintenance facility that dates back to 1897.

The Railtown 1897 SHP Interpretive Center, the authentic roundhouse and shops, and the Depot Store (a railroad specialty gift shop) are among the park's unique year-round offerings. Steam train rides are offered on weekends during the spring, summer, and fall.

This one-of-a-kind attraction combines industrial heritage and railroad history with the lore of Hollywood. Known as "The Movie Railroad," Railtown 1897's survival has been influenced by its popularity with the film industry. Because Hollywood's movie studios had discovered the railroad's steam engines, great scenery, and country ambiance, the Historic Jamestown Shops and Roundhouse were not demolished, nor were the remaining steam locomotive and historic passenger and freight cars scrapped.

Since 1897 the historic locomotives and railroad cars preserved here have appeared in more than 200 films, television productions, and commercials. Still a popular Hollywood location site, Railtown 1897 has been called "the most photographed railroad in the world." Petticoat Junction, The Wild, Wild West, High Noon, The Virginian, and Unforgiven were all filmed here.

The Railtown 1897 roundhouse has an operating turntable, a functional blacksmithing area, and a belt-driven machine shop in which locomotives and cars are inspected, repaired, and rebuilt—just as they have been for the past century. Self-guided and guided tours are available. The complex also includes several related historic structures, a collection of Hollywood "props," a large picnic area and an Interpretive Center.

In spring, summer and fall, climb aboard a vintage steam-powered excursion train on weekends at Railtown 1897. Enjoy a six-mile, 40-minute round-trip ride through the scenic Sierra foothills, in vintage passenger coaches pulled by an authentic steam locomotive.

SCHEDULES AND FARES
Railtown 1897 State Historic Park is open Tuesdays through Sundays year round, except Thanksgiving Day, Christmas Day, and New Year's Day. Steam-powered excursion trains depart on weekends from April through October. Please call or check website for current schedules and fares.

EQUIPMENT
No. 28 2-8-0 Sierra Railroad
No. 3 4-6-0
No. 5 combine
No. 6 coach
No. 2 former Feather River Shay
Southern Pacific commuter coaches

CONTACT
Railtown 1897 State Historic Park
5th Street & Reservoir Road
Jamestown, CA 95327
209-984-3953
www.railtown1897.org

ROARING CAMP RAILROADS
Felton, CA

In the 1880s, small but powerful steam locomotives hauled timber out of the redwood forests of California's coastal mountains. Today, these steam engines are no longer used for logging but continue to operate at Roaring Camp Railroads in Felton, carrying passengers over trestles through the big trees, whistling and chugging along, just as they did more than a century ago.

The grounds of Roaring Camp contain a general store, a depot, an opera house, the smallest covered bridge in America, a tiny one-room schoolhouse, loggers' skid sheds, and an engine house. The main attractions are its two railroads: Roaring Camp's Steam Train climbs on a narrow-gauge track through virgin redwood forests and the Santa Cruz Beach Train travels on a standard gauge track along the scenic San Lorenzo River gorge to the beach of Santa Cruz. Seeing the redwoods up close is one of the reasons people visit Roaring Camp.

Roaring Camp's railroad history began in 1875 when the narrow-gauge Santa Cruz & Felton Railroad was established. It gained fame as the Picnic Line, carrying freight and weekend tourists from Alameda to Felton to see the big trees. Presidents Ulysses S. Grant and Theodore Roosevelt were among its distinguished passengers.

SCHEDULES and FARES
Trains operate year-round but schedules vary seasonally for the steam and beach trains. Adult fares are generally under $25. There is a fee for parking. Please call or check website for current schedules and fares.

EQUIPMENT
7 narrow gauge steam locomotives (four are operating)
Kahuku No. 3, a Baldwin 0-4-2T
Tuolumne No. 2, a 2-truck Heisler locomotive, 1899
Dixiana No. 1, a 2-truck Shay, 1912
Sonora No. 7, a 3-truck Shay
Open-air excursion cars and covered cars that are authentic antiques or replicas of rare passenger coaches

CONTACT
Roaring Camp Railroads
P.O. Box G-1
Felton, CA 95018
831-335-4484
info@roaringcamp.com
www.roaringcamp.com/

Photos: John Poimiroo

SACRAMENTO SOUTHERN RAILROAD
Sacramento, CA

The Sacramento Southern Railroad is a place where guests can climb aboard a train of vintage passenger coaches and open-air gondolas, led by a steam locomotive, for a six-mile 40-minute round-trip ride along the Sacramento River. For a first-class experience (and an extra fare), guests can ride in air-conditioned luxury aboard the El Dorado, the SSRR's beautifully restored first-class observation car.

The Sacramento Southern Railroad (SSRR) began shortly after the turn of the 20th century. The SSRR was built to serve the rich farmlands of California's Sacramento-San Joaquin Delta region. The first line, of nearly 25 miles, opened in 1912 between Sacramento, Freeport, Hood, and Walnut Grove. Workers extended the line another 7.5 miles in 1929, to Isleton.

In 1984 the first season of regular Sacramento Southern Railroad excursion service began. This volunteer-operated program of the California State Railroad Museum today carries over 60,000 guests annually; 12,000 school children enjoy weekday rides aboard seasonal "School Trains," and learn about immigration and 19th century train travel as a part of their experience at the California State Railroad Museum.

SCHEDULES AND FARES

Trains operate every weekend from April through September. Trains depart from the Central Pacific Freight Depot located on Front Street between J and K Streets in Old Sacramento (just two blocks south of the California State Railroad Museum). Please call or check website for current schedules and fares.

CONTACT

Sacramento Southern Railroad
At California State Railroad Museum
111 "I" Street
Sacramento, CA 95814
916-445-7387
916-445-6645
www.californiastaterailroadmuseum.org

Photos: Sacramento Southern Railroad

SIERRA RAILROAD/SACRAMENTO RIVER TRAIN
Woodland, CA

Launched in July 2005, the Sacramento River Train is one of the nation's newest dinner trains. Still, the equipment and railroad have a long history.

The Sacramento River Train operates on the 16-mile "Woodland Branch," which was constructed in 1911 by the Northern Electric Company. The idea was to link the fertile farmlands of Yolo County to the developing city of Sacramento. In 1941, when the Uinted States entered World War II, passenger operations came to an end.

Powered now by diesel locomotives, the Sacramento Northern Railway continued to move a high volume of freight over the line until the early 1960s. Slowly, the various rail spurs were torn up along the route, and eventually only the industries in Woodland remained. The Western Pacific Railroad acquired the Woodland Branch and merged with the Union Pacific in 1984.

The Yolo Shortline Railroad Company was created in 1991 and purchased the Woodland Branch. In 2003 the Yolo Shortline merged with the Sierra Railroad Company under the Sierra name. The excursion train was renamed the Sacramento River Train. The 8,000-foot-long Fremont Trestle is a highlight among the things you will experience along the way.

SCHEDULES and FARES
The Sacramento River Train operates year-round. Fares vary according to the excursion. Please call or check website for current schedules and fares.

EQUIPMENT
The Sacramento River Train features three open-air cars and three enclosed air-conditioned coaches. Two of the coaches were from the previous train. The third coach was provided by the Sierra Railroad Dinner Train.

CONTACT
Sacramento River Train
East Main and E Street
Woodland, CA 96766
800-866-1690
www.SacramentoRiverTrain.com

Photos: Sierra Railroad - Sacramento River Train

SIERRA RAILROAD/SIERRA RAILROAD DINNER TRAIN
Oakdale, CA

The Sierra Railroad was formed in 1897 to connect the Central Valley to the Gold Country. As the third oldest railroad in North America, the Sierra continues to haul freight, carry passengers, make Hollywood movies, and play an important role in California. Thomas S. Bullock believed that a railroad to the Sierra Nevada foothills was sorely needed and financially feasible.

Besides carrying freight and passengers, the Sierra became famous as "The Movie Railroad" for making over 300 movies, commercials, and television shows. In the 1970s the railroad launched an industry when it operated the nation's first dinner train.

Today, the Sierra Railroad Dinner Train provides visitors an opportunity to travel on the historic Sierra Railroad while enjoying a delicious meal, beautiful countryside, and a wide range of entertainment. Every week of the year, the dinner train offers romantic dinners, fun murder mysteries, lunches, Sunday brunches, Wild West shows, wine tasting, and much more.

SCHEDULES and FARES
The Sierra Railroad Dinner Train operates year-round with 200-plus trips. Fares vary according to excursion chosen. Please call or check website for current schedules and fares.

CONTACT
The Sierra Railroad Dinner Train
220 South Sierra Avenue
Oakdale, CA 95361
800-866-1690
209-848-2100
http://www.sierrarailroad.com/dinnertrain/

Photos: Sierra Railroad - Sierra Railroad Dinner Train

SIERRA RAILROAD /THE SKUNK TRAIN
Fort Bragg, CA

A ride on the Skunk Train is definitely a step back in time. All of our trains arrive at Northspur Station, the midpoint of the line, a large redwood grove on the banks of the Noyo River. Whether you leave Fort Bragg on the rugged Mendocino Coast or Willits on Highway 101 in inland Mendocino County, your trip will take you through mountain tunnels, over bridges and across the Coastal Mountain Range. Train schedules vary by season, and we invite you to come ride, relax, and see the redwoods. The Skunk Train, then a part of California Western Railroad, was officially recognized in 2001 as the last railroad in America to haul U.S. mail to eighteen remote residents along the line. Mail is delivered six days a week, so you just might see a delivery on your trip.

Founded by Charles R. "C. R." Johnson in 1885, the Skunk train hauled logs from the forest to Johnson's sawmill, the Union Lumber Company. Passenger service started in 1904, and in 1925 the California Western Railroad became known as the "Skunk Train." The nickname stems from the vintage motor-cars. With the combination of the fumes from the gasoline engines and pot-bellied stoves, the locals used to say "You can smell 'em before you can see 'em": hence the name "Skunk." The Sierra Railroad bought the Skunk Train in 2004, saving the line from bankruptcy.

SCHEDULES and FARES
There are Skunk Train excursions scheduled year-round. Please call or check website for current schedules and fares.

EQUIPMENT
1925 M-100 built by the Edwards Railcar Company
1935 streamlined M-300 built by the American Car & Foundry Company
1955 EMD GP-9 diesel engines
The Grand Old Lady, Engine No. 45, a 1924 Baldwin 2-8-2 Mikado
Engine No. 45 sports a color scheme like no other out there in operation--
brilliant colors that are simply stunning in a backdrop of towering redwoods

CONTACT
Skunk Train Fort Bragg Depot
Foot of Laurel Street
Fort Bragg, CA 95437
or
Skunk Train Willits Depot
299 East Commercial Street
Willits, CA 95490
866-45-SKUNK
www.skunktrain.com

Photos: Sierra Railroad - The Shunk Train

SOCIETY FOR THE PRESERVATION OF CARTER RAILROAD RESOURCES
Fremont, CA

In 1880 the Society for the Preservation of Carter Railroad Resources (SPCRR) was the South Pacific Coast Railroad, a narrow gauge railroad that steamed south across the marshes and farms of Alameda and Santa Clara Counties, then wound through the Santa Cruz Mountains until it reached the ocean at Santa Cruz.

The SPCRR carried lumber from the mountains and produce from the valley to build and feed the growing cities of Oakland and San Francisco. It carried commuters, travelers, and tourists from small farm towns and logging camps to big cities. It maintained a fleet of locomotives, baggage cars, passenger cars, boxcars, flatcars, and cabooses from shops in Newark, California.

Today the SPCRR is a railroad museum located in Ardenwood Historic Farm Regional Park in Fremont, California. The SPCRR restores equipment representative of those bygone days. Its collection contains 13 cars from the 1870s and 1880s. Most of the cars were built by the Carter Brothers in Newark. The SPCRR is actively restoring three cars and has

four cars in service. It has 1.5 miles of track and operates a recreation of the original SPCRR's Centerville Branch at Ardenwood. Draft horses pull an 1885 North Pacific Coast RR flatcar set up as a picnic car on scheduled runs through farm fields and
eucalyptus groves.

SCHEDULES and FARES
The South Pacific Coastal Railroad is open Tuesday through Sunday. Please call or check website for current schedules and fares.

EQUIPMENT
Oakland Railroad 12 - 1887
Mt. Diablo & San Jose 21 - 1989
South Pacific Coast 47 - 1881
Nevada Central 253 - 1874
Diamond and Caldor 64
South Pacific Coast 10, 44 and 472 - 1880
Southern Pacific 1010 - 1882
North Shore 1725
ASARCO 2 - 1940
No.4 Old Mission Cement
Solvent Recovery 588

CONTACT
SPCRR
P.O. Box 783
Newark, CA 94560
866-417-7277
www.spcrr.org

Photos: SPCRR

WESTERN PACIFIC RAILROAD MUSEUM/PORTOLA RAILROAD MUSEUM
Portola, CA

The Portola Railroad Museum is home to one of the most comprehensive collections of locomotives and rolling stock from a single railroad system. Operated by the Feather River Rail Society, the PRM is dedicated to presenting the history of the Western Pacific Railroad and its subsidiaries, the Sacramento Northern Railway and Tidewater Southern Railway.

The museum itself is an authentic Western Pacific locomotive facility. The site includes a 220-foot-long, 16,000-square-foot diesel locomotive shop, built in 1954, and the Western Pacific Portola Hospital, built starting in 1912. The facility has two and a half miles of trackage and offers caboose train rides on summer weekends.

Unlike other museums, the Portola Museum encourages visitors to climb up in the cabs of locomotives, to sit in the engineer's seats, and to browse through the many cabooses and passenger cars that are on display. The PRM even offers a "Rent-a-Locomotive" program, where visitors can run a locomotive under the supervision of an engineer.

Portola is located 5,000 feet high in the Sierra Nevada range. Portola has long been a railroad town and has served the Western Pacific and now Union Pacific as a crew-change point for decades.

SCHEDULES and FARES
The museum is open from Memorial Day weekend to Labor Day weekend. Please call or check website for current schedules and fares.

EQUIPMENT
36 diesel locomotives
2 steam engines
100 freight and passenger cars

CONTACT
Feather River Rail Society
700 Western Pacific Way
or

P.O. Box 608
Portola, CA 96122
530-832-4131 (museum)
530-832-4532 (reservations)
www.wplives.org

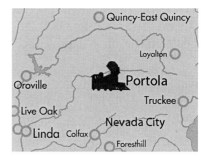

Photos: Western Pacific Railway Museum / Portola Railroad Museum

WESTERN RAILWAY MUSEUM
Suisun, CA

The Western Railway Museum began in 1946 after a group of rail enthusiasts banded together to save an old Oakland streetcar. The group became the Bay Area Electric Railroad Association. As a result of their efforts, visitors can now ride historic streetcars and interurban electric trains from all over California and other western states.

Streetcars loop the shaded picnic grounds, and there are restored cars you may tour. Interurban cars run over the restored main line of the old Sacramento Northern Railway, a 9.5-mile journey to Gum Grove Station. The association adopted the name "Western Railway Museum in 1984. Today the museum is one of the few places in the world that re-creates an authentic interurban trip on the original rails.

SCHEDULES and FARES
The Western Railway Museum is open on weekends year-round. There are extended hours during the summer months. Adult admission is generally around $10. Please call or check website for current schedules and fares.

EQUIPMENT
The museum has more than 50 historic cars on display.

CONTACT
Western Railway Museum
5848 State Highway 12
Suisun City, CA 94585
707-374-2978
www.wrm.org

Photos: Western Railway Museum

YOSEMITE MOUNTAIN SUGAR PINE RAILROAD
Fish Camp, CA

High in the Sierra Nevada Mountains just south of Yosemite National Park, travelers will thrill to the sights and sounds of steam-powered narrow gauge railroading. The Yosemite Mountain Sugar Pine Railroad operates excursion trains through the scenic Sierra National Forest over old tracks once used for logging trains at the turn of the century. Vintage Shay locomotives power the "Logger Steam Train" for the one-hour narrated trip through the magnificent pine forests at the 5000 foot elevation. Antique model "A" gasoline engines power the trolley-like Jenny Railcars over the same route when steam trains are not scheduled.

On Saturday and Wednesday evenings in the summer, steam whistles, barbecue smoke, and old-fashioned music fill the air during the Moonlight Special. Barbecued New York steaks and all the trimmings are served up at the station, along with music by the Sugar Pine Trio. Then it's "All Aboard" for the Logger Steam Train trip through the woods to the campfire. The beautiful evening sky forms the backdrop for the return trip up the mountain with the long, lonesome steam whistle bringing back the bygone days of railroading at its best.

SCHEDULES and FARES
Departure times vary throughout the year. Adult fares are generally under $50 depending on the excursion. Group excursions, field trips and special events are available. Please call or check website for current schedules and fares.

EQUIPMENT
Shay No. 15 was built in 1913 and weighs 60 tons.
No. 10, built in 1928, weighs 83 tons and is the heaviest operating narrow gauge Shay locomotive today.
Railcars once used to provide transportation for logging and track repair crews have been refurbished and are now operated for passenger excursion.

CONTACT
Yosemite Mountain Sugar Pine Railroad
56001 Yosemite Hwy 41
Fish Camp, CA 93623
559-683-7273
www.ymsprr.com

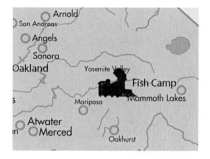

Photos: Yosemite Mountain Sugar Pine Railroad

Did You Know...

In 1838 the Boston & Worcester Railroad was the first railroad to charge commuter fares in the U.S.

COLORADO

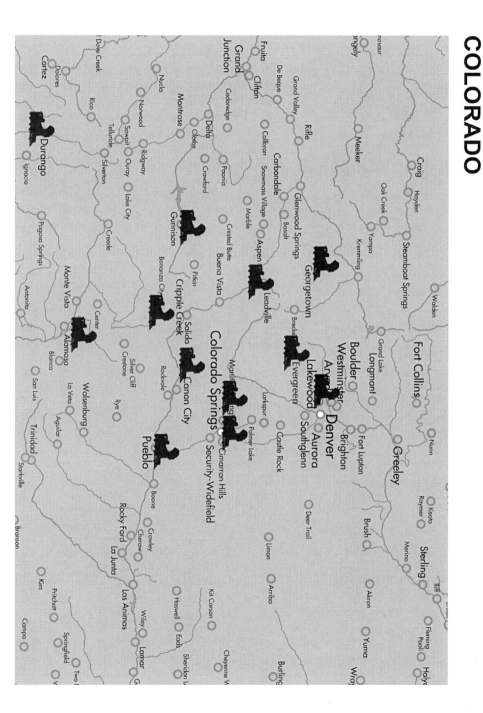

COLORADO RAILROAD MUSEUM
Denver, CO

The Colorado Railroad Museum houses the largest collection of Colorado narrow gauge equipment anywhere. In the depot museum one can look through thousands of antique photographs, artifacts, and documents relating to the history of the Colorado railroad. The lower level of the museum is home to the "Denver and Western" model train and the exhibition hall. The hall houses static and seasonal displays of all kinds. There is also a general store that has hundreds of books, DVD's, magazines, posters, etc. relating to railroads of all types. Also, don't forget to take a look at the renowned reference library which houses of 10,000 railroad-specific books, pamphlets, periodicals, photographs, slides, and films.

The Denver Garden Railway Society runs a garden railway on Saturday mornings, year-round. Once a month, the steam trains run as well.

SCHEDULES AND FARES:
The museum is open year round except Thanksgiving, Christmas and New Year's Day. Visit the website for fare information.

EQUIPMENT:
The 15 acres around the depot displays all of the railroad equipment including narrow and standard gauge steam and diesel locomotives, passenger cars, cabooses and a roundhouse that boasts a 90-foot "Armstrong" turntable.

CONTACT:
Colorado Railroad Museum
17155 W. 44th Avenue
Golden, CO 80403
303-279-4591 or 800-365-6263
www.coloradorailroadmuseum.org
Info@ColoradoRAILROADMuseum.org

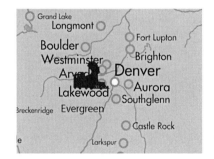

CRIPPLE CREEK AND VICTOR NARROW GAUGE RAILROAD
Cripple Creek, CO

Take a trip back in time to the lusty pioneer days of railroading when you board the Cripple Creek and Victor Railroad. The locomotive is a 15-ton iron horse of the 0-4-0 type, typical of the time when steam engines played a crucial role in winning the West. Surrounded by the pillaring smoke of the engine and the clanging of working steam and steel, you're treated to a four-mile journey of spectacular views and interesting stories that only a dynamic gold town could produce.

The 45-minute trip begins at the old Midland Terminal Depot. The track goes south out of Cripple Creek, passes the old Midland Terminal Wye over a reconstructed trestle, and ends near the deserted mining camp of Anaconda before making its return trip. Along the way, you'll pass many historic mines and stop at special points of interest, including Echo Valley.

SCHEDULES and FARES
The Cripple Creek and Victor Narrow Gauge Railroad is open from May through October. Adult fares are generally under $12. Please call or check website for current schedules and fares.

EQUIPMENT
No. 1, 1902 Orenstein and Koppel 0-4-4-0
No. 2, 1936 Henschel 0-4-0
No. 3, 1927 Porter 0-4-0 tank type
No. 4, 1947 Bagnall 26-ton 0-4-4 OT type

CONTACT
Cripple Creek & Victor Narrow Gauge Railroad
5th & Bennett Avenue
Cripple Creek, CO 80813
719-689-2640
719-689-3256 (fax)
ccnvgrr@aol.com
www.cripplecreekrailroad.com

Photos: Cripple Creek and Victor Railroad

DENVER AND RIO GRANDE
US NATIONAL PARK SERVICE
Gunnison, CO

At the mouth of Cimarron Creek stands a reminder of the railroading days. Locomotive No. 278, its coal tender, a boxcar, and a caboose stand stopped on the last remaining railroad trestle along the Black Canyon of the Gunnison route. The trestle is a steel deck span bridge. It was constructed in 1895, replacing the original wooden Howe truss design trestle. The "new" bridge's four spans incorporated a metal Pratt truss and three girder sections brought from other locations on the Denver and Rio Grande line. As originally designed and constructed, the trestle itself was 288 feet in length. Telegraph lines (reconstructed) can be seen extending from the ties on the south side of the trestle. It was common, for many years, to see trestles used in this manner for stringing telegraph lines along railroad routes.

The locomotive and the other cars have been restored to look as they would have in 1940. This locomotive was retired in 1952 and given to the city of Montrose, as a gift, by the D&RG railroad. It has been on lease to the National Park Service since 1973, along with the tender and caboose. In 1976, the trestle was placed on the National Register of Historic Places, because of its significance as the last remaining structure representing the history of the narrow gauge railroad in the Black Canyon of the Gunnison. Today, the Cimarron Canyon railroad exhibit can help us understand and appreciate the accomplishments of the trains that ran the Black Canyon of the Gunnison.

SCHEDULES and FARES
The Cimarron Visitor Center is open from Memorial Day through Labor Day. The exhibits at the loading yard, the visitor center, and the locomotive on the trestle are open on a self-guiding basis year-round. Please call or check website for current schedules and fares.

EQUIPMENT
No. 278, C16 2-8-0 mainline freight, Baldwin 1882
(No. 278 was used on part of the D&RG's main line, on the Crested Butte Branch, and in the rail yards of Gunnison for over 70 years.)
Boxcar, built in 1903 (rebuilt in 1923)
Caboose, built in the mid-1880s

CONTACT
Curecanti National Recreation Area
102 Elk Creek
Gunnison, CO 81230
970-641-2337
www.nps.gov/cure

Photos: Denver and Rio Grande

DURANGO & SILVERTON NARROW GAUGE RAILROAD and MUSEUM
Durango, CO

Take a ride on a historic, coal-fired, steam-powered train through the back-country wilderness of the San Juan Mountains of Southwest Colorado and relive the sights and sounds of yesteryear. The Denver & Rio Grande arrived in Durango in August of 1881 and construction on the line began in the fall of that same year. By July of 1882, the tracks to Silverton were completed. The line was constructed to haul silver and gold ore from the mountains, but passengers soon realized it was the view that was truly precious. This scenic line has been in continuous operation ever since. Named "one of the World's Top Ten Train Rides" by the American Society of Travel Writers.

Today's passengers enjoy the rare and authentic experience of a trip on a steam train as it winds its way through the mountains and spectacular scenery. One of the most recognized highlights of the trip is the Highline, a ledge carved out of granite cliffs 400 feet above the Animas River. Imagining the construction of this section of track back in 1882 conjures up some heroic and engineering feats. The D&SNGRR received a National Historic Civil Engineering Landmark Award in 1968.

The train travels 45 miles to Silverton from May - October and 26 miles to the Cascade Canyon Wye from late November - early May. An additional highlight of the trip is a trip to the D&SNGRR Museum (open on days the train is operating), located in the Durango roundhouse, and a stop at the Freight Yard and Silverton Depot museum (open in the summer months only). Both museums feature large collections of railroad memorabilia from the area: old photographs, lanterns, china, railroad locks, full-size locomotives, coaches, or other historic rolling stock, and much more. Admission to both museums is included with the purchase of a train ticket.

SCHEDULES and FARES
Trains to Silverton run early May - late October. The Winter Cascade Canyon Train runs late November - early May. Schedules and fares vary according to excursion and class of service. Please call or check our Web site for current schedules and information.

EQUIPMENT
No. 473, 2-8-2 type, K-28 class Alco, 1923
No. 476, 2-8-2 type, K-28 class Alco, 1923
No. 478, 2-8-2 type, K-28 class Alco, 1923
No. 480, 2-8-2 type, K-36 class Baldwin, 1925
No. 481, 2-8-2 type, K-36 class Baldwin, 1925
No. 482, 2-8-2 type, K-36 class Baldwin, 1925
No. 486, 2-8-2 type, K-36 class Baldwin, 1925
No. 42, 2-8-0 type, C-17 class Baldwin, 1887
No. 493, 2-8-2 type, K-37 class Baldwin, 1902

CONTACT
Durango & Silverton Narrow Gauge
Railroad and Museum
479 Main Avenue
Durango, CO 81301
970-247-2733 (reservations)
877-872-4607 (toll free)
970-259-0274
www.durangotrain.com

Photos: Durango & Silverton Narrow Gauge Railroad

GEORGETOWN LOOP MINING & RAILROAD PARK®
Georgetown, CO

The Georgetown Loop Mining and Railroad Park® brings Colorado History to life in a fun adventure that will thrill the entire family. The entire Park is a designated National Historic Site. It has rolling stock dating back to the nineteenth century.

The Georgetown Loop operates both historic steam and diesel locomotives. The beauty of the rugged Colorado Rocky Mountains surrounds you as an old time steam locomotive chugs its way up the canyon and over the Devil's Gate High Bridge. Their open air cars offer an unobstructed view of everything along the line. In the fall and winter they operate their enclosed heated coaches for the comfort of their guests. Departures are available from the historic Silver Plume Depot at 9200 ft. or the Devil's Gate Depot from historic Georgetown. Gift shops at both ends of the line offer outstanding selections of railroad-themed items, books, books clothing, snack foods, and hot & cold drinks.

The railcar barn at the Silver Plume Depot contains old railcars from the late 1800s and early 1900s, including a restored RPO car. There is usually some kind of maintenance work being performed at the engine house that you can peak in on to see what real railroaders do.

The optional guided silver mine tour of the historic Lebanon Silver mine takes visitors back over 400 feet into Republican Mountain. Here you will see what the miners saw including the Morningstar glory hole. The tour also includes the mine manager's office, the changing room, tool room, and blacksmith's shop.

The Georgetown Loop offers many expanded activities including wine & hors d'oeuvres, dinner, 4th of July, Oktoberfest, pumpkin festival, and Santa's North Pole Adventure trains. They also host special activities like family reunions, birthday parties, weddings, club outings, wedding receptions, corporate functions, and Bar/Bat Mitzvahs. They can also offer full service catering for events.

SCHEDULES AND FARES:
The railway operates from May 1 – Dec. 30. Fares vary according to the excursion but are normally in the $20 to $30 dollar range. Please call ahead for reservations and current fares.

EQUIPMENT:
1884 Cooke Steam Locomotive (in restoration)
1929 Baldwin Steam Locomotive
1926 Baldwin Steam Locomotive (in restoration)
1955 General Electric 45 Ton Diesel
1946 Porter 85 Ton Diesel
1880-1920 Denver and Rio Grande cars

CONTACT:
Georgetown Loop Railroad
P.O. Box 249
Georgetown, CO 80444
(888) 456-6777
www.georgetownlooprr.com
info@historicrailadventures.com

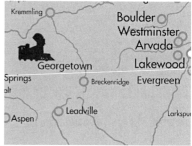

LEADVILLE, COLORADO & SOUTHERN RAILROAD
Leadville, CO

Tucked away in a magnificent alpine valley at the base of Colorado's highest peak is the historic mining town of Leadville. Among the spectacular views you'll find a hidden gem: the Leadville, Colorado & Southern Railroad. Originating in "the highest incorporated city in North America," the LC&S travels along the old Denver, South Park & Pacific and Colorado & Southern lines to the Continental Divide.

Your journey begins at the renovated depot, originally completed in 1893 for the Colorado, Leadville & Gunnison rail line. This is where you purchase your ticket for the 2.5 hour train trip. During the 22.5-mile trip, you'll marvel at the breathtaking panoramas across the Arkansas River Valley, following that river to an elevation of 11,200 feet over an old narrow gauge roadbed converted to standard gauge in the 1940s. Your experience is enhanced by colorful and humorous narratives of Leadville's fascinating past, a past rich with railroading and mining history.

SCHEDULES and FARES
The Leadville & Southern Railroad is open from Memorial Day weekend through September. Adult excursion fares are generally under $30. Please call or check website for current schedules and fares.

EQUIPMENT
1955 EMD GP9 No. 1714
EMD GP9 No. 1918

CONTACT
Leadville, Colorado & Southern Railroad
327 E. Seventh Street
Leadville, CO 80461
719-486-3936
719-486-0671
info@leadville.train
www.leadville-train.com

Photos: Leadville Colorado & Southern Railroad

Did You Know...

The Durango & Silverton Narrow Gauge Railroad has carried over $300 million in precious metals.

The Durango & Silverton Railroad uses 10,000 gallons of water per round-trip and 12,000 pounds of coal; the coal is shoveled one shovelful at a time.

Fact by: Durango and Silverton Narrow Gauge Railroad

MANITOU & PIKES PEAK COG RAILWAY
Manitou Springs, CO

The most asked question about the Manitou & Pikes Peak Cog Railway just might be: "What is a cog railway?" Unlike conventional railways that use adhesion or wheel friction for locomotive power, the cog railroad uses a gear or meshing system. The result is a train that can climb a much steeper grade. You still find most cog or rack railways in Switzerland, but the Manitou & Pikes Peak Cog Railway is the highest in the world. It is the highest railway of any kind in North America and boasts of a perfect safety record.

One of the tourists to visit Pikes Peak in the 1880's was Zalmon Simmons, inventor/founder of Simmons Beautyrest Mattress. He made the trip on a mule. He loved the view but wanted a more comfortable way to experience it, so he ultimately supplied the capital to build the railroad.

It is an 8.9-mile ride that last just over three hours. Passengers travel along Ruxton Creek in Engleman Canyon. There are boulder fields on either side of the train. Before getting above the timberline, you pass through beautiful trees, some believed to be over 2,000 years old. You just might see mule deer grazing or bighorn sheep foraging. The views of Pikes Peak are breathtaking and once on top, you'll have 30-40 minutes to see skyscrapers in downtown Denver or the Continental Divide (on clear days).

SCHEDULES and FARES
The Manitou & Pikes Peak Cog Railway runs from early April to late October. Pets are not allowed. Adult fares are generally under $35.00. Please call or check website for current schedules and fares.

EQUIPMENT
Our rolling stock includes 4 Swiss railcars powered by Cummins Diesel Engines.

CONTACT
Manitou & Pikes Peak Cog Railway
515 Ruxton Avenue
Manitou Springs, CO 80829
719-685-5401
719-685-9033 (fax)
info@CogRailway.com
www.cograilway.com

Photos: Manitou & Pikes Peak Railway

PIKES PEAK HISTORICAL STREET RAILWAY FOUNDATION/
COLORADO SPRINGS & INTERURBAN RAILWAY
Colorado Springs, CO

The Pikes Peak Historical Street Railway Foundation, a nonprofit organization, was formed in 1982 to restore and operate electric trolleys in Colorado Springs and Manitou Springs. In 1990, an original Colorado Springs streetcar, built in 1901, was donated to the foundation.

In 1995, the foundation learned of the availability of a number of post-World War II President's Conference Committee (PCC) cars from Philadelphia. With the acquisition, the foundation has linked the three historic districts in the area. Today visitors can watch the restoration in progress, view equipment in the storage yard, and ride one of the restored trolleys on museum grounds.

SCHEDULES and FARES
Guided tours can be scheduled on Tuesdays through Fridays. Please call or check website for current schedules and fares.

EQUIPMENT
17 Interurban cars dating back to 1901

CONTACT
Pikes Peak Historical Street Railway
Foundation
P.O. Box 544
Colorado Springs, CO 80901
719-475-9508
719-475-2814 (fax)
cstrolley@juno.com
www.coloradospringstrolleys.com

Photos: Pikes Peak Historical Street Railway Foundation

PUEBLO RAILWAY MUSEUM
Pueblo, CO

Volunteers at the Pueblo Railway Museum want to make history come alive by displaying and operating rail equipment. It is a train watchers' paradise, with more than 25 trains passing alongside the museum yard daily. The museum offers train rides on special occasions.

Historically, Pueblo has always played a major role in railroading. All rail manufactured in the western U.S. still originates in Pueblo, just as it has done since 1881. Pueblo is also home to the exclusive railroad-testing facility for North America and one of few in the world. All new locomotives and rolling stock, some from abroad, are tested here for performance and safety. The facility is owned by the U.S. Department of Transportation and operated by a private company. It is home to the massive AT&SF No. 2912, the largest steam locomotive of its type built, and three operating GP-7 diesel locomotives.

SCHEDULES and FARES
The museum is open all year, Tuesday through Saturday. There is no entrance fee, but donations are welcome. Please call or check website for current schedules and fares.

EQUIPMENT
ATSF No. 2912, Baldwin 1944
Colorado and Wyoming GP-7s Nos. 102, 103, and 104, built in 1952
Trolley No. 1245
Express mail/boxcar No. 2649, Great Northern, built in 1946
Crane, diesel, U.S. Army No. 289, 1951
Amtrack No. 5410 coach, 1946
Dining car - BNSF No. 95, 1868
Kitchen car - BNSF No. 95, 1864
Tool car - BNSF No. 95, 1859
C&W No. 100
C&S No. 10538, 1969
Missouri Pacific (MP) No. 1234
D&RGW No. 1432
C&W No. 03
D&RGW boxcars Nos. 67508, 67996, built in 1946
D&RGW boxcar, narrow gauge, wood car 36', ca. 1900

CONTACT
Pueblo Railway Museum
200 West B Street
Pueblo, CO 81003-3483,
719-251-5024 (tour information)
719-544-1773 (office)
Info@Pueblorailway.org
www.pueblorailway.org

Photos: Pueblo Railway Museum

ROYAL GORGE ROUTE
Canon City, CO

Travel is an event upon the Royal Gorge Route Railroad, Colorado's first and most scenic full-service streamliner. This is a grand train on an epic adventure along the tumbling waters of the legendary Arkansas River deep within the granite cliffs of the Royal Gorge. Classes of service hark back to a time when travel was an elegant and leisurely affair, which has earned the train its reputation as the premier excursion railroad in the country.

Choose from multi-course chef-prepared meals, wine tastings or murder mystery dinners in the meticulously restored dining or observation dome rail cars or travel in classic coach style and visit the well-outfitted concession and lounge cars for any number of goodies.

The Royal Gorge Route Railroads 1950's era streamlined, air-conditioned locomotives ferry more than 100,000 passengers each year for a 24-mile round trip up the rails through the dramatic Royal Gorge and below the famous Hanging Bridge, soaring bald eagles and blue herons. If you're lucky, you might even spot a big horn sheep.

The Railroad is located 45 minutes southwest of Colorado Springs and just under 2 hours southwest of Denver.

SCHEDULES AND FARES
The Royal Gorge Route Railroad runs from late May to early October, with limited scheduling from November through April. You may choose from parlor class, vista dome, lunch, dinner, murder mystery, or winemaker's dinner trains. Reservations are recommended. Please call or check website for current schedules and fares.

CONTACT
Royal Gorge Route Railroad
401 Water Street
Canon City, CO 81212
1-888-RAILS-4U
719-276-4000
719-269-8907 (fax)
www.royalgorgeroute.com
www.royalgorgereservations.com

Photos: Royal Gorge Route Railroad

RIO GRANDE SCENIC RAILROAD
Alamosa, CO

The Rio Grande Scenic Railroad is located in historic Alamosa, Colorado a town is that was literally built in a day to service the coming railroad. Legend has that the men who worked the new rail line had breakfast in old Garland City that morning, and were later served dinner in the very same building that evening - in Alamosa.

The Rio Grande Scenic Railroad is a great way to see the grandeur of Colorado. The San Luis Express crosses La Veta Pass - a legendary pass in railroading circles that marks the highest point at which any standard gauge rail line crosses the Rockies in Colorado. the Rio Grande Scenic Railroad also gives visitors the opportunity to extend their trip by connecting with the Cumbres & Toltec Scenic Railroad in Antonito.

The Rio Grande Scenic Railroad shares a depot with the San Luis & Rio Grande Railroad (freight), and is close to city parks, hotels, restuarants, pubs, cafes, and other attractions. Passengers can enjoy shopping and dining in Alamosa after de-boarding the train.

SCHEDULES and FARES
The railroad runs daily with both steam and diesel locomotives. There are special excursion trains throughout the year, including the *Moonlight in the Mountains, Cinco de Mayo,* and *Firecracker Express* trains. Please call or check website for current schedules and fares.

EQUIPMENT
SP-1744, 2-6-0 Mogul steam locomotive, built in 1901
LS&I, 2-8-0 Consolidation steam locomotive, built in 1910
SLRG-8577, General Electric B-39-8E diesel locomotive
Dome, open-window, and air conditioned cars
Parlor car

CONTACT
Rio Grande Scenic Railroad
601 State Street
Alamosa, CO 81101
877-726-RAIL
info@riograndescenicrailroad.com
www.riograndescenicrailroad.com

CONNECTICUT

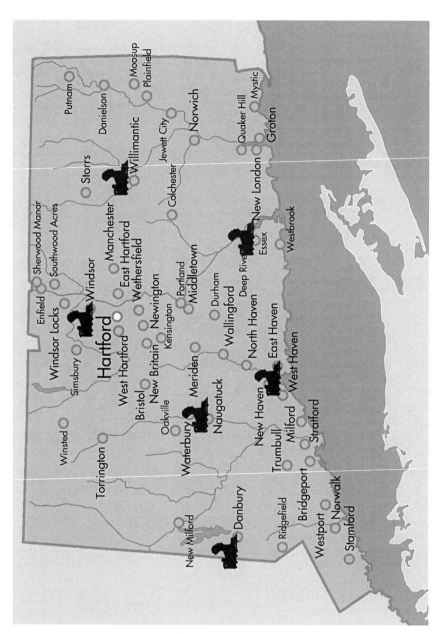

CONNECTICUT EASTERN RAILROAD MUSEUM
Willimantic, CT

The Connecticut Eastern Railroad Museum is located within the Town of Willimantic, CT. Here you will find the reconstructed railroad village of Columbia Junction. Within this village is the six stall Columbia Junction Roundhouse along with a Boston bridge Works 60' Armstrong Turntable. Phase one of the roundhouse reconstruction is now complete and on-going interior reconstruction is continuing. The original Chaplin Station built in 1872 was moved to the village in 1991 and is fully restored. The Groton Freight House once stood next to the mainline opposite the Groton Tower in Groton, CT.

Dismantled in February 1998, it was brought to the museum. A new roof was added before the building was moved to its current location near the turntable in late 1999, is has been fully restored. The New haven Railroad Section House sat abandoned in the Willimantic freight yard for years. In need of serious repairs, it was moved to the museum in 1992 and has been fully restored. Built in the 1920's, the Versailles Operator's Shanty was constructed

for the New York, New Haven & Hartford Railroad. Its original use was a telegrapher's shanty and later became a Block Operator's Shanty. It was moved in derelict condition to the museum in 2000. It has been fully restored and is used as the museum's ticket booth.

SCHEDULES AND FARES:
The Connecticut Eastern Railroad Museum is open to the public from May to the end of October each year. We are also open on certain holidays that fall during the above months. Admission is as follows: Adults - $5.00, 8-12 Years - $1.00, under 8 Years – FREE

EQUIPMENT:
Locomotive Rolling Stock:
New Haven Railroad 1750 HP Dual-mode FL9 – #2023
Central Vermont Alco S4 1000 HP Diesel Switcher – #8081
Northeast Utilities General Electric 25 Ton Locomotive –
Long Island Railroad #400, Connecticut Eastern Railroad Museum #400 44 Ton Locomotive
Pfizer SW8 900 HP Diesel-Electric Switcher
New Haven Terminal General Electric 45 Ton Diesel-Electric Locomotive
Baldwin Oil Fired 0-4-0T Steam Engine #10

Freight and Passenger Rolling Stock:
Maine Central Railroad #10 Railbus
Trackmobile Model 95TM Car Mover
NY, NH & H Railroad Baggage Car #3841
(2) NY, NH & H 8600 Series Coaches
NY, NH & Hartford Steel Caboose C-618
NY, NH & H Crane Hook Carrier Car #F-213
Central Vermont End Cupola Caboose #4029
Central Vermont Center Cupola Caboose Number 4052
Central Vermont Wooden Box Car #43022
Central Vermont 40' Wooden Flat car #4287
Grand Trunk Western Box Car #515747
RMC McWilliams Spot Tamper Model F
CERM Lever Pump Car #94
Budd SPV 2000 Metro-North Commuter RR #293 Self propelled Vehicle
Yankee Silver Smith Dining Car #104
1972 Dodge Penn Central Flat Bed, Boom Crane Truck
Gradall Boom Excavator

CONTACT:
Connecticut Eastern Railroad Museum
55 Bridge St, Willimantic, CT 06757
860-456-9999
www.cteastrrmuseum.org
info@cteastrrmuseum.org

CONNECTICUT TROLLEY MUSEUM
East Windsor, CT

Founded in October 1940, the Connecticut Electric Railway Association, Inc., is the owner and operator of the Connecticut Trolley Museum and is the nation's oldest incorporated organization dedicated to the preservation of the trolley era.

The association owns more than 70 pieces of rolling stock, dating to 1869, approximately half is housed in five storage barns. The museum is located on a 17-acre facility, and the right of way is a 3.2-mile portion of the original Rockville branch of the Hartford and Springfield Street Railway Company. A three-mile, 20-minute round-trip streetcar ride through the Connecticut countryside with an educational narrative is provided to the museum's visitors during their visit. Museum visitors can visit the Connecticut Fire Museum at no additional charge.

SCHEDULES and FARES
The Connecticut Trolley Museum is open March through December. Please call or check website for current schedules and fares.

EQUIPMENT
70 pieces of rail equipment, dating to 1869. Many have been restored and are in operation. Early-20th-century electric engines are run during special events.

CONTACT
Connecticut Trolley Museum
58 North Road (Route 140)
East Windsor, CT 06088-0360
860-627-6540
860-627-6510 (fax)
www.ct-trolley.org

Photos: Alfred J. Gruhler, Frank Rossano

DANBURY RAILROAD MUSEUM
Danbury, CT

The Danbury Railway Museum is located in the historic station and rail yard in Danbury, Connecticut. The museum features over 50 pieces of equipment representing almost a dozen northeastern railroads. There are many one-of-a-kind pieces, including the New Haven RR Mack FCD rail bus and a fully operating turntable.

Along with railroad history, your visit includes a guided tour of the rail yard and equipment as well as exhibits and operating layouts in the station.

SCHEDULES and FARES

The Danbury Railway Museum is open year-round. For an additional fee you can ride the train in the rail yard. Special events are also available. Please call or check website for current schedules and fares.

EQUIPMENT

12 locomotives
3 self-propelled passenger vehicles
6 cabooses
11 passenger equipment
22 freight cars

CONTACT

Danbury Railway Museum
120 White Street
Danbury, CT 06813-0090
203-778-8337
203-778-1836 (fax)
www.danbury.org/drm

Photos: Danbury Railway Museum

ESSEX STEAM TRAIN & RIVERBOAT
Essex, CT

Sit back, relax, and take in all the sights on a 2.5-hour excursion aboard the Essex Steam Train & Riverboat, one of Connecticut's most popular attractions.

Named by the Nature Conservancy as "one of the last great places on earth," the scenic Connecticut River Valley is a favorite recreation area for residents and tourists alike. The 1920s steam locomotive and authentically restored vintage coaches travel north from historic Essex Station along the west bank of the river to Deep River Landing, where passengers transfer to the multi-decked riverboat.

The one-hour cruise up the unspoiled Connecticut River passes many interesting sites, including Goodspeed Opera House, the unusual swing bridge in Haddam, and the famous Gillette Castle. The boat returns to Deep River Landing, and the train makes the return trip to Essex.

Learn about local history and folklore and discover Connecticut's flora and fauna as the narrated train and boat ride take you through the picturesque countryside. On your train ride choose either an up-close view of our land and riverscape in the open car, or sit back and relax in the plush parlor car. Refreshments are available in the train's parlor car and on the boat.

Ride and Dine In old-fashioned elegance alongside Connecticut's scenic river aboard the Essex Clipper Dinner Train, Connecticut's only dinner train. This excursion lasts about two hours.

Essex Station includes a working railroad yard with antique locomotives and cars, a gift shop, and a snack bar. Both the Essex and the Deep River stations are listed on the National Register of Historic Places.

SCHEDULES and FARES
The Essex Steam Trains run from May to October generally Wednesday through Sunday. Please call or check website for current schedules and fares.

EQUIPMENT
6 locomotives
12 coaches
8 others

CONTACT
The Valley Railroad Company
One Railroad Avenue
Essex, CT 06426
800-ESS-EXTRAIN
860-767-0103
860-767-2021 (engine house)
860-767-0104 (fax)
valley.railroad@snet.net
www.essexsteamtrain.com

Photos: Essex Steam Train & Riverboat

NAUGATUCK RAILROAD
Thomaston, CT

The Railroad Museum of New England established its railroad-operating subsidiary, the Naugatuck Railroad Company, in the late 1980s to operate 19.5 miles of track from Waterbury.

You begin your 20-mile round-trip journey at the 1881 Thomaston Station and follow the scenic Naugatuck River south to Waterville.

Along the way, you'll enjoy the beauty of the unspoiled Mattatuck Forest and the Black Rock cliffs; you will also pass among massive brass mills, sentinels of New England's rich industrial heritage. As you head back to the north, you'll cross the face of the spectacular Thomaston Dam, high above the spillway and river valley below, a true trip highlight!

SCHEDULES and FARES
Trains start running on Memorial Day weekend. A variety of themed train rides are scheduled throughout the year. Please call or check website for current schedules and fares.

EQUIPMENT
New Haven RS-3 No. 529
New Haven U25B No. 2525
Naugatuck GP-9 No. 1732
Canadian open-window heavyweight coaches from the 1920s
The Railroad Museum of New England has an extensive collection of rolling stock, some of which is on display at the Thomaston Depot.

CONTACT
Naugatuck Railroad
East Main Street
P.O. Box 400
Thomaston, CT 06787-0400
860-283-RAIL
www.rmne.org

Photos: Naugatuck Railroad

SHORE LINE TROLLEY MUSEUM
East Haven, CT

The Shore Line Trolley Museum incorporated in 1945 as the Branford Electric Railway Association. Founded to preserve the unique heritage of the trolley car, the museum has a collection of close to 100 vintage vehicles. The museum credits its volunteers with creating a multi-sensory voyage into the past, from the mournful growl of the motors, to the smell of the electric arc, to the feel of rattan seats and varnished hardwood detailing.

The Shore Line Trolley Museum operates the Branford Electric Railway, a National Historic Site. The railway is the oldest continuously operating suburban trolley line in the United States. Your ride will take you on a three-mile loop that includes views of wooded areas, marshes and shoreline.

SCHEDULES and FARES
The Shore Line Trolley operates on select weekends throughout the year. It runs daily from June to August. Your fare is good on all streetcars for the entire day. Please call or check website for current schedules and fares.

EQUIPMENT
The Shore Line Trolley Museum maintains several collections which preserve the history and heritage of the Trolley Era. The museum owns nearly 100 vintage transit vehicles. Five of those cars carry passengers on the excursion.

CONTACT
Shore Line Trolley Museum
17 River Street
East Haven, CT 06512
203-467-6927
www.bera.org

Photos: Shore Line Trolley

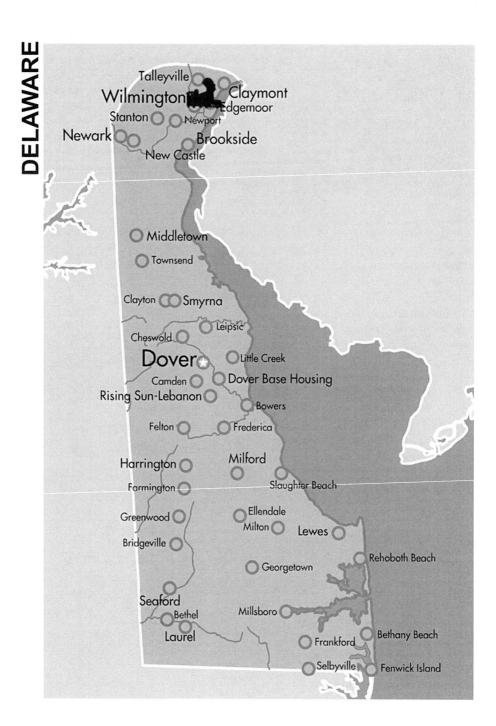

DELAWARE

Talleyville
Wilmington Claymont
            Edgemoor
Stanton Newport
Newark
            Brookside
     New Castle

Middletown

Townsend

Clayton Smyrna

Cheswold Leipsic

Dover Little Creek

Camden Dover Base Housing
Rising Sun-Lebanon
            Bowers
Felton Frederica

Harrington Milford

Farmington Slaughter Beach

Greenwood Ellendale
            Milton Lewes
Bridgeville
            Rehoboth Beach
         Georgetown

Seaford
     Bethel Millsboro
     Laurel   Bethany Beach
            Frankford
               Selbyville Fenwick Island

WILMINGTON & WESTERN STEAM TOURIST RAILROAD
Wilmington, DE

Once operated by the B&O Railroad, the Wilmington & Western Steam Tourist Railroad is the oldest continuously operating short-line railroad in Delaware. It has served the Red Clay Creek Valley since 1872 by carrying passengers, mail, and freight. The Wilmington & Western Railroad is currently owned and operated by Historic Red Clay Valley, Inc. (HRCV), a local nonprofit organization. This all-volunteer railroad, listed on the National Register of Historic Places, travels 10.2 miles, beginning from Greenbank, Delaware, to its current terminus of Hockessin, Delaware. Your ride is designed to take you back to a simpler time when water-powered mills dotted the landscape.

SCHEDULES and FARES
The Wilmington & Western Steam Tourist Railroad makes hour-long excursion runs from April through December on Saturdays and Sundays. Please call or check website for current schedules and fares.

EQUIPMENT
No. 58 Atlanta, Birmingham & Atlantic 1907 Baldwin 0-6-0
No. 98 Alco steam 4-4-0, American Locomotive, 1909 (currently under restoration, completion date: Spring 2003)
No. 92, 1910 Canadian National Locomotive Co. 2-6-0
Nos. 114 & 8408, SW-1 EMD switchers
1929 PRR railcar (Doodlebug)

CONTACT
Greenbank Station
2201 Newport Gap Pike, Route 41 North
Wilmington, DE 19808
302-998-1930
302-998-7408 (fax)
schedule@wwrr.com
www.wwrr.com

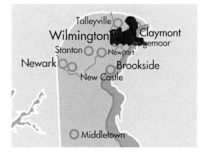

Photos: Wilmington & Western Railroad

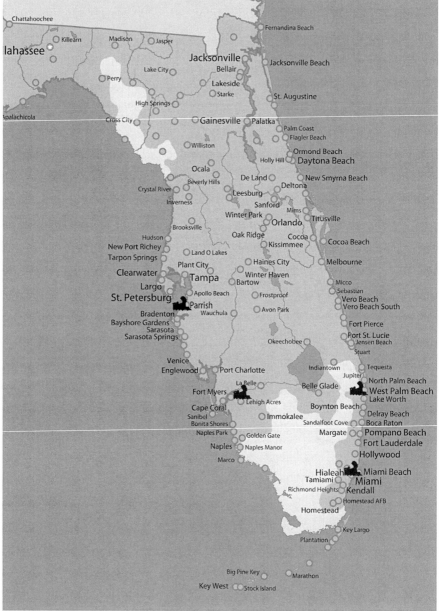

FLAGLER MUSEUM
Palm Beach, FL

Henry Flagler founded Standard Oil in 1870 with John D. Rockefeller and Samuel Adams. In his 50s, Flagler became interested in Florida. He bought what would eventually become the Florida East Coast Railway Company. Before Flagler bought the organization, the railroad stretched only between South Jacksonville and St. Augustine and lacked a depot sufficient to accommodate travelers to his St. Augustine resorts. Flagler built a modern depot facility as well as schools, hospitals and churches. Before he died, his Florida East Coast Railway linked the entire east coast from Jacksonville to Key West. A true standout at the Museum is Flagler's private railcar. It looks like a Gilded Age railway palace and is housed in the new Flagler Kenan Pavilion

SCHEDULES and FARES
The Flagler Museum is open on Tuesdays through Sundays, year-round. It is closed on Thanksgiving, Christmas, and New Year's Day. Admission for adults is under $20. Please call or check website for current schedules and fares.

CONTACT
Flagler Museum
One Whitehall Way
Palm Beach, FL
561-655-2833
561-655-2826 (fax)
flagler@paradista.net
www.flaglermuseum.us

FLORIDA GULF COAST RAILROAD MUSEUM, INC.
Parrish, FL

The Florida Gulf Coast Railroad Museum, Inc. was founded in 1981 to acquire, protect, preserve and operate interesting and historic examples of railroad equipment, artifacts and other aspects of railroad history, with an emphasis on those that served Florida.

A trip to the museum (which bills itself as "the museum where you ride the exhibits!") includes a 13-mile trip on diesel-powered excursion trains with open-air coaches, an air-conditioned coach, lounge cars, and cabooses. There is even an opportunity for you to be in charge as part of the rent-a-locomotive program.

SCHEDULES and FARES
The museum currently operates diesel-powered trips every weekend, year-round. Trains depart from their station on 83rd Street East in Parrish, behind the Post Office. Special weekend events are planned year-round. Adult fares are generally around $10. Please call or check website for current schedules and fares.

EQUIPMENT
US Army GP7s, Nos. 1822 and 1835
Southern Railway Baggage mail car 142
Pennsylvia RR 804 Alco RS3
FGC 100, GE 44-ton diesel-electric
Sleeper/lounge car, Cape Tormentine
Coaches Nos. 3518 and 3572 DL&W MU cars
Louisville & Nashville tavern lounge, "Kentucky Club"

CONTACT
Florida Gulf Coast Railroad Museum, Inc.
P.O. Box 355
Parrish, FL 34219
877-869-0800
941-776-0906 (fax)
TRAININFO@fgcrrm.org
www.fgcrrm.org

Photos: Florida Gulf Coast Railroad Museum

Did You Know...

An eight car passenger train traveling at 100 km/h requires about 1,070 meters to stop. When traveling at 130 km/h, a stopping distance of about 1,825 meters is required.

THE GOLD COAST RAILROAD MUSEUM
Miami, FL

The Gold Coast Railroad Museum was formed in 1957, in an effort to preserve history. It all began a year earlier, when a University of Miami business student convinced his university that the land it was leasing from the Naval Air Station Richmond would be best used as a learning facility for future engineers. Three miles of track made it the perfect location for an operating steam engine.

Two of the earliest pieces added to the collection were the "Ferdinand Magellan," the private railroad car built for President Franklin Roosevelt, and the Florida East Coast Railway locomotive No. 153, the engine that pulled the rescue train out of Marathon, Florida after the 1935 hurricane.

SCHEDULES and FARES
The museum is open year-round except for scheduled maintenance. Train rides (link trains, standard gauge, and cabs) are offered on the weekend for an additional fee. Please call or check website for current schedules and fares.

EQUIPMENT
The Gold Coast Railroad has more than 30 pieces of rolling stock including:
Florida East Coast Railway (FEC) Steam Locomotive No. 153
Florida East Coast Railway (FEC) Steam Locomotive No. 113
Steam engine No. 9, "saddle tank" engine
Crown locomotive 24"-gauge 4-4-0 No. 3

CONTACT
The Gold Coast Railroad, Inc.
12450 S.W. 152nd Street
Miami, FL 33177
888-60-TRAIN
305-253-0063
305-233-4641 (fax)
webmaster@goldcoast-railroad.org
www.goldcoast-railroad.org

Photos: Gold Coast Railroad Museum

SEMINOLE GULF RAILWAY
Ft. Myers, FL

Since 1987, the Seminole Gulf Railway has been the premier provider of integrated freight transportation and logistics in southwest Florida. Still, it is probably best known today as the home of the Murder Mystery Dinner Train. This 3.5-hour journey takes you north toward Punta Gorda, crossing the Caloosahatchee on a 1-mile trestle and bridge that also crosses the intercoastal waterway. Your five course meal is prepared on board in the railcar kitchen.

If shorter rides are more to your liking, you can opt for an excursion ride. This daytime trip north through Fort Myers takes you across the same 1-mile Caloosahatchee trestle and bridge system spanning the intercoastal waterway, to Bayshore, with views visible only by rail.

SCHEDULES and FARES

The excursion train runs from December through August. The ride is not offered on Christmas Day, New Year's Day, Easter Sunday, Mother's Day, Father's Day, Memorial Day, July 4th, Labor Day, or Thanksgiving. The dinner train departs Wednesdays through Saturdays year-round. Please call or check website for current schedules and fares.

EQUIPMENT

Diesel-electric locomotives built between 1956 and 1958
"Marco," stainless steel combined kitchen and dining car, built by Budd in 1949
"Sanibel," built in 1937 as a Canadian long-distance coach, now a dining car
"Gasparilla," built by Pullman in 1949, originally for use as a sleeper car.
"Captiva," built in 1937 as a Canadian long-distance coach

CONTACT

Seminole Gulf Railway
4410 Centerpoint Drive, Suite 207
Ft. Myers, FL 33916
800-SEM-GULF
239-275-8487
Carl@semgulf.com
www.semgulf.com

Photos: Seminole Gulf Railway

Did You Know...

An approaching train activates flashing light signals and gates approximately 20 seconds before the train reaches the crossing.

SOUTHWEST FLORIDA MUSEUM OF HISTORY
Ft. Myers, FL

Housed in the former Atlantic Coastline Railroad Depot, the museum is home to the history of Southwest Florida. Land of Giants Paleo-Florida is the newest exhibit, exposing the visitor to 50-foot sharks and the giant land mammals of the Ice Age. Calusa Indians, Seminole Indians, Spanish explorers, and early settlers are just a few of the people you will meet as you view our exhibits. A recovered P-39 fighter plane, a pioneer "cracker" house, a 1926 La France fire pumper, and a 1929 private Pullman railcar are also part of the tour. The museum displays various fascinating traveling exhibits throughout the year.

SCHEDULES and FARES
The museum is open on Tuesdays through Saturdays and is closed on most holidays. Admission for adults is under $10. Please call or check website for current schedules and fares.

EQUIPMENT
No. 6242 Pullman Standard Car & Manufacturing Co. "Esperanza", 1929/30

CONTACT
Southwest Florida Museum of History
2300 Peck Street
Fort Myers, FL 33901
239-332-5955
239-332-6637 (fax)
museuminfo@cityfotmyers.com
www.cityftmyers.com/museums/

Photos: Southwest Florida Museum of History

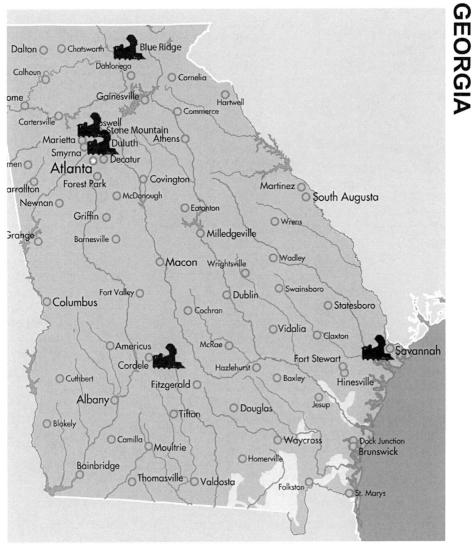

Dalton ○   ○ Chatsworth   Blue Ridge

Calhoun   Dahlonega
                        ○   ○ Cornelia

ome   Gainesville
                                        Hartwell
                                    ○ Commerce

Cartersville   swell
                        Stone Mountain
    Marietta   Duluth   Athens ○
    Smyrna
men ○   Atlanta   Decatur

arrollton   Forest Park   Covington
    Newnan ○   ○ McDonough   Martinez ○
                                            ○ South Augusta
        Griffin ○   ○ Eatonton
                                        ○ Wrens
Grange
        Barnesville ○   ○ Milledgeville

                    ○ Macon   Wrightsville   ○ Wadley
                                    ○
    Fort Valley ○   ○ Swainsboro
○ Columbus   ○ Dublin
                    ○ Cochran   ○ Statesboro

                                ○ Vidalia
                                        Claxton
    ○ Americus   McRae ○
    Cordele   Fort Stewart   Savannah
    ○ Cuthbert   Hazlehurst ○
            Fitzgerald ○   ○ Baxley   Hinesville
    Albany ○
                ○ Tifton   ○ Douglas   Jesup
    ○ Blakely

        ○ Camilla   ○ Waycross   Dock Junction
                Moultrie   Brunswick
    Bainbridge   ○ Homerville
            ○ Thomasville ○ Valdosta
                                Folkston   St. Marys

BLUE RIDGE SCENIC RAILWAY
Blue Ridge, GA

Nestled in the mountains of Georgia's Chattahoochee National Forest, historic Blue Ridge, called the "antique capital" of northwest Georgia, awaits you with a visit to the past on the Blue Ridge Scenic Railway.

The railroad's route was originally built as the narrow gauge Marietta & North Georgia Railroad. Construction began in Marietta in 1877 and reached Blue Ridge in 1886. The route consists of a 26-mile round trip on 100-year-old track through historic Murphy Junction along the beautiful Toccoa River. You begin at the depot in Blue Ridge, a depot built in 1905 and now on the National Register of Historic Places. Enjoy the lush and unspoiled mountain scenery as you head to McCaysville, Georgia, where you stop to stretch your legs and explore the community, along with nearby Copperhill, Tennessee. Then it's back on board to Blue Ridge, a total 3.5-hour journey.

The more adventurous can take a trip on the Ocoee Rail Adventure, offered by

the Blue Ridge Scenic Railway and Rolling Thunder River Company. You board the train at Blue Ridge and are met by Rolling Thunder representatives at the McCaysville platform. Then you're treated to a wild adventure on the Ocoee River or a more leisurely tubing trip down the Toccoa. At the end of your river trip, you're transported back to your vehicle at Blue Ridge.

SCHEDULES and FARES
Blue Ridge Scenic Railway is open from May to November. The Christmas Train is one of the excursion highlights of the year. Fares vary, depending on excursion but are generally under $36. Please call or check website for current schedules and fares.

EQUIPMENT

No. 8704, Model GP18, 1750 HP, built 1960
No. 7562, Model GP10, 1850 HP, built 1979.
Nos. 2929 and 697, open-air cars
Nos. 105, 106, 2705, 549, 206, 332, 150, and 2975, vintage coaches from the
1930s and 1940s

CONTACT

Blue Ridge Scenic Railway
241 Depot Street
Blue Ridge, GA 30513
800-934-1898
706-632-9833
info@brscenic.com
www.brscenic.com

Photos: Blue Ridge Scenic Railway

VISA MasterCard DISCOVER

ROUNDHOUSE RAILROAD MUSEUM
Savannah, GA

The Roundhouse Railroad Museum is part of
Savannah's Central of Georgia Railway National
Landmark District, the oldest and most complete
antebellum railroad manufacturing and repair facility
still in existence in the United States. The Central of
Georgia Railway began construction on the site in
1845, and today 13 of the original structures are still
standing, including the 125-foot smokestack and the
roundhouse with its operating turntable.

The Roundhouse Railroad Museum is evidence of the
city of Savannah's
goal to interpret the
history of the railroads in Georgia and their
influence on the growth of the state. It now has
exhibits in several of the structures on site,
including steam engines, locomotives, and
railroad rolling stock.

SCHEDULES and FARES

The Roundhouse Railroad Museum is open year-round. It is closed Thanksgiving, Christmas Day, and New Year's Day. Group tours and private use of the facility are available. Special events include Blues and Barbecue in April and a Labor Day celebration. Admission for adults is generally under $5. Please call or check website for current schedules and fares.

EQUIPMENT

No. 223, Wrightsville & Tennille, built in 1907
"Old Maude," 1886
Georgia Power "goat," the only operating steam locomotive at the museum
Melbourne Tramways type W5 car No. 756

CONTACT

Roundhouse Railroad Museum
601 West Harris Street
Savannah, GA 31401
912-651-6823
912-651-3194 (fax)
www.chsgeorgia.org

Photos: Roundhouse Railroad Museum

SAM SHORTLINE EXCURSION TRAIN
Cordele, GA

The name "SAM Shortline" comes from the original railroad's name: the Savannah, Americus and Montgomery, and from the name of the line's founder and president, Colonel Samuel Hugh Hawkins, a prominent 19th-century Sumter County capitalist.

The SAM Shortline was one of the railroads that emerged after the Civil War. Today it brings tourists to southwest Georgia to relive history. One of your stops might be the Georgia Veterans State Park, one of Georgia's most-visited state parks. You may even spot a former President, because SAM rolls through Jimmy Carter's hometown of Plains. The train runs from Cordele west to Archery. There are six rail depots with historic destinations along the way.

SCHEDULES and FARES

The SAM Shortline runs all year, rain or shine. For safety reasons you must wear closed-toe shoes or sandals with back straps. Rain gear is always a good idea on this ride. Reservations can be made on-line or by calling. Please call or check website for current schedules and fares.

EQUIPMENT

HOG's locomotives, primarily No. 1209 and No. 1309, modified EMD GP-9's Passenger cars Norfolk and Western and Pennsylvania Railroad heritage. Samuel H. Hawkins tavern-observation car No. 1508, Budd, 1939.

CONTACT

SAM Shortline Excursion Train
105 East 9th Avenue
Cordele, Ga 31010
229-276-0755
877-GA-RAILS (toll free)
229-276-0816 (fax)
www.samshortline.com

Photos: SAM Shortline Excursion Train

Did You Know...

The average locomotive weighs 110 tons, and the average loaded boxcar weighs 70 tons.

SOUTHEASTERN RAILWAY MUSEUM
Duluth, GA

For more than 32 years, the Southeastern Railway Museum has provided visitors with "hands-on" living-history lessons about the railroad. More than 90 pieces of rolling stock, including Pullman cars and classic steam locomotives, await the inspection and enjoyment of young and old alike.

Ride in restored cabooses behind either steam (during summer and fall) or diesel locomotives on the museum's onsite track. Stand next to the massive driving wheels of the locomotive that once pulled passenger trains to Key West, Florida, on the "railroad that went to the sea." Tour the business car that helped bring the Olympics to Atlanta. Pose on the platform of the private car once used by President Warren G. Harding. All this and much more.

SCHEDULES and FARES

The Southeastern Railway Museum is open on Thursdays, Fridays, and Saturdays. Various special events are scheduled throughout the year. Admission for adults is under $10. Please call or check website for current schedules and fares.

EQUIPMENT
Over 90 pieces on display, including diesel locomotives, steam locomotives/tenders, passenger and private cars, RPO/baggage cars, freight cars, cabooses, and maintenance-of-way equipment

CONTACT
Southeastern Railway Museum
3595 Peachtree Road
Duluth, GA 30096
770-476-2013
770-926-6095
admin@srmduluth.org
www.srmduluth.org

Photos: Southeastern Railway Museum

STONE MOUNTAIN SCENIC RAILROAD
Stone Mountain, GA

Enjoy the beauty and grandeur of the world's largest mass of exposed granite from the comfort of open-air train cars when you climb aboard the Stone Mountain Scenic Railroad. Located in Stone Mountain Park, this railroad gives riders the chance to get a breathtaking perspective of this truly majestic natural wonder, located just 16 miles east of Atlanta. This 3,200-acre park is considered the "Eighth Wonder of the World," because it boasts the world's largest high-relief carving (depicting three heroes of the American confederacy)--a true marvel of western engineering!

You depart from a scale replica of the main train depot from late 19th-century downtown Atlanta. The depot is located in the area called Crossroads. Not only can you enjoy the ride, you can also take advantage of a walk-up trail when you stop at Confederate Hall. But watch out! Don't let your guard down as you are enjoying the grandeur and beauty of the mountain; you never know what will happen as you watch the action in the seasonal live train show!

SCHEDULES and FARES
In season, guests can enjoy the 30-minute ride on the scenic railroad by purchasing the park's one-day all-attraction pass, or by purchasing an individual-attraction ticket. Vehicle entry to Stone Mountain Park is $8 cash. Although Stone Mountain Park is open year-round, the park offers limited attractions during the off-seasons (January to March) and weekdays from August to December. Please call or check website for current schedules and fares.

CONTACT
Stone Mountain Park
Highway 78 East
Stone Mountain, GA 30087
800-317-2006
770-498-5690
www.stonemountainpark.com

Photos: Stone Mountain

HAWAII

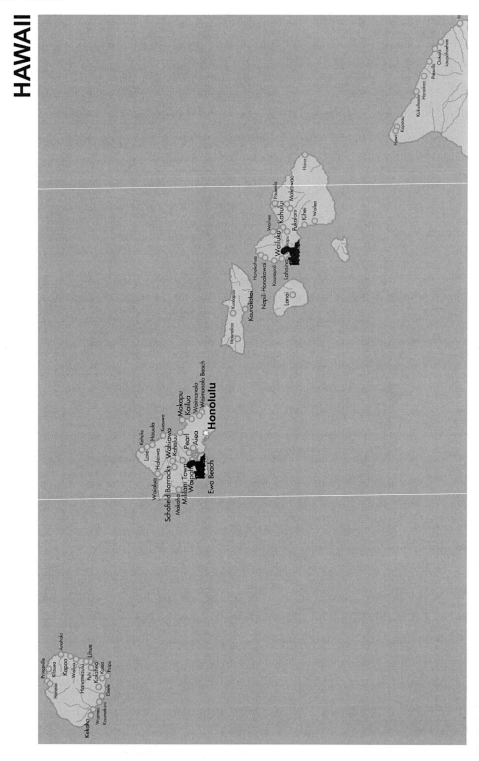

HAWAIIAN RAILWAY SOCIETY
Ewa, HI

Step into a page of Hawaii's history when you board a Hawaiian Railway train in old Ewa. The Hawaiian Railway Society was formed over 30 years ago by a group of rail enthusiasts. The society is an educational, nonprofit organization with a twofold mission: first to save, restore, and protect as much of Oahu's old railroad equipment as possible; second, to keep this page of Hawaii's history alive through narrated train rides. The income it derives from train fares and gift shop sales goes toward maintaining and extending the track, restoring vintage railroad equipment, and expanding the operation. Someday the society hopes to have an authentic replica of a train station, an engine house, and a museum.

On the second Sunday of every month, the restored parlor/observation car is put on the passenger train for the general public. This car was designed and built in Honolulu in 1900 for Benjamin F. Dillingham, the owner of the railroad. The car was restored in 1995. They suggest that you make reservations because there is room for only 14 passengers.

A picnic area is available for passengers to use before or after their ride, or they may take both food and beverages on board. The picnic area is great for holding birthday parties and other special occasions.

SCHEDULES and FARES
Train rides down Hawaii's historical railroad tracks are available year-round. Departures are on Sunday for the 90-minute ride. Adult fares are around $10. Please call or check website for current schedules and fares.

EQUIPMENT
Whitcomb diesel-electric, 1944
Ewa No. 1 Baldwin steam, 1890s
Kauila No. 6, coal, 1889
W.A. Co. No. 6, the only steam locomotive built in the Hawaiian Islands
Parlor/observation car 64, 1900

CONTACT
Hawaiian Railway Society
P.O. Box 60369
Ewa Station
Ewa, HI 96706
808-681-5461
808-681-4860 (fax)
info@hawaiianrailway.com
www.hawaiianrailway.com

Photos: Hawaiian Railway

Did You Know...

Elijah J. McCoy, a brilliant African-American mechanical engineer, invented an automatic lubricator cup (or drip cup) for steam locomotives and other machines. It worked so well that inspectors, when checking in a new piece of machinery, would ask, "Is that the real McCoy?"

Fact by: Steamtown Historic National Site

LAHAINA KAANAPALI RAILROAD (The Sugar Cane Train)
Lahaina, Maui, HI

The Lahaina Kaanapali Railroad welcomes nearly a half-million passengers each year on a scenic and nostalgic journey into Maui's past. The ride on the Sugar Cane Train, which lasts about an hour, runs six miles between the historic whaling town of Lahaina and the Kaanapali Beach Resort. Highlights include Hahakea Trestle, a 325-foot-long bridge rising 35 feet above a stream bed, and views of mountains, and Molokai and Lanai islands. During the winter you just might see a pod of humpback whales off the Kaanapali coast. LKRR's conductors provide entertaining and historical narrations, so you don't miss anything along the way.

One hundred years ago, railroads were used primarily for hauling sugar cane to the mills, and transporting workers between their homes and the cane fields. Today, Hawaii's railroads have disappeared almost entirely. The Sugar Cane Train transports visitors from the Maui of yesteryear to the beauty and charm of Maui today.

SCHEDULES and FARES
The Sugar Cane Train runs year-round. Dinner trains run on Thursdays. Fares range from $19 to $80. Please call or check website for current schedules and fares.

EQUIPMENT
Stars of the LKRR, Anaka and Myrtle are steam locomotives restored to resemble the 1890s engines that once hauled sugar cane to the mill and workers to the cane fields--hence the nickname "Sugar Cane Train."

CONTACT
The Lahaina Kaanapali Railroad
975 Limahana Place, No. 203,
Lahaina, Maui, HI 96761
800-499-2307
808-667-6851
808-661-8389 (fax)
www.mauisteamtrain.com

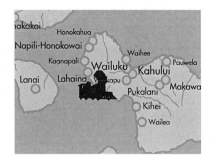

Photos: Lahaina Kaanapali & Pacific Railroad

Did You Know...

Roundhouses were essential to steam railroading. Most steam locomotives required servicing about every 150 to 200 miles when they were new.

Fact by: Steamtown National Historic Site

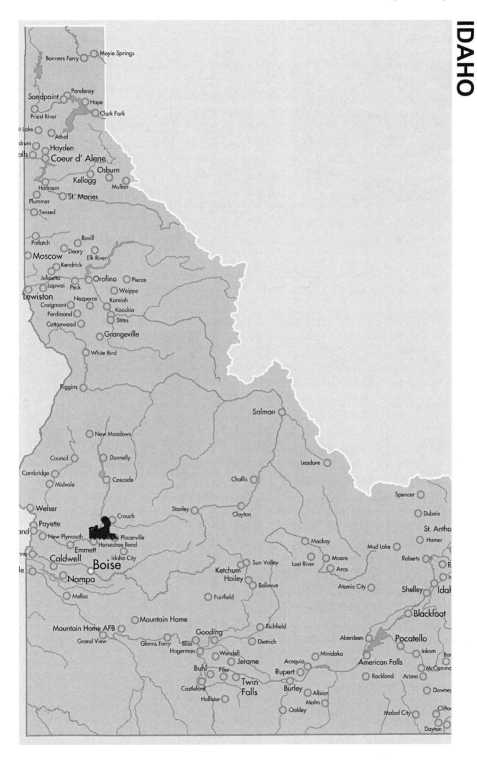

THUNDER MOUNTAIN LINE
Meridian, ID

The Thunder Mountain Line takes you back to the simpler things in life. Your train offers amazing scenery as it winds around a narrow canyon along the beautiful Payette River. Depending on your route, the train will venture through sagebrush-covered hillsides, pristine forests, mountain meadows, and range lands. As you roll out of the station, you will travel along the same mountain trails as the settlers did in the early part of the century. Watch carefully along the route for fox, deer, elk, blue heron, osprey, and bald eagles.

The Thunder Mountain Line offers several different routes throughout the year. Each train ride is a 2.5 to 3 hour mountain railroading experience.

The history of the Thunder Mountain Line dates back more than a century. The railroad was originally intended to serve the Thunder Mountain Mining District, which was full of gold and ore. The Idaho Northern was incorporated on December 18, 1897, by Colonel W. Dewey and presumed later to be in the camp of the Union Pacific.

Small towns and depots were established along the railroad tracks to support the local timber industry. Smaller logging railroads reached into the rich timber valleys and connected with Idaho Northern's main line. The Union Pacific operated this branch line as part of its Oregon Short Line Division until the Idaho Northern and Pacific Railroad purchased the railroad in 1993. Until recently, the railroad had continued to be supported by the timber industry.

SCHEDULES and FARES
The Thunder Mountain Railway runs from April to December, depending on the excursion. The depot is open on Wednesday through Sunday. Fares vary according to excursion. Please call or check website for current schedules and fares.

EQUIPMENT
EMD FP10
1965 GP 35
1955/1956 Pullman passenger cars   3
1955/1956 parlor cars   3
Open-air cars   4

CONTACT
Horseshoe Bend Depot
120 Mill Road
Horseshoe Bend, ID 83629
877-432-7245
208-793-4425
208-887-9663 (fax)
www.thundermountainline.com

Photos: Thunder Mountain Line

Did You Know...

In 2001, the heaviest train in the world was a freight train in Australia. It was 4.6 miles long and weighed 95,000 tons. That is as heavy as 2.8 million ten-year-olds or more than 27,000 elephants.

ILLINOIS

FOX RIVER TROLLEY MUSEUM
South Elgin, IL

The Fox River Trolley Museum offers education through demonstration. Visitors are treated to a nostalgic trip back to an era when the electric trolley car was a vital part of American life. You'll ride an old-time trolley car on a four-mile trip along the banks of the scenic Fox River and the Blackhawk Forest Preserve. The museum operates a variety of antique trolleys, many from lines long vanished, over trackage that once connected Carpentersville, Elgin, Aurora, and Yorkville.

The Fox River Line dates back to 1896. Originally the interurban line was part of the Elgin, Aurora and Southern Traction Company and ran about 40 miles along the Fox River from Carpentersville to Yorkville. Time, money problems and even problems with the Environmental Protection Agency could have spelled the demise of this railway, but a small group of loyal rail fans struggled to keep the memory of the line alive. In 1961 they began what would become the Fox River Trolley Museum.

SCHEDULES and FARES
The Fox River Trolley Museum is open from mid-May to early November. It is open also open on Memorial Day, Independence Day, and Labor Day. Fares are generally under $5 for adults. Please call or check website for current schedules and fares.

EQUIPMENT
Our rolling stock includes more than 25 trolleys from companies including Aurora, Elgin and Fox River Electric Company; Chicago Surface Lines; Chicago; Aurora & Elgin; South Shore Lines; and the Soo Line.

CONTACT
Fox River Trolley Museum
361 South LaFox Street (Illinois Route 31)
South Elgin, IL 60177
847-697-4676
info@foxtrolley.org
www.foxtrolley.org

Photos: Fox River Trolley Museum

ILLINOIS RAILWAY MUSEUM
Union, IL

The Illinois Railway Museum calls itself America's largest railway museum. Volunteers started building it decades ago on a farm. Initially the idea was to preserve just one piece of rolling stock. Now some say it has turned into the ultimate experience for a railroad historian. Its main-line trackage was laid on the vacant right-of-way of the Elgin & Belvidere Electric railway.

At one time in our nation's past, the railroad industry was the largest private employer. Among its employees were various special interest groups devoted to activities such as taking railroad pictures or publishing books on railroads, building railroad models, or just "riding the rails." The Illinois Railway Museum is probably the ultimate railroad historian special-interest group.

Visitors to the museum are welcome to join in the education, restoration and preservation efforts. Only one prerequisite is recommended: a sincere interest in some aspect of railroading.

SCHEDULES and FARES
The Illinois Railway Museum is open from April through October. Your ticket is good for unlimited rides. On some days the museum grounds are open but the trains do not run. Adult fares are generally $10 and under. Please call or check

website for current schedules and fares.

EQUIPMENT
Over the past 49 years, the Illinois Railway Museum has acquired over 375 pieces of equipment.

CONTACT
Illinois Railway Museum
7000 Olsen Road
Union, IL 60180
800-BIG-RAIL
815-923-4000
www.irm.org

Photos: Illinois Railway Museum

MONTICELLO RAILWAY MUSEUM
Monticello, IL

Relive the days of glorious rail travel with a 7-mile round trip ride on former Illinois Central and Illinois Terminal trackage as part of your visit to the Monticello Railway Museum. Passengers can board at the museum site or at the 1899 Wabash Depot in downtown Monticello. Layovers are encouraged at sites, where there are railroad cars to walk through and many pieces of rolling stock to inspect.

One unique piece in the museum's collection is the Nautilus, a fish-transport car used to carry exotic species of marine life from the oceans to the Shedd Aquarium in Chicago, Illinois. There are wooden and steel tanks of many shapes and sizes, many with labels such as "octopus" and "eel." When it was in service, the Nautilus had to be as near the front of the train as possible to lessen the side-to-side movement that might cause the fish to develop motion sickness.

SCHEDULES and FARES

The Monticello Railway Museum is open on weekends and most holidays from May through October. You can leave from either the museum site or the Wabash Depot. Fares are generally under $10 for adults. Please call or check website for current schedules and fares.

EQUIPMENT

The museum features almost 100 pieces of rolling stock.

CONTACT

Monticello Railway Museum
993 Iron Horse Place
Monticello, IL 61856
217-762-9011
mrm@prairienet.org
www.prairienet.org/mrm

Photos: Monticello Railway Museum

Did You Know...

The engineer drives the locomotive using the throttle lever, brakes and reversing gear. He/She is in charge of the locomotive. The conductor, however, is in charge of the train.

Facts by: Steamtown National Historic Site

MUSEUM OF SCIENCE AND INDUSTRY
Chicago, IL

The Pioneer Zephyr is the centerpiece of the museum's permanent exhibit: All Aboard the Silver Streak. Walk through the train, take a guided tour, and learn about the science that made this famous train come to life.

The streamlined Pioneer Zephyr experienced about one-third less drag than did steam engines of the time. Less drag meant higher speeds. Thus, the Zephyr embarked on its famous "Dawn-to-Dusk" run from Denver to Chicago on May 26, 1934. The Zephyr rode 1,015 miles nonstop at an average speed of 77.5 miles per hour, sometimes reaching speeds of 112.5 miles per hour. Thirteen hours and five minutes after leaving Denver, the Zephyr pulled into the Halsted Street Station in Chicago, breaking the record for the longest nonstop run at the fastest average speed.

The museum's exhibit, "The Great Train Story" illustrates how modern railroads operate in the United States. The exhibit highlights four operations of the railroad: grain transport, movement of raw materials, intermodal operations, and passenger transportation. Modeled in HO scale, trains travel between Chicago and Seattle, through the Great Plains and the Rocky Mountains. The exhibit covers more than 3,000 square feet, has thousands of scale miles of track, and features more than 35 model trains.

SCHEDULES and FARES
The museum is open all year except for December 25. Times of operation change throughout the year. Adult admission is under $15. Please call or check website for current schedules and fares.

EQUIPMENT
- Mississippi, the second-oldest locomotive in the United States
- Empire 999, the first machine to break the 100-mph barrier
- York locomotive replica, the first coal-burning locomotive built in the United States
- Stevens locomotive replica, which demonstrated the potential of locomotive travel in the 1820s
- Rocket locomotive, whose design contributed to the evolution of the modern steam locomotive

CONTACT
Museum of Science and Industry
57th Street and Lake Shore Drive
Chicago, IL 60637-2093
773-684-1414
www.msichicago.org

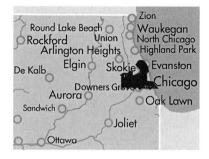

Photos: Museum of Science and Industry

SILVER CREEK & STEPHENSON RAILROAD
Freeport, IL

The Silver Creek & Stephenson Railroad is housed in the Silver Creek Depot, built from the original plans of an Illinois Central depot. This collection includes lanterns, locks and keys, whistles, sounders, tickets, and couplers. The Stephenson County Antique Engine Club bought the four miles of right-of-way adjacent to the depot 20 years ago, when the Chicago, Milwaukee, St Paul & Pacific Railroad went bankrupt. The four-mile trip takes passengers through Illinois farmland, virgin timber, and the "Indian Gardens." You will also travel over a 30-foot cement and stone pier bridge. The train travels on salvaged track laid by members of the Stephenson County Antique Engine Club. Your train may be pulled by the railroad's signature Heisler steam locomotive. It is believed to be one of only three that remain in operation in the world.

SCHEDULES and FARES
The Silver Creek & Stephenson Railroad is open on select holidays and weekends from May through October. Expect to pay under $10 for an adult fare. Please call or check website for current schedules and fares.

EQUIPMENT
Heisler 2, 36-ton, coal-fired, built in 1912
Brookville 5, 14-ton, gasoline/diesel, built in 1945
Plymouth 2303, 23-ton, 60-HP, gasoline, 1938
Wood caboose, built in 1889 (reportedly the oldest in Illinois)
Cupola caboose, built in 1948

CONTACT
Silver Creek & Stephenson Railroad
2945 W. Walnut Road
Freeport, IL 61032
815-232-2306
815-235-2198 (day of operation)
www.thefreeportshow.com

Photos: Silver Creek & Stephension Railroad

Did You Know...

A large hard-working steam locomotive can use up to 6 tons of coal in about an hour. This means a fireman (the one who shovels the coal) might shovel 200 pounds of coal a minute. This is why railroads invented automatic stokers.

Facts by: Steamtown National Historic Site

INDIANA

Michigan City
Hammond   Gary   La Porte   Elkhart   Angola
                              South Bend
                                          Ligonier
Crown Point   Hebron   Plymouth
                        Knox
North Judson   Warsaw
                        Rochester   New Haven
                                              Fort Wayne
     Rensselaer   Huntington
              Logansport   Wabash   Decatur
                        Peru   Berne
     Fowler   Delphi
                        Marion
     Lafayette   Kokomo   Portland

          Frankfort   Elwood
          Noblesville Anderson   Muncie
Crawfordsville   Lebanon
                        Carmel   New Castle
          Speedway   Lawrence
     Rockville   Indianapolis
              Greenwood   Knightstown
     Brazil   Franklin   Shelbyville Connersville
Terre Haute   Edinburgh   Carthage   Brookville
                                  Greensburg
          Bloomington   Columbus
     Sullivan
          Bloomfield   North Vernon
                    Seymour
          Bedford
                        Austin   Madison
Vincennes   Washington
              French Lick   Paoli
Cuzco   Norton
     Fort Branch   Huntingburg   New Albany

Evansville

CARTHAGE, KNIGHTSTOWN AND SHIRLEY RAILROAD
Knightstown, IN

The Carthage, Knightstown & Shirley Railroad (CK&S for short) is a nostalgic, wheel-clacking, whistle-blowing excursion back into an earlier time. The one-hour trip is a unique way to "get away from it all." A good selection of railroad memorabilia and refreshments may be found in the charming old depot next to the Knightstown Antique Mall. The adjacent platform gives easy access to the passenger car and a neat old Santa Fe caboose complete with a cupola that is reached by a ladder. Equipped with ramps, an open-air car can accommodate up to 20 wheelchairs.

The train travels a five-mile stretch of the old Cleveland, Cincinnati, Chicago, and St. Louis Railroad. Heading south out of Knightstown, it crosses the National Road (U.S. 40), and passes under the old "Pennsy" railroad bridge. Passengers get a great perspective of rural Indiana, ranging from cornfields and cool woodland ravines, to the picturesque Big Blue River. Nearing the end of the line at Carthage, the train slows giving everyone a good look at a working saw mill with stacks of cut trees, ready to be worked into boards. On selected days, you might find yourself a victim of a train "robbery," or enjoying other themed trips on Mother's Day, Knightstown Jubilee Days, Labor Day, or Pumpkin Patch Runs.

SCHEDULES and FARES
The CK&S train departs Knightstown from May to October, including Memorial Day and Labor Day. Excursion times vary. Fares are generally under $10 for adults. Please call or check website for current schedules and fares.

EQUIPMENT
No. 215, a 44-ton GE
Several coaches and cabooses

CONTACT
The Carthage, Knightstown
and Shirley Railroad
112 West Carey Street
Knightstown, IN 46148
765-345-5561
800-345-2704 (Indiana only)
www.cksrailroad.com

Photos: Carthage Knightstown & Shirley Railroad

HOOSIER VALLEY RAILROAD MUSEUM
North Judson, IN

The public is invited to walk around the railroad museum and view the various railroad locomotives, railroad cars, and displays inside caboose No. 99 and the depot. Visitors may also take a short caboose ride through the railroad museum, boarding at the depot. While at the depot please browse the historic photo exhibit in the waiting room and then visit the unique gift shop stocked with specialty items relating to railroading. Museum volunteers are available to assist you and answer any of your questions.

The mission of Hoosier Valley Railroad Museum is to bring together people who are interested in maintaining the history and heritage of railroading, and to create and maintain a working railroad museum and display site developed from donated railroad equipment and other railroad-related items.

Established in 1988, the railroad museum began with a dream of creating a working railroad museum and restoring a former Chesapeake & Ohio steam locomotive: No. 2789. The "Kanawha," as the C&O Railway referred to their 2-8-4 wheeled locomotives, was brought to North Judson from Peru, Indiana, where the locomotive sat on display in the City Park adjacent to the old C&O shops.

The PRR, NYC, Erie and C&O railroads at one time all intersected and interchanged in North Judson. On abandoned former Erie Railroad right-of-way in North Judson, volunteers and soon-to-be members of the Hoosier Valley

Railroad Museum started relaying track and building switches and spents years accumulating abandoned track around the surrounding communities. The track work or physical plant of the railroad museum then began to take shape.

SCHEDULES and FARES
There is no admission charge to the Hoosier Valley Railroad Museum. It is open and staffed on Saturdays. Short train rides are available from May through September. Please call or check website for current schedules and fares.

EQUIPMENT
5 locomotives
7 cabooses
5 coaches
Various other flatcars and troop cars

CONTACT
Hoosier Valley Railroad Museum
P.O. Box 75
North Judson, IN 46366-0075
574-896-3950
http://hvrm.railfan.net

Photos: Hoosier Valley Railroad Museum

INDIANA RAILWAY MUSEUM/
FRENCH LICK, WEST BADEN & SOUTHERN RAILROAD
French Lick, IN

Join the excitement and fun as the French Lick, West Baden & Southern Railroad takes you on a ride into the scenic rolling hills of southern Indiana. The ride, which takes almost two hours, rolls you through 20 miles of the Hoosier National Forest, limestone rock-cuts, and the 2,200-foot Burton Tunnel, one of the longest railroad tunnels in the state. Trains depart from the French Lick Depot--the original limestone Monom railroad station to Cuzco, Indiana (near Patoka Lake), and then return.

But beware: On certain weekends, you might find yourself facing some Wild West bandits set on stealing the treasures of the train!

Your train ride is made possible by the Indiana Railway Museum. Workers have moved the museum location three times since it opened in 1961. Currently the museum and its display of rolling stock and artifacts call French Lick their home.

SCHEDULES and FARES
The Indiana Railway Museum/ French Lick, West Baden & Southern Railroad operates from April through November. Train robberies occur on elected days in April, May, July, August, September, and October. Adult fares are generally under $15. Please call or check website for current schedules and fares.

EQUIPMENT
No. 3, 1947 General Electric 80-ton diesel locomotive
No. 208, 1912 Baldwin 2-6-0
No. 97, 1925 Baldwin 2-6-0
No. 4, Alco RS-1 diesel
No. 313, trolley built in 1930 in Portugal

CONTACT
Indiana Railway Museum/
French Lick, West Baden & Southern Railroad
1 Monom Street
French Lick, IN 47432
800-74-TRAIN
812-936-2405
www.indianarailwaymuseum.org

Photos: Indiana Railway Museum

INDIANA TRANSPORTATION MUSEUM
Noblesville, IN

A visit to the Indiana Transportation Museum is a must for anyone who wants to see Indiana's railroad history preserved, learn more about the history of the railroad, and experience rail travel as it used to be. Just 20 minutes north of downtown Indianapolis, the museum operates 38 miles of track once known as the Indianapolis & Peru, and more recently as the Nickel Plate Road. The Atlanta Express runs on the main line, from Hobbs Station (located at the museum) to Atlanta, Indiana, which is located 11 scenic miles north of Noblesville. The Hamiltonian, a dinner train, whisks riders from Fishers Station to one of two restaurants in either Atlanta or Cicero, Indiana.

Along with the train ride, the museum offers a number of shop facilities where restoration and maintenance of its equipment and display items take place. You'll also see a variety of locomotives, passenger coaches, a dinner coach, and cabooses. Don't miss the Railway Post Office car, an early electric engine used by the Singer Company, and several hand-operated railroad vehicles. On special occasions, the Henry M. Flagler private car is open for tour.

SCHEDULES and FARES
The Indiana Transportation Museum is open on Saturdays and Sundays. Cab rides are available on most trains for an additional fee. Entrance fees for adults are generally under $5. Please call or check website for current schedules and fares.

EQUIPMENT
USRA Light Mikado ITM No. 587
EMD F-7 and FP-7, GP-9, GP-7L, and SW-1
ITM Nos. 83, 96, 200, 426, 99, 91 and 50
Baldwin VO-1000
GE 44-ton
IPL fireless cooker
Twin Branch No. 4
Budd coaches
FEC No. 90 (Flagler Car)
Pullman sleeper
C&O 90876
NKP 770

CONTACT
Indiana Transportation Museum
325 Cicero Road
Noblesville, IN 46061
317-773-6000
nkp58@iquest.net
www.itm.org

Photos: Indiana Transportation Museum

NATIONAL NEW YORK CENTRAL RAILROAD MUSEUM
Elkhart, IN

A real timetable to the past, the National New York Central Railroad Museum in Elkhart, Indiana, recaptures the days when locomotives were symbols of progress and ambassadors of good will across the country. With one of the largest rail yards in America, this museum was founded in 1987 to preserve both local and national railroad heritage.

As you enter the museum through a 1915 passenger coach, you're introduced to a time line of local railroad history, beginning in 1833 with the Lake Shore and Michigan Southern Railroad. Follow history back to 1914, when the New York Central gained control of the railroad. At the end of the coach, you are led into the museum's 100-year-old freight house complex. Don't miss your chance to bring railroad history alive by taking advantage of the numerous hands-on exhibits.

SCHEDULES and FARES
The National New York Central Railroad Museum is open year-round. It is closed on Mondays and all major holidays. Adult entrance fees are generally below $5. Please call or check website for current schedules and fares.

EQUIPMENT
NYC 3001 L3a Mohawk Alco 1940
NYC 4085 E8 EMD, 1953
PRR 4882 GG1
CSS No. 15
Various passenger and freight cars and cabooses

CONTACT
National New York Central Railroad Museum
721 S. Main Street
Elkhart, IN 46515
574-294-3001
574-295-9434 (fax)
info@nycrrmuseum.org
www.nycrrmuseum.org

Photos: National New York Central Railroad

TRAINTOWN
New Haven, IN

Volunteers with the Fort Wayne Railroad Historical Society saved the Nickel Plate Road locomotive 765 from becoming a rusting monument at a city park. They restored it to operating condition in 1979. For the next 14 years the 765 ran special excursions. It also had a brush with fame in two feature films.

From 1993 to 2005, volunteers rebuilt the 765. It cost $750,000, and there were more than 13,000 volunteer hours involved. In 2006, 765 operated under its own power for a series of tests and performed flawlessly.

The society's offices and museum are located on a site dubbed Traintown. The plan is to build a working replica of the Nickel Plate Depot and to restore a second locomotive: the Lake Erie and Fort Wayne six coupled steam locomotive No.1.

Volunteers with the Fort Wayne Railroad Historical Society saved the Nickel Plate Road locomotive 765 from becoming a rusting monument at a city park. They restored it to operating condition in 1979. For the next 14 years the 765 ran special excursions. It also had a brush with fame in two feature films.

From 1993 to 2005, volunteers rebuilt the 765. It cost $750,000, and there were more than 13,000 volunteer hours involved. In 2006, 765 operated under its own power for a series of tests and performed flawlessly.

The society's offices and museum are located on a site dubbed Traintown. The plan is to build a working replica of the Nickel Plate Depot and to restore a second locomotive: the Lake Erie and Fort Wayne six coupled steam locomotive No.1.

SCHEDULES AND FARES
Traintown offers an "Engineer for an Hour"
program and caboose rentals. Trains run on Saturdays. Traintown is open every Saturday. Please call or check website for current schedules and fares.

EQUIPMENT
Nickel Plate Road locomotive 765
Lake Erie and Fort Wayne six-coupled steam locomotive No. 1.
Tool/crew car No. 701, St. Louis Car Company, 1953
Water canteen 765A, former 1900-series L&N Berkshire tender, 1949
Nickel plate caboose 451, Morrison-International Car Company, 1962
Nickel plate caboose 141, LE&W, 1960
Norfolk & Western 200-ton crane No. 540019, 1922
Nickel plate boxcar X-50448, Haskell & Barker, 1902

CONTACT
Traintown
15808 Edgerton Road
New Haven, IN 46774
260-493-0765
www.765.org

Photos: Fort Wane Railroad Historical Society

WHITEWATER VALLEY RAILROAD
Connersville, IN

Spend a glorious afternoon aboard the Whitewater Valley Railroad. This railroad first reached Connersville in 1867, following the route of the Whitewater River and Canal. The Whitewater River formed a natural trade route for the Indians and for early settlers. Today's operating railroad museum began weekend passenger excursions in 1974.

You can enjoy an excursion, too. Just be ready to depart the Connersville depot at 12:01 p.m. (EST) and head to historic Metamora, Indiana. Here, you'll have a two-hour layover that allows you to explore this restored canal town and stop by the working grist mill. While you're in Metamora, you can take a short shuttle trip to view the surrounding country-side. Then it's back on the train at 3:30 p.m. for your 1.5-hour return trip. But watch out: Depending on when you visit, your train may be subject to a holdup by the Delaware Rangers!

SCHEDULES and FARES
The Whitewater Valley Railroad operates from May through October on weekends and at other times during the year for special events. Fares vary according to your excursion. Please call or check the website for current schedules and fares.

EQUIPMENT
CUT 25, switcher
NYC 9339, switcher
ARMCO 709, switcher
B&O 320, switcher
M&W 8, switcher
MILW 532, roadswitcher
WWRR 210, switcher
WWRR 2561, gas mechanical

CONTACT
Whitewater Valley Railroad
455 Market Street
Connersville, IN 47331
765-825-2054
www.whitewatervalleyrr.org

Photos: Whitewater Valley Railroad

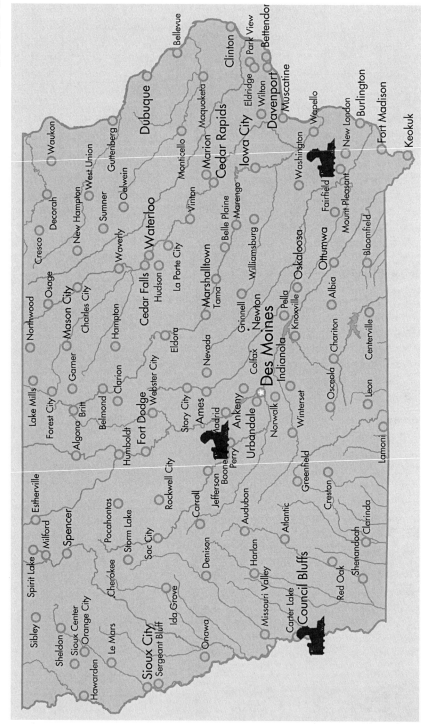

IOWA

BOONE & SCENIC VALLEY RAILROAD
Boone, IA

The trains of the Boone & Scenic Valley Railroad traverse some of the most beautiful countryside in Iowa as they wind their way to the bottom of the Des Moines River Valley at Fraser. Regular excursion trains, dinner trains, dessert trains and picnic trains make the 15-mile round trip. You will live a bygone time as you board 1920s-era coaches or dining cars of the 1950s. You are traveling some of the most beautiful countryside in Iowa. Travel writers have refered to the area as the "Grand Canyon" of the midwest. The Bass Point Creek High Bridge, at 156 feet high and 784 feet long, is the highest interurban, steel railroad trestle in the United States.

While waiting for the train you can enjoy the new James H. Andrew Railroad Museum & History Center, located adjacent to the depot. This museum houses one of the largest and most unique railroad collections in the country. A must see stop for the discremenating railfan.

SCHEDULES and FARES
The Depot and James H. Andrew Railroad Museum & History Center are open year-round. The exursion trains run Saturdays in May and then daily Memorial Day weekend through the end of October. Dinner trains run Friday nights April through the Satuday night before Thanksgiving and Saturday nights June through October. Fares vary from $3 to $55.

EQUIPMENT
The Railroad boasts a large collection of engines, trollys and cars. Their JS8419 steam locomotive was the last commercially produced steam locomotive in the world/

CONTACT
Boone & Scenic Valley Railroad
225 10th Street
Boone, IA 50036
1-800-626-0319
515-432-4249
info@bsvrr.com
www.scenic-valleyrr.com

Photos: Boone & Scenic VAlley Railroad

MIDWEST CENTRAL RAILROAD
Mount Pleasant, IA

Midwest Central Railroad features steam powered trains, located in Mount Pleasant, Iowa. They house educational displays and a 1.25 mile full-circle track that runs during reunions. The railroad also has a gift shop and a "steam school" for those wishing to learn more about steam-powered locomotives. The MCRR volunteers maintain 3 engines, numerous rail cars, tracking, and buildings to the delight of any railway enthusiast. The Midwest Electric Railway also operates during events, and operates streetcars on a loop.

SCHEDULES AND FARES:
Select events throughout the year offered, including the Old Threshers Reunion. Check the website for upcoming events and fares.

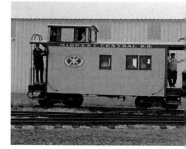

EQUIPMENT:
Various Engines, Cabooses, Coaches, Hand Carts and other rolling stock on the grounds, and many project pieces that are being restored.

CONTACT:
Midwest Central Railroad
405 E. Threshers Road
Mount Pleasant, IA, 50322
319.385.2912
www.mcrr.org

UNION PACIFIC RAILROAD MUSEUM
Council Bluffs, IA

The Union Pacific Railroad Museum houses one of the oldest corporate collections in the nation. It includes artifacts, photographs, and documents that trace the development of the railroad and the American West. The collection dates to the mid-1800s. A survey of the early rail equipment and artifacts from the construction of the nation's first transcontinental railroad tells the story of one of the world's construction marvels.

The completion of the transcontinental railroad in 1869 by the Union Pacific and its constituent railroads shaped the landscape and geography of the American West.

SCHEDULES and FARES
The Union Pacific Railroad Museum is open year-round. Admission is free. Please call or check website for current schedules and fares.

EQUIPMENT
Challenger No. 3985
Steam locomotive No. 844
Streamliner

CONTACT
Union Pacific Railroad Museum
200 Pearl Street
Council Bluffs, IA 51503
712-329-8307
www.uprr.com/aboutup/history/museum
/index.shtml

Photos: Union Pacific Railroad Museum

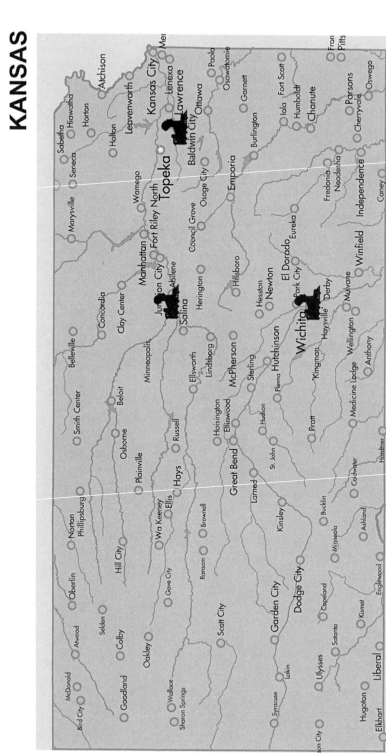

ABILENE & SMOKY VALLEY RAILROAD
Abilene, KS

Take the Abilene & Smoky Valley Railroad for a 1.5-hour, 10-mile round trip from historic Abilene to Enterprise, Kansas. Pass through the Smoky Hill River Valley in a restored 100-year-old coach/diner or an open-air observation car pulled by a 1945 Alco S1 diesel-electric locomotive. Cross the Smoky Hill River on a high steel-span bridge.

In 1866, J. G. McCoy, a pioneer western cattle shipper, conceived the idea of making Abilene the shipping point for Texas cattle on the Kansas Pacific Railway. Over the next five years, as many as three million Texas longhorns arrived in Abilene, led by Jesse Chisholm by way of "The Chisholm Trail." The cattle were shipped back east by the railroad.

The railroad again played a role in American history, when Dwight D. Eisenhower left by train for West Point to begin his famous military career. The rails were used extensively by "Ike" as he campaigned for President of the United States. He often visited his hometown during his years of service as Allied Commander during World War II and later as the President of the United States. President Eisenhower's body was returned to Abilene by rail for his burial at the Eisenhower Center in 1969.

In 1993, a group of railroad volunteers demonstrating their love for trains started an excursion train.

SCHEDULES and FARES
The Abilene & Smoky Valley Railroad Association offers regular excursions from Memorial Day through Labor Day. The trains also run on weekends during the months of May, September, and October. Rides on dinner trains, private charters, and the Silver Flyer rail bus are also available. Fares vary according to excursion. Please call or check website for current schedules and fares.

EQUIPMENT
1919 Baldwin 4-6-2 "Pacific"
1945 Alco S1
1945 GE 44-ton
1945 Whitcomb 45-ton side-rod

122 Kansas

CONTACT
Abilene & Smoky Valley Railroad
200 S. Fifth Street
Abilene, KS 67410
888-426-6687
785-263-1077 (fax)
info@asvrr.org
www.asvrr.org

Photos: Abilene & Smoky Valley Railroad

GREAT PLAINS TRANSPORTATION MUSEUM
Wichita, KS

The Great Plains Transportation Museum is the railroad museum of Kansas. The museum opened its doors to the public in December 1986 with a small outdoor collection of rolling stock and a small indoor display of artifacts and memorabilia pertaining to railroad operations. Since that time, the museum has expanded by acquiring additional rolling stock and artifacts through donations from area railroads and individuals. Volunteers staff the museum and work on the restoration projects and maintenance.

Visitors can roam the grounds on a self-guided hands-on tour; they can stand next to any of the rolling stock to get a perspective on size and components; and they can get into most of the equipment and view what the engineer or conductor sees. The caboose collection varies from a wooden style built in 1904 to an all-steel style built in 1982, virtually the last year that cabooses were built.

SCHEDULE and FARES
The Great Plains Tranportation Museum is open year-round on Saturdays and some Sundays. It is closed on Christmas Day. Special-event bookings are available. Adult admission fees are generally around $5. Please call or check website for current schedules and fares.

EQUIPMENT
No. 3768, ATSF 4-8-4 type steam locomotive, 1938
No. 93 ATSF model FP45 diesel electric, 1967
Frisco wooden caboose, 1904
Burlington caboose, 1929
CKR caboose, 1981
Missouri Pacific caboose, 1950
Rock Island caboose, 1967
Santa Fe drovers' car

CONTACT
Great Plains Transportation Museum, Inc.
700 E. Douglas
Wichita, KS 67202-3506
316 263 0944
www.gptm.us

Photos: J. Harvey Koehn

MIDLAND RAILWAY
Baldwin City, KS

Board the Midland Railway in Baldwin City (just look for the grain elevator; the depot is right next door!) for a leisurely 11-mile round trip to the former site of Norwood, Kansas. Traveling in vintage railcars on line originally constructed in 1867, you'll pass through scenic eastern Kansas farmlands and woods. The railway, which is staffed entirely by volunteers, features over 50 pieces of rolling stock. A unique offering of the Midland Railway Historical Association is a program for Scouting-type organizations. The Railroading Weekend includes working on the track, riding the train, and managing equipment in order to earn a railroading merit badge.

SCHEDULES and FARES
The Midland Railway operates from Memorial Day weekend through October. Special Friday runs, in April, May, September, and October, are by reservation only. Please call or check website for current schedules and fares.

EQUIPMENT
No. 1, GE diesel-electric, built in 1938
No. 652, E-8 diesel-electric, built in 1952
No. 2123 0-4-0 steam tank engine, built in 1928

CONTACT
Midland Railway
1515 High Street
Baldwin City, KS 66006-0005
800-651-0388
913-371-3410
785-594-6982 (operating hours)
www.midland-ry.org

Photos: Midland Railway

Did You Know...

The fastest train in the world is the TGV in France. It can go up to 322 mph. That is four and a half times faster than a car on a highway.

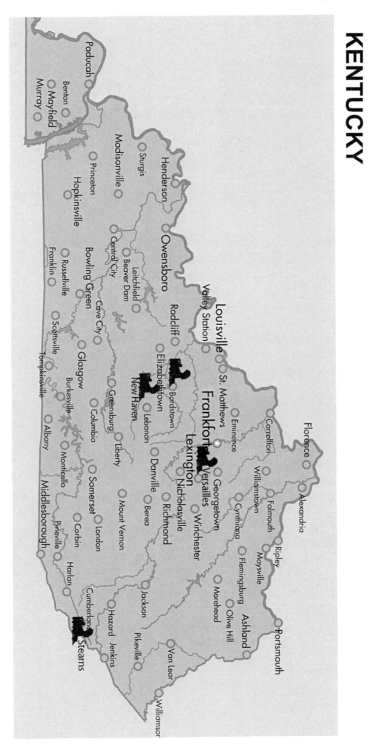

BIG SOUTH FORK SCENIC RAILWAY
Stearns, KY

In 1902 Justus Stearns of Ludington, Michigan bought 30,000 acres of virgin timberland in southern Kentucky. When coal was discovered soon afterward, the Stearns Coal & Lumber Company was in business. The company built the town of Stearns to serve as the hub of a logging and mining empire. In the 1920's Stearns built the Kentucky and Tennessee Railway as well as the world's first all-electric sawmill.

The Big South Fork Scenic Railway is still part of the Kentucky & Tennessee Railway. At one time the K&T stretched over 20 miles and operated 12 steam locomotives. It carried freight and workers for the coal and lumber industries. In the 1950s when the coal mines started dying off, Stearns Coal & Lumber started selling off its assets. The last coal car left the mines in 1987.

Today's train excursion takes you back in time down into the Big Fork Valley and to a 1902 coal camp. It is a three-hour round trip. Volunteers are currently trying to extend the line.

SCHEDULES and FARES
The Big Fork Scenic Railway operates from March through December, with peak season being May through September. Per the railway's website: The railway reserves the right to cancel trains and change equipment without prior notice. Please call or check website for current schedules and fares.

EQUIPMENT
15+ steam locomotives
IHB 2016 and IHB 2096, Indiana Harbor Belt Railroad
3 canopy cars
No. 113 Stearns Coal & Lumber Co., 47-ton Heisler

CONTACT
Big South Fork Scenic Railway
100 Henderson Street
Stearns, KY 42647
800-GO-ALONG
606-376-5330
606-376-5332 (fax)
info@bsfsry.com
www.bsfsry.com

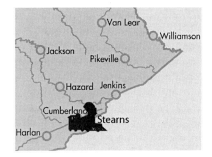

Photos: Big South Fork Scenic Railway

BLUEGRASS RAILROAD MUSEUM
Versailles, KY

Located on 5.5 miles of track between Versailles, Kentucky, and the Kentucky River, the Bluegrass Railroad Museum offers you the chance to journey through the Bluegrass region of Central Kentucky. The line was built in the 1880s by the Louisville Southern Railroad and became part of the Southern Railway in 1894.

Although the museum is located just 15 miles from Lexington, Kentucky, you'll feel as though you've stepped back in time as your train ride takes you over gently rolling hills and through picturesque farmland. You'll enjoy seeing beautiful thoroughbred horse farms, herds of grazing cattle, and Kentucky wildflowers in bloom. After your 1.5-hour, 1.5-mile ride, visit the museum's display car to view interesting railroad displays.

SCHEDULES and FARES
The Bluegrass Railroad Museum is open every weekend from June through October. Adult fares are generally under $10. Group rates are available. Please call or check website for current schedules and fares.

EQUIPMENT
GP9, acquired from Consol
Alco MRS1s Nos. 2043 and 2086
Fairbanks Morse H12-44 1849
L&N caboose No. 1086

CONTACT
Bluegrass Railroad Museum
175 Beasley Road
Versailles, KY 40383
800-755-2476
859-873-2476
webmaster@bgrm.org
www.bgrm.org

Photos: Bluegrass Railroad Museum

KENTUCKY RAILWAY MUSEUM
New Haven, KY

Located in the heartland of Kentucky, the Kentucky Railway Museum is one of the oldest rail museums in the United States.
Founded in Louisville in 1954, KRM now owns 17 miles of the former Louisville & Nashville Lebanon branch, with a passenger boarding area in Boston, Kentucky. New Haven is located 12 miles south of historic Bardstown, very near the junction of Interstate 65 and the Bluegrass Parkway.

Your 90-minute journey will be powered by first-generation diesels, and on select weekends an operating 1905 steam locomotive welcomes visitors. No. 152 is the only operating steam locomotive in the state of Kentucky. This trip takes you through the scenic Rolling Fork River Valley, just as it did in those long-ago days when America moved by rail. Our train depot houses our museum, which has a collection of artifacts and memorabilia from days past.

SCHEDULES and FARES

The museum is open year-round. Trains run from March through December. Regular fares include museum and model train center visits. There is an additional fee for locomotive cab rides and steam weekends. Please call or check website for current schedules and fares.

EQUIPMENT

No. 152 steam, 1905
Santa Fe No. 2546
Monon No. 32

CONTACT

Kentucky Railway Museum
P.O. Box 240
New Haven, KY 40051
800-272-0152
502-549-5470
kyrail@bardstown.com
www.kyrail.org

Photos: Kentucky Railway Museum

MY OLD KENTUCKY DINNER TRAIN
Bardstown, KY

My Old Kentucky Dinner Train operates on the Bardstown branch of the Louisville-Nashville Railroad. This branch was built in the 1850s and connects Bardstown with the main north/south line running from Louisville to Nashville. It is one of the earliest branches of the Louisville & Nashville Railroad. In 1986, only 20 miles of track remained between Bardstown and Bardstown Junction, where the branch line intersects with the main line, now owned by CSX Railroad. This branch was purchased by R. J. Corman Railroad Corporation as a short-line railroad in 1986 and began its freight operation in 1987. My Old Kentucky Dinner Train made its inaugural run in July 1988.

The pre-Civil War 1860s train station is open one hour prior to departure times for ticketing. Until 1953 it served as both a freight depot and a passenger station. It is constructed of native limestone and is the last dry-laid depot in Kentucky. The depot is listed on the National Register of Historic Places.

SCHEDULES and FARES
My Old Kentucky Dinner Train offers 2.5-hour lunch and dinner excursions year-round. Murder Mystery and children's excursions are also available. Fares generally range from $30 to $100 depending on the excursion. Please call or check website for current schedules and fares.

EQUIPMENT
No. 1940 & No. 1941 FP7-A
Nos. 7, 11, .21, and 777 Budd diner, circa 1940

CONTACT
My Old Kentucky Dinner Train
602 North Third Street
Bardstown, KY 40004
866-801-3463 (toll free)
502-348-7300
www.kydinnertrain.com

Photos: My Old Kentucky Dinner Train

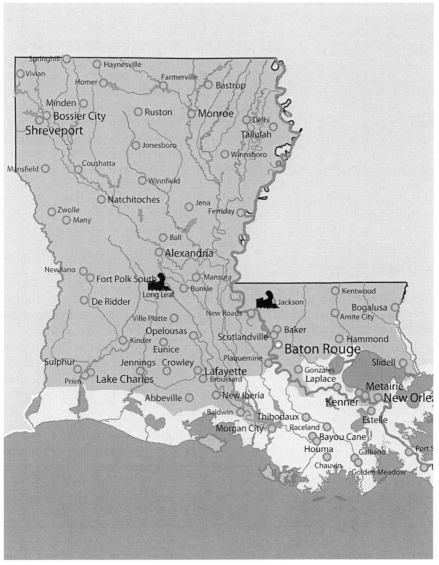

LOUISIANA

OLD HICKORY RAILROAD
Jackson, LA

The Old Hickory Railroad is one of the earliest railroads in America. It was part of the Clinton and Port Hudson Railroad, which included a spur into Jackson. The present train was built in 1964 and brought to Jackson in 1998. It features a live steam narrow gauge locomotive traveling a scenic 6.2-mile route with stops at four historic sites in Jackson. It took over two years to get the railroad up and running, but modern-day enthusiasts have been enjoying the ride since 2000, when the railroad began its weekend excursions.

A live steam locomotive pulls two open coaches on the journey back in time through the historic town of Jackson. The city was named after Andrew Jackson in 1816, in honor of his victory over the British in the Battle of New Orleans. The town has over 120 historic buildings, many relating to its early importance as a center of higher education, banking, and government.

SCHEDULES and FARES
The Old Hickory Railroad operates on weekends from mid-March to mid-November. Note that rides may be canceled due to inclement weather. Model trains run on the second and fourth Saturdays of the month. Special events are scheduled throughout the year and are posted to the website, as scheduled. Fares are generally under $10. Please call or check website for current schedules and fares.

EQUIPMENT
Narrow gauge steam locomotive
Model railroad display, including O, HO, N, S, and G scale

CONTACT
Old Hickory Railroad
P.O. Box 297
Jackson, LA 70748
225-634-7397
225-634-3337 (fax)
Harv707@aol.com
www.louisianasteamtrain.com

Photos: Old Hickory Railroad

SOUTHERN FOREST HERITAGE MUSEUM
Long Leaf, LA

The Southern Forest Heritage Museum honors the great sawmills found throughout the South during the latter part of the 19th and early part of the 20th centuries. The long-leaf yellow pine forests extended from Virginia on the east to Texas on the west. The railroads were the only way to get the logs from the piney woods to the mills and then to market. The mill at Long Leaf, Louisiana, operated from 1892 to 1969 and is a rare survivor of that era. Visitors to the museum get a chance to see the famed Corliss steam engine with a 12-foot flywheel. The Corliss steam engine drove the planer mill machinery until its function was replaced by electric motors in the 1950s.

According to the Library of Congress, "this 57-acre museum, representative of the many sawmill towns that once flourished throughout the South, offers a unique opportunity to glimpse the golden age of lumbering and saw milling." Artifacts date back to the early 1900s. Give yourself two hours to see everything and take a ride on the rail motorcar from the commissary to the roundhouse.

SCHEDULES and FARES

The Museum is open year-round, except on Easter, Thanksgiving, and Christmas Day. Admission and fares are generally under $10. Please call or check website for current schedules and fares.

EQUIPMENT
Clyde 4-line rehaul skidder, 1919
Engine 202, 2-6-0 wood burning steam locomotive, 1913
Engine 400, 4-6-0 , coal and later oil-burning locomotive, 1919

CONTACT
Southern Forest Heritage Museum
P.O. Box 101
Long Leaf, LA 71448
318-748-8404
longleaf@centurytel.net
www.forestheritagemuseum.org

Photos: Southern Forest Heritage Museum

MAINE

Madawaska
Fort Kent
Van Buren
Loring AFB
Caribou
Fort Fairfield
Presque Isle
Houlton
Millinocket
East Millinocket
Lincoln
Milo
Calais
Dover-Foxcroft
Dexter
Old Town
Madison
Orono
Farmington
Bangor
Brewer
Skowhegan
Unity
Hampden
Mexico
Buckport
Ellsworth
Wilton
Waterville
Boothbay
Livermore Falls
Belfast
Winthrop
Augusta
Bar Harbor
Norway
South Paris
Camden
Farmingdale
Auburn
Lewiston
Alna
Thomaston
Lisbon Falls
Bath
Brunswick
Westbrook
Yarmouth
Saco
Portland
Sanford
Biddeford
Kennebunkport

BOOTHBAY RAILWAY VILLAGE
Boothbay, ME

The Boothbay Railway Village is dedicated to being a living museum of railroading, antique automobiles, small towns, and rural life, with an emphasis on Maine between 1850 and 1950.

Climb aboard trains pulled by Henschel narrow gauge steam engines, built in Europe between 1913 and 1938, for a tour around this re-created historic village. During your ride on these coal-fired, narrow gauge steam trains, you'll pass more than 24 re-created structures containing historical exhibits, including the Thorndike and Freeport railroad stations. Don't miss the Maine Narrow Gauge photo display, the Summit Station, coal bin, water tower, crossing tower, train shed, model railroad exhibit, and much more. You depart the train at an exceptional antique vehicle display, housing more than 50 vehicles from 1907 to 1949.

SCHEDULES and FARES
The Boothbay Railway Village is open to visitors from Memorial Day to mid-October. Adult fares are generally under $10. Special-event fares may vary. Please call or check website for current schedules and fares.

EQUIPMENT
Four Henschel 0-4-0T locomotives, Nos. 12313, 22486, 24022, and 24023, built between 1913 and 1938
Baldwin steam locomotives Nos. 14283 and 14522, built in 1895
Plymouth gasoline locomotive, built in 1929
Variety of boxcars, coaches, freight cars, and cabooses

CONTACT
Boothbay Railway Village
Route 27
Boothbay, ME 04537
207-633-4727
207-633-4733 (fax)
staff@railwayvillage.org
www.railwayvillage.org

Photos: Boothbay Railway Village

DOWNEAST SCENIC RAILROAD
Ellsworth, ME

This line, built by Colonel John N. Greene with the financial backing of the Maine Central Railroad, was to become the premier passenger line in New England, hosting the notable and noteworthy of the day as they traveled to the then burgeoning summer resorts on Mount Desert Island aboard the Mount Desert Limited which later became the Bar Harbor Express. The Downeast Scenic Railroad offers two trips per day on Saturdays and Sundays through the season. Their round-trip tour travels from Ellsworth, Maine, on the historic Calais Branch Line to Ellsworth Falls and then to Washington Junction and back to Ellsworth. The ten-mile trip takes approximately 90 minutes.

At the core of the Downeast Scenic Railroad Project is the rehabilitation of the Washington Junction/Ellsworth to Green Lake section of the Calais Branch Line to create a 24-mile round- trip excursion ride. This stretch of the Calais Branch Line provides exceptional views of wetland marshes, glacial erratica including massive boulders, river and stream crossings, Little Rocky Pond and Green Lake. While working on this stretch of the line we have

observed many forms of wildlife including osprey, Blue herons, Bald Eagles, moose, deer, snapping turtles, beavers, and bears, just west of Green Lake Road!

EQUIPMENT:
Engine 54, 1948 70 Ton GE
Engine 1055, 1950 Alco
Engine 53, Davenport
Caboose 2608
Several Passenger cars

SCHEDULES AND FARES:
Trains will depart at 10:30am and 1:30pm each weekend and holiday starting with the Memorial Day weekend 2012
Fares:
Adults $13.00
Children 3-12 years $7.00
Children under 2 years of age and not occupying a seat ride at no charge.

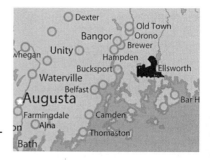

CONTACT:
Our ticket agent: Cadillac Mountain Sports [Boarding is directly behind store]
34 HIgh Street
Ellsworth, Maine 04605
1-866-449-7245

MAINE EASTERN RAILROAD
Rockland, ME

Maine Eastern Railroad, also known as the "Maine Line" operates excursions on restored vintage railcars through the mid-coast of Maine, between Brunswick and Rockland. Come aboard the Art Deco era railcars and enjoy the comfort of safety and hospitality. The fleet boasts 54 and 58 seat coaches, a restored dining car with a full-service food and beverage line. The two-hour, 57-mile trip runs in both directions and provides first-class service. Stations serviced include Rockland, Wiscasset, Bath, and Brunswick.

SCHEDULES AND FARES:
Service runs May through the Fall Wednesday through Sunday, and in December for holiday events. Fares vary by station. Check the website for further details and for reservations.

EQUIPMENT:
The railroad has a collection of beautifully restored streamliner stainless steel railcars from the 1940s and 1950s era.

CONTACT:
Maine Eastern Railroad
4 Union St, Rockland, ME 04841
866.637.2457
www.maineeasternrailroad.com
info@maineeasternrailroad.com

MAINE NARROW GAUGE RAILROAD COMPANY AND MUSEUM
Portland, ME

The Maine Narrow Gauge Railroad Company and Museum gives visitors a view of Portland's working waterfront. Take a trip back in time and enjoy magnificent views of Portland's working waterfront aboard antique railcars pulled by hard-working steam and diesel locomotives. Discover the unique trains that linked rural Maine to the rest of the world. Trains run every hour on the hour.

During the last half of the 19th century, Maine had a unique system of railroads that ran on rails that were only two feet apart. Eventually there were five of these trains serving rural areas in the central and western part of the state. In 2006, volunteers performed maintenance on a one-mile section of track along the waterfront. All the work has to be done by hand, as it was in 1879.

SCHEDULES and FARES
The Maine Narrow Gauge Railway is open from February to December (the schedule is limited during the winter). It is closed on Thanksgiving, Christmas Day, and New Year's Day. Adult fares are generally around $10. Please call or check website for current schedules and fares.

EQUIPMENT
4 steam locomotives dating back to the 1920s
Edaville diesel No. 1

CONTACT
Maine Narrow Gauge Railroad
Company and Museum
58 Fore Street
Portland, ME
207-828-0814
mngrr@maine.rr.com
www.mngrr.org

Photos: Maine Narrow Gauge Railroad

SEASHORE TROLLEY MUSEUM
Kennebunkport, ME

The Seashore Trolley Museum, located on approximately 300 acres of land in beautiful Kennebunkport, Maine, is home to the most comprehensive collection of street railway vehicles in the world. As the first private organization to save transit equipment anywhere in the world, the museum was founded as a not-for-profit organization in 1939 by eight young men with a dream of preserving this piece of history. The museum now houses over 250 mass-transit vehicles from all over the world. The collection includes a streetcar from almost every major city in the U.S. that had a trolley system, as well as representative cars from foreign countries such as Canada, England, Germany, Italy, Australia, New Zealand, and Japan. Many of these vehicles have been restored to operating condition and are used daily during the operating season on the museum's main line.

The museum's main line is situated on a part of the original roadbed of one of Maine's premier interurban trolley systems, the Atlantic Shore Line Railway, a trolley line that ran from Biddeford to Kennebunkport, Kittery, and Sanford, Maine. The main line is part of the line that was open for service from 1904 to 1927. Visitors of all ages now enjoy a 3.5-mile round trip through the countryside from the Visitor's Center to Talbott Park and return, occasionally spotting a moose or a deer. Normally, two to five different restored streetcars are operating each day.

The Town House Shop is "Where the Magic Happens." Here visitors watch restoration in progress as museum personnel and volunteers painstakingly restore streetcars to as close to the original condition as possible. Whenever possible and practical, workers use the same methods as those used by the street railway companies and builders.

SCHEDULES and FARES
The museum is open for weekend excursions during the spring. From Memorial Day to mid-October, it is open every day. Adult fares are generally under $10 for the whole day and include unlimited rides. Please call or check website for current schedules and fares.

EQUIPMENT

No. 10, New Bedford, MA, Union Street Railway, horse car
Manchester, NH, Manchester Street Railway, VIP parlor car, "City of Manchester"
No. 31, Biddeford, ME, Biddeford & Saco Railway, open car
No. 2, Montreal, Canada, Montreal Tramways, observation car
No. 4547, Brooklyn, NY, Brooklyn Rapid Transit, convertible car
No. 4387, Stoneham. MA, Eastern Mass. Street Railway, semiconvertible car,
No. 18, Földalatti subway car, Philadelphia, PA.
No. 62, Philadelphia & West Chester Railway, car
No. 1700, Sydney, Australia, car
No. 966, New Orleans Public Service, car
No. 48, "The Liberty Bell Limited" San Francisco, CA, O'Farrell & Hyde Street, cable car
No. 631, New York City, Third Avenue Railway System car

CONTACT

Seashore Trolley Museum
195 Log Cabin Road
Kennebunkport, ME 04046
207-967-2712
207-967-0867 (fax)
carshop@gwi.net
www.trolleymuseum.org

Photos: Mathew D. Cosgro, Seashore Trolley Museum,

Did You Know...

The steepest Cogwheel railway in the world is in Switzerland. It has a gradient of 48% and goes over Mount Pilatus.

WISCASSET, WATERVILLE, AND FARMINGTON RAILWAY
Alna, ME

The Wiscasset, Waterville, and Farmington Railway began as an idea in the 1830s when the townspeople of Wiscasset, Maine, wished to revive their dying seaport with a railroad connection. The legislature wanted to connect the area by railroad to Quebec. The Kennebec and Wiscasset Railroad was chartered in 1854 to build Wiscasset's connection to other railroads. Little action was taken until the 1890s when a few wealthy locals revived the dream and the Kennebec and Wiscasset's successor, the Wiscasset and Quebec Railroad, was formed. To save on construction and operation costs, the planners decided that the W&Q would be a two-foot gauge road. Over the years the railroad saw good times and bad, but really started to fall on hard times in the 1930s and 1940s.

What we see today is the result of a group of rail fans who never gave up. They collaborated with the Connecticut family that had obtained some of the equipment from the old railroad and brought it back to Maine. You can enjoy a scenic, 4-mile round trip.

The museum is located at the site of the old Sheepscot station in Alna, with main line track running north from Cross Road, on the original roadbed.

SCHEDULES AND FARES
The museum is open on Saturdays year-round, and Sundays between Memorial Day and Columbus Day, and at other times by appointment. Trains operate only on weekends unless there is a special event. Please call or check website for current schedules and fares.

EQUIPMENT
9 historical railcars and locomotives dating back to the 1880s
3 combines
4 passenger coaches

CONTACT
The Wiscasset, Waterville,
and Farmington Railway
P.O. Box 242
Alna, ME 04535
207-882-4193

Photos: Wiscasset, Waterville & Farmington Railway

MARYLAND

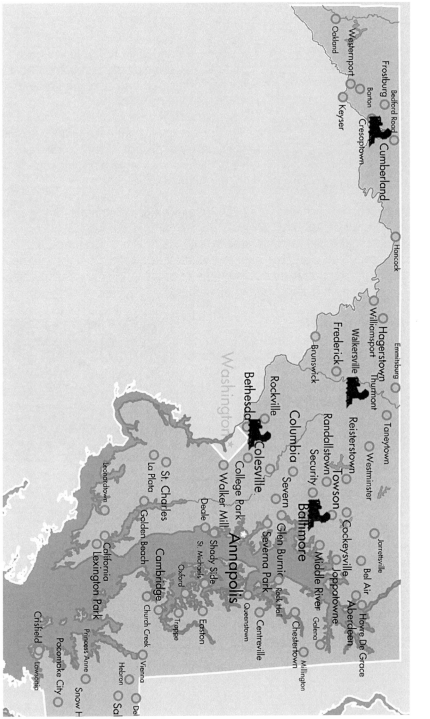

Oakland
Westernport
Barton
Keyser
Cresaptown
Frostburg
Bedford Road
Cumberland
Hancock

Washington

Emmitsburg
Williamsport
Hagerstown
Thurmont
Taneytown
Walkersville
Reisterstown
Westminster
Frederick
Brunswick
Randallstown
Towson
Cockeysville
Jarrettsville
Security
Middle River
Joppatowne
Bel Air
Rockville
Columbia
Severn
Glen Burnie
Aberdeen
Havre De Grace
Bethesda
Colesville
College Park
Severna Park
Rock Hall
Chestertown
Galena
Millington
Walker Mill
Baltimore
Leonardtown
St. Charles
La Plata
Deale
Shady Side
Annapolis
Queenstown
Centreville
California
Golden Beach
Cambridge
St. Michaels
Oxford
Easton
Lexington Park
Church Creek
Trappe
Cristfield
Princess Anne
Hebron
Vienna
Pocomoke City
Towsonia
Snow H
Sal
Del

BALTIMORE & OHIO RAILROAD MUSEUM
Baltimore, MD

The Baltimore and Ohio Railroad Museum reportedly has the oldest, most comprehensive collection of railroad history in the Western Hemisphere. Its roster of 19th and 20th-century railroad equipment, original shop buildings, and surviving tracks helps present virtually every aspect of American railroad development and its impact on our society, culture, and economy.

The B&O collection, which includes over 200 pieces of rolling stock dating back to 1827, is situated on 40 acres of land. Visitors can ride the rails of history along the first commercial railroad track in America. While visiting the B&O Railroad Museum, you may also want to visit the Ellicott City Station. It is the oldest surviving railroad station in America, and was the original terminus of the first 13 miles of commercial railroad in the country.

SCHEDULES and FARES

The museum is open year-round except for Easter Sunday, Memorial Day, Independence Day, Labor Day, Thanksgiving Day, Christmas Eve, Christmas Day, New Year's Eve, and New Year's Day. The museum normally offers train rides from April to December. The trains do not run in inclement weather. Adult fares are generally under $15. Add $2 to any admission price and visit both the B&O Railroad Museum and the Ellicott City Station. Please call or check website for current schedules and fares.

EQUIPMENT
No. 3684, GM-EMD GP-40
No. 5605, GM-EMD GP-7
No. 6607, GM-EMD GP-9
No. 6944, GM-EMD GP-30
Western Maryland No. 195, Alco RS-3, 1953
Western Maryland No. 236, GM-EMD F-7A, 1952
Western Maryland No. 81, GM-EMD BL-2, 1948

CONTACT
B&O Railroad Museum
901 W. Pratt Street
Baltimore, MD 21223
410-752-2464
www.borail.org

Photos: B & O Railroad Museum

NATIONAL CAPITAL TROLLEY MUSEUM
Colesville, MD

The National Capital Trolley Museum was founded in 1959, when the District of Columbia decided to end trolley service. The museum opened to the public in 1969 at its present location in Northwest Branch Park in Montgomery County, Maryland.

The museum's mission is to preserve and interpret the history of Washington's electric street railways. The museum holds its collections in trust for the public and is accountable to the public it serves. A 1.25-mile trolley ride is available.

The museum's volunteers have constructed and maintained a visitor's center, car houses, and a demonstration railway. These volunteer efforts continue with maintenance and on-going development of the museum's facilities.

SCHEDULES and FARES
The National Capital Trolley Museum is open year-round. Please call or check website for current schedules and fares.

EQUIPMENT
CTCo 07 snow sweeper, 1898
CTCo 0522 closed motor, 1898
CTCo 0509 work car, 1899
WA&MtV 51, snow sweeper, 1905
WRECo 650 semiconvertible center-door, 1912

EQUIPMENT Cont.
CTCo 766 closed, 1918
CTCo 1053 streamliner, 1935
DCTS PCC, 1937
CTCo 1430 PCC, 1943
DCTS 1540 PCC, 1045

CONTACT
National Capital Trolley Museum
1313 Bonifant Road
Colesville, MD 20905-5955
301-384-6088
301-384-2865 (fax)
www.dctrolley.org

Photos: National Capital Trolley Museum

WALKERSVILLE SOUTHERN RAILROAD
Walkersville, MD

Take a leisurely ride through the picturesque Maryland countryside on the Walkersville Southern Railroad, established in 1991 on the old PRR Frederick Secondary, which was built in 1869. The pace is relaxed, with speeds limited to 10 miles per hour. Choose to ride on either the open-air excursion car, the refurbished troop carrier, the remodeled passenger car, or the caboose.

You depart Walkersville and go through Walkersville Community Park, then past Fountain Rock, the site of a 100-year-old lime kiln. Coal for heating the limestone was brought in by rail, and the finished product was shipped back out to farmers locally and taken north into Pennsylvania. This was once a major industry for this area, and remnants of the old railroad operation are still visible.

The ride continues through the woods and then into beautiful Maryland farm country. You pass Barrick's Farm, established in the early 1820s. On a clear day, you can see the Catoctin Mountains. On your way back to the Walkersville Station, you cross the Monocacy River over a reconstructed railroad bridge.The original was washed out in 1972 when Hurricane Agnes hit the area.

SCHEDULES and FARES
The train operates on weekends from May through October. Special events include Midweek Matinees, Mystery Trains, Nature Trains, Band Concert and BBQ Trains, Bunny Train, Fireworks Specials, and Santa Trains. Regular adult fares are generally under $10. Please call or check website for current schedules and fares.

EQUIPMENT
No. 1, 18-ton Plymouth, built in 1942
No. 2, 25-ton Davenport, built in 1939
No. 101, Model 40, 40-ton, built in 1942
No. 12, 55-foot troop sleeper
85-foot crew dormitory car

CONTACT
Walkersville Southern Railroad
34 W. Pennsylvania Avenue
Walkersville, MD 21793-0651
877-363-WSRR
www.wsrr.org

Photos: Walkersville Southern Railroad

WESTERN MARYLAND SCENIC RAILROAD
Cumberland, MD

The Western Maryland Scenic Railroad (WMSR), located in Cumberland, Maryland, is a part of the dying history of railroading. The scenic train operates both steam and diesel engines.

As Maryland's only steam excursion, "Mountain Thunder" is a beautiful example of living history. This 1916 Baldwin 2-8-0-steam locomotive was originally in service from 1916 to 1956. When the engine was taken out of use, it was discarded in an old coal mine. While in the mine vandals set it on fire and burned the tender out of portions of the engine. The Western Maryland Scenic Railroad bought the engine and reconstructed it. The train pulled out of the shop, once again operational, in 1994.

The WMSR also has two diesel locomotives. Both diesels were built in the 1960s for the Chessy Railroad. In the 1990s, the diesels were purchased so that the WMSR could alternate the diesel and steam engines. Today one of the diesel locomotives is painted with the Western Maryland Railway fireball logo. The second diesel is painted purple with the NFL's Baltimore Ravens' logo.

As the train climbs through the spectacular scenery of the Allegheny Mountains, passengers can listen to a narration of the excursion. The train pulls its passengers through natural cuts in the mountains, such as the Narrows. There are two horseshoe curves and one hairpin turn. Keep a lookout for Brush Tunnel a 900-foot-long tunnel built through Piney Mountain. The run will take you 16 miles to Frostburg, where you will have a 90-minute layover.

SCHEDULES and FARES
The Western Maryland Scenic Railroad, open from May through December, runs Excursion, Mystery and Specialty Trains. Please call or check website for current schedules and fares.

EQUIPMENT
1916 Baldwin 2-8-0
2 1960s-era diesel locomotives

CONTACT
Western Maryland Scenic Railroad
13 Canal Street
Cumberland, MD 21502
1-800-TRAIN-50
wmsrinfo@wmsr.com
www.wmsr.com

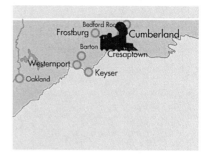

Photos: Western Maryland Scenic Railroad

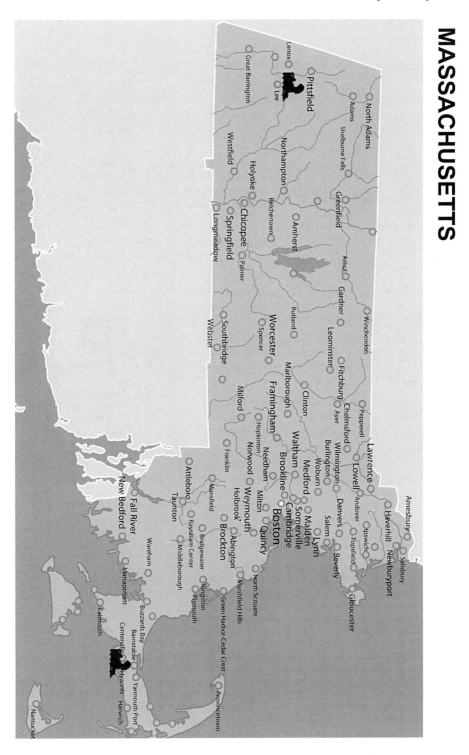

MASSACHUSETTS

Lenox
Great Barrington
Lee
Pittsfield
North Adams
Adams
Shelburne Falls
Westfield
Northampton
Greenfield
Athol
Holyoke
Belchertown
Amherst
Longmeadow
Springfield
Chicopee
Palmer
Webster
Southbridge
Spencer
Rutland
Gardner
Winchendon
Worcester
Leominster
Fitchburg
Ayer
Pepperell
Clinton
Marlborough
Framingham
Milford
Hopkinton
Franklin
Needham
Waltham
Brookline
Norwood
Attleboro
Taunton
New Bedford
Fall River
Mansfield
Raynham Center
Middleborough
Wareham
Mattapoisett
Centerville
Falmouth
Hyannis
Nantucket
Barnstable
Buzzards Bay
Yarmouth Port
Harwich
Provincetown
Green Harbor-Cedar Crest
Mansfield Hills
Kingston
Plymouth
Bridgewater
Abington
North Scituate
Brockton
Holbrook
Weymouth
Quincy
Milton
Boston
Cambridge
Somerville
Malden
Medford
Lynn
Salem
Beverly
Gloucester
Woburn
Burlington
Wilmington
Danvers
Chelmsford
Lowell
Lawrence
Andover
Topsfield
Ipswich
Haverhill
Newburyport
Amesbury
Salisbury

BERKSHIRE SCENIC RAILWAY
Lenox, MA

On summer weekends and holidays, Berkshire Scenic Railway offers two ninety-minute round trips from Lenox Station to Stockbridge and a forty-five-minute round trip from Lenox Station to Lee, narrated along the way by a conductor.

The museum resumed tourist excursion service over 10 miles of track owned by the Housatonic Railroad in the spring of 2003.
During 2005 the museum repainted locomotive 8619 in an adaptation of the New York, New Haven and Hartford switching locomotive paint scheme. Three passenger cars that match our existing fleet of 1920s-era coaches were leased from the Commonwealth of Massachusetts and were moved to Lenox from Holyoke, where they had been stored. Two have been returned to service.

The museum continues to connect with the free trolleybus operated by the Berkshire Regional Transit Authority, allowing connections to other Berkshire-area attractions from the museum's excursion trains.

SCHEDULES and FARES
Fares are charged for the round-trip train ride. There is no charge for admission to the museum in the station. Fares are subject to change without notice. Excursions can be canceled without notice. Please call or check website for current schedules and fares.

EQUIPMENT
Locomotives:
No. 67
No. 0954
No. 8619
No. 9128
Passenger Cars:
Nos. 310, 328, 329, 341, and 1444
Nos. 3204, 3224, and 4301
Maintenance-of-Way Equipment:
No. 8315
No. HF-01

CONTACT
Berkshire Scenic Railway
10 Willow Creek Road
Lenox, MA 01240-2608
413-637-2210
marketing@berkshirescenicrailroad.com
www.berkshirescenicrailroad.org

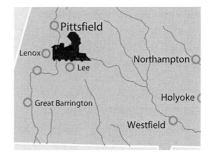

Photos: Berkshire Scenic Railway

CAPE COD CENTRAL RAILROAD
Hyannis, MA

The Cape Cod Central Railroad operates several trains over a 46-mile trip from Hyannis to the Cape Cod Canal and return. Its premier attraction is the Cape Cod Dinner Train, which has received national acclaim by being featured on the Food Network. This train offers a leisurely scenic three-hour ride and a five-course gourmet meal in nostalgic and vintage dining cars.

Variations for food service include the Cape Codder Luncheon Train and the Family Supper Train. The meals are prepared on board prior to each trip, and are served by a friendly and attentive staff. Advance reservations are necessary for the food trains.

The railroad also operates a two-hour daily narrated excursion train from Hyannis out along the sand dunes of Cape Cod Bay, past cranberry bogs and salt marshes, then on to the banks of the Cape Cod Canal. This has been rated one of the ten best train rides in the country by *USA Today*. The railroad is particularly popular for group functions.

SCHEDULES and FARES

In addition to its daily excursion train, the Cape Cod Central Railroad operates dinner, lunch, and family supper trains. Adult fares range from $15 to $60. Please call or check website for current schedules and fares.

EQUIPMENT

New York Central RS-3, 1951
2 Bayline Railroad chopnose GP-7s, 1952
3 Long Island RR coaches (for excursion train), 1964
3 Ex-Canadian National and Ex-VIA coaches, 1938
Ex-Illinois Central parlor/lounge car, 1917

CONTACT

Cape Cod Central Railroad
252 Main Street
Hyannis, MA 02601
508-771-3800
888-797-RAIL (toll free)
508-771-1335 (fax)
www.capetrain.com

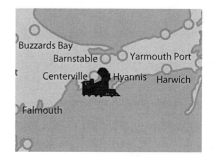

Photos: Cape Cod Central Railroad

Did You Know...

The longest possible journey on one train can be taken between Moscow and Vladivostok in Russia, on the Trans-Siberian Express. The journey is 5,857 miles long.

MICHIGAN

COOPERSVILLE & MARNE RAILWAY
Coopersville, MI

The Coopersville & Marne Railway takes you on a ride through family-owned farmlands on antique passenger cars. You will cross over an open-deck girder bridge, four creeks and one road bridge before you arrive at the Village of Marne. It is an 1.25-hour ride taking you back to a simpler time in transportation. During the trip, the conductor describes points of interest while train music from the 1800's plays throughout the cars. Wildlife such as deer, wild turkeys, hawks, and eagles may be seen along the way, as well as farm animals.

The Coopersville & Marne Railway Company was incorporated on July 13, 1989. Initially, those involved wanted to buy the right-of-way between Coopersville and Marne, preserving the track for future use. Over the years it has turned into a full-fledged excursion line with a new train-boarding area and a small depot in downtown Coopersville.

SCHEDULES and FARES
Coopersville & Marne Railway trains run from April through December. Regular and themed excursions are available. Adult fares are generally around $10. Please call or check website for current schedules and fares.

EQUIPMENT
SW9 switcher locomotive, No. 7014
5 coaches
Red caboose, 1940s

CONTACT
Coopersville & Marne Railway
P.O. Box 55
Coopersville, MI 49404
616-997-7000
www.coopersvilleandmarne.org

Photos: Coopersville & Marne RR

THE HENRY FORD
Dearborn, MI

Visitors to Greenfield Village have the opportunity to explore 300 years of history as the sights, sounds, and sensations of America's past come alive. And you can explore this town on the Weiser Railroad, a vintage steam locomotive that makes stops throughout the village along its three-mile route. Start at Railroad Junction, where you can explore Smiths Creek Depot and the Detroit, Toledo & Milwaukee Roundhouse.

Greenfield Village was the result of Henry Ford's desire to create a showcase for the best and brightest stories on how our country was built. This 88-acre setting is the largest indoor/outdoor museum complex in America. There is also a fully equipped roundhouse on site.

SCHEDULES and FARES
Greenfield Village is open from April 15 to December 31. Please call or check website for current schedules and fares.

EQUIPMENT
The Fair Lane, built in 1920-21 by the Pullman Company in Kensington, IL.
C & O Allegheny No. 160, built in 1941

CONTACT
The Henry Ford
20900 Oakwood Blvd.
Dearborn, MI 48124-4088
313-982-6100
313-982-6150 (recorded information)
313-271-2455 (TDD)
www.hfmgv.org

Photos: Henry Ford Museum & Greenfield Village Museum

HUCKLEBERRY RAILROAD AT CROSSROADS VILLAGE
Flint, MI

The Huckleberry Railroad was so named because it ran so slow; a person could jump off the train, pick huckleberries and jump back on the train with minimum effort.

The Huckleberry Railroad began its history in 1857 as part of the Flint Pere Marquette Railroad Company. The Flint Pere Marquette Railroad Company was organized on June 22, 1857. The branch of the Pere Marquette from Flint to Otter Lake (15 miles) was constructed under the Flint River Railroad Charter and opened in 1872. It was later known as the Otter Lake Branch. Eventually the track was extended to another 4.5 miles from Otter Lake to Fostoria, for a total of 19.5 miles from Flint to Fostoria.

Pere Marquette was absorbed by the C&O (Chesapeake and Ohio) Railroad. The C&O merged and other railroad lines merged with the B&O to become the Chessie System. The Chessie System is now CSX.

Currently, the Huckleberry Railroad owns 7 locomotives. Of the 7 locomotives, #2 and #464 are the primary locomotives that serve the Huckleberry Railroad. The Huckleberry Railroad #2, formally known as #152 locomotive, is a 4-6-0 (wheel arrangement) built in June of 1920 by Baldwin Locomotive Works of Philadelphia, PA for the Alaska Engineering Commission (AEC). The AEC purchased #2 and the Tanana Valley Railroad to further its task of building the Alaska Railroad. Each and every coach, caboose, and car is very unique in its origins and history. Ride the Huckleberry Railroad and see history come to life!

SCHEDULES AND FARES:
The railroad runs Memorial through Labor Day, in October for Halloween Ghosts and Goodies, and in December for Christmas at Crossroads Holiday Magic.

EQUIPMENT:
As of January 2003, the Huckleberry Railroad own and operate 7 locomotives, two cabooses, one hopper car, and motor car (Speeder).

CONTACT:
Huckleberry Railroad at Crossroads Village
6140 Bray Rd, Flint MI 48505
260.316.0529
http://geneseecountyparks.org/huckleberry_
railroad.htm

MICHIGAN TRANSIT MUSEUM
Mount Clemens, MI

Get your seat on a 1920s interurban rapid-transit car and take a ride through the Selfridge Air National Guard Base. The train leaves Joy Park for a 45-minute ride on a route laid out in the early 1900s, when it served the sugar beet mill of the Mt. Clemens (Franklin) Sugar Company. On your ride, you'll see small industrial developments, farmland, and suburban areas. Give yourself at least an hour to explore the Selfridge Military Air Museum.

You'll also want to visit the Mount Clemens Depot Museum, originally built for the Chicago, Detroit & Canada Grand Trunk Junction Railway. It was here in 1862 that young Thomas Edison saved the station agent's small child from certain death when he pulled her off the tracks and out of the path of a rolling boxcar. In appreciation, the station master taught Edison telegraphy. Many of Edison's early inventions came from what he learned at the depot.

SCHEDULES and FARES
The Michigan Transit Museum is open year-round on weekends. Adult fares are generally under $10. Special trains are available. For an additional fee, you can also visit the Air Museum. You must have photo identification for Air Museum entrance. Please call or check website for current schedules and fares.

EQUIPMENT
No. 1807, built in 1941 by the American Locomotive Company
EL cars Nos. 442 and 4450, built in 1924 by the Cincinnati Car Company for the Chicago Transit Authority
No. 77058, caboose built near the turn of the century
No. 4040 RS-4
Other streetcars under restoration

CONTACT
Michigan Transit Museum
200 Grand Avenue
Mt. Clemens, MI 48046
586-463-1863
www.michigantransitmuseum.org

Photo: Michigan Transit Museum

OLD ROAD DINNER TRAIN/MYSTERY DINNER TRAIN (ADRIAN & BLISSFIELD RAILROAD)
Blissfield, MI

This excursion is more comedy than drama, but it still involves a murder mystery. The depot is in Blissfield on the Adrian & Blissfield Railroad. You can also catch a ride on a mystery dinner train from Charlotte near Lansing. Either way, you will be taking a leisurely trip through the countryside. The excursion will take from two to three hours, depending on where you board. Expect fine dining, entertainment, and audience participation on this 12-mile round trip.

The show is rated PG-13 and would be considered adult-oriented humor. All tables seat four guests and are elegantly appointed with white linens, crystal, and china. We may combine couples into a table of four, in traditional railroad dining car practice.

SCHEDULES and FARES
The Old Road Dinner Trains/Mystery Dinner Train departs on selected Fridays, Saturdays, and Sundays. Reservations are required. Please call or check website for current schedules and fares.

EQUIPMENT
2 GP9 locomotives
CONTACT
Old Road Dinner Train
301 E. Adrian Street (US-223)
Blissfield, MI 49228
888-467-2451 (toll free)
517-486-5979
abrrdp@tc3net.com
www.murdermysterytrain.com

Photos: Old Road Dinner Train

SOUTHERN MICHIGAN RAILROAD SOCIETY, INC.
Clinton, MI

On August 9, 1838, the first train rolled into Tecumseh, Michigan; 164 years later, the Southern Michigan Railroad Society continues to operate a train along "The Clinton Branch Line." The nickname stuck after tracks from Jackson to Clinton were abandoned and removed between 1963 and 1965. "The Southern Michigan Railroad Society, Inc." was formed in 1982 with the express purpose of bringing the Clinton Branch back to its original glory and increasing awareness of railroading history.

SMRS offers a variety of passenger train tours between the towns of Clinton and Tecumseh. The railroad crosses the River Raisin twice as it winds its way through scenic countryside from Clinton to the railroad's southernmost terminal at Raisin Center.

SCHEDULES and FARES

The Southern Museum Railroad Society is open from May through September. Special events and charters are available. Children under 16 must be accompanied by an adult. Adult fares are generally under $15. Please call or check website for current schedules and fares.

EQUIPMENT

1943 Western Maryland GE 44-ton center-cab
1960 prototype General Motors GMDH-3
1947 New York Central mill gondola
1926 Chicago South Shore & South Bend Railroad car No. 1
1947 NYNH former PC cupola caboose

CONTACT

The Southern Michigan Railroad Society, Inc.
320 S. Division Street
Clinton, MI 49236
517-456-7677
www.southernmichiganrailroad.org

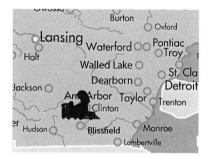

Photos: Southern Michigan Railroad Society

Did You Know...

The longest railway station in the world is Grand Central Station in New York. It has 44 platforms.

MICHIGAN STATE TRUST FOR RAILWAY PRESERVATION, INC.
Owosso, MI

The Michigan State Trust for Railway Preservation, Inc., maintains and operates steam locomotives as educational tools to enhance the programs of the Steam Railroading Institute. They strive to educate the public about steam-era railroad technology and its impact on the culture and economy of the Great Lakes region by safely operating, preserving, exhibiting, and interpreting historic railroad equipment.

The preservation's excursion trains currently feature operationing locomotives Nos. 1225 and 75. The restoration of Nos. 76 and 10 was ongoing. The locomotives will visit communities to demonstrate the equipment and technology of the steam era. The North Pole Express, hauled by No. 1225 and used as the basis for the movie *Polar Express*, operates trips to the "North Pole" over four weekends in November and December, and quickly sells out. Please call for availability of tickets.

The Steam Railroading Institute is the base of operations for the Pere Marquette No. 1225 and Flagg Coal Company No. 75. It provides the necessary support mechanisms, offices, mechanical maintenance, archives, and exhibit storage, a museum where the craft of locomotive maintenance is demonstrated and taught.

SCHEDULES and FARES
The Michigan State Trust for Railway Preservation/Steam Railroading Institute Visitor Center is open from Memorial Day through Labor Day. During December, the North Pole Express runs. The steam locomotive No. 75 operates from Memorial Day through Labor Day. Please call or check website for current schedules and fares.

EQUIPMENT
Pere Marquette steam locomotive No. 1225
Flagg Coal Co. steam locomotive No. 75
Mississsipian Railway steam locomotive No. 76
Detroit & Mackinac diesel locomotive No. 10
Ann Arbor Caboose No. 2839
Pere Marquette caboose No. A909
NCCX 1701, former PM No. 361 troop sleeper
50' PM boxcar No. 72332
C&O combine car
C&O "City of Ashland" Pullman sleeper

CONTACT
Michigan State Trust for Railway
Preservation, Inc.
P.O. Box 665
Owosso, MI 48867-0665
989-725-9464
989-723-1225 (fax)
tjgaffney@mstrp.com
www.mstrp.com

TRAIN TRAVEL, INC.
Walled Lake, MI

Train Travel, Inc., has been providing rail entertainment experiences for over twenty-three years and continues its tradition of providing unique rail-themed escursions.

Michigan Star Clipper Dinner Train
Experience America's premiere dinner train, where you enjoy a chef-prepared five-course meal with live entertainment while traveling in beautifully restored passenger cars from the golden days of railroad travel.

Walled Lake Scenic Railway
Enjoy a unique rail experience on vintage pre-WWII, open-air passenger cars. Each train has a different theme. Come enjoy an old-fashioned train ride with friends and loved ones.

Pullman Palace Bed & Breakfast
The Pullman Palace Bed & Breakfast is the perfect complement to your Michigan Star Clipper Dinner Train experience. Spend the night in our historic and beautifully restored first-class sleeping car, Vista Cavern, or our Kentucky Thoroughbred car. Reserve early as space is limited.

Steel Wheels Entertainment Train

The Steel Wheels Entertainment Train is located on Track "59 North" at the historic 1887 Walled Lake depot. It offers a unique club setting aboard authentic railroad cars providing Comedy Club nights and music. Steel Wheels is also available for uniquely designed off-site corporate meetings, receptions, and other group functions.

SCHEDULES and FARES

The dates that the trains run vary according to the excursion you choose. Please call or check website for current schedules and fares.

EQUIPMENT

Electromotive F-9
Star Clipper lounge
Meadow Rose car
Michigan Spruce car
Vista Chef, kitchen car
Kentucky Thoroughbred lounge
Vista Cavern
Vista Power
Caboose No. 62

CONTACT

Train Travel, Inc.
840 North Pontiac Trail
Walled Lake, MI 48390
248-960-9440
248-960-9444 (fax)
www.rail-road.com

Photos: Train Travel, Inc.

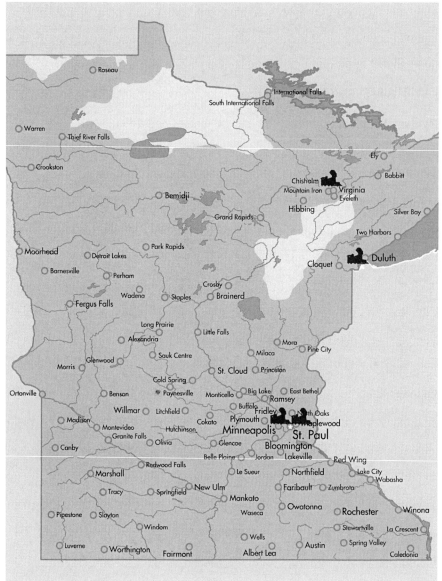

MINNESOTA

Roseau

International Falls
South International Falls

Warren
Thief River Falls

Ely

Crookston

Chisholm Babbitt
Mountain Iron Virginia
Bemidji Eveleth
Hibbing
Grand Rapids Silver Bay

Two Harbors

Park Rapids
Moorhead Detroit Lakes
Cloquet Duluth
Barnesville Perham

Crosby
Wadena Staples Brainerd
Fergus Falls

Long Prairie Little Falls
Alexandria Mora
Pine City
Glenwood Sauk Centre Milaca
Morris
Cold Spring St. Cloud Princeton
Ortonville Benson Paynesville Monticello Big Lake East Bethel
Ramsey
Willmar Litchfield Buffalo Fridley North Oaks
Madison Cokato Plymouth Maplewood
Montevideo Hutchinson Minneapolis St. Paul
Granite Falls
Canby Olivia Glencoe Bloomington
Belle Plaine Jordan Lakeville
Redwood Falls Red Wing
Marshall Le Sueur Northfield Lake City
Wabasha
Tracy Springfield New Ulm Faribault Zumbrota
Mankato
Pipestone Slayton Waseca Owatonna Rochester Winona
Windom Stewartville La Crescent
Wells
Luverne Worthington Austin Spring Valley
Fairmont Albert Lea Caledonia

JACKSON STREET ROUNDHOUSE MUSEUM
St. Paul, MN

Jackson Street Roundhouse Museum is housed in a former Great Northern Railroad Roundhouse, built in 1907, and commissioned by James J Hill to service passenger locomotives. Between 1959 and 1985 it was converted to non railroad uses, the tracks and turntable were removed and both have been replaced. The turntable is operable and rides are offered on it weather permitting.

Visitors can roam the roundhouse and the outdoor grounds, take a short caboose ride pulled by a switcher engine and participate in interactive exhibits. Tours of the roundhouse where equipment restoration takes place are also available.

SCHEDULES AND FARES:
The museum is open Wednesdays and Saturdays year round and Sundays during Santa's Train Shop in December. Tickets range from $5-10 for admission.

EQUIPMENT:
10 Locomotives
16 Passenger Cars
20 Freight Cars
6 Cabooses

CONTACT:
193 Pennsylvania Ave E
St. Paul, MN 55130
651-228-0263
www.mtmuseum.org/jsrh.shtml

LAKE SUPERIOR RAILROAD MUSEUM
Duluth, MN

The Lake Superior Railroad Museum has one of the largest collections of railroad cars, locomotives, and other pieces in the country: from antique steam locomotives to green Pullman coaches to rare cabooses to elegant parlor cars to old diesel engines. The museum has been educating and displaying artifacts since 1892. Some of the highlights of your visit will include a look at the William Crooks and the Mallet; two steam powered locomotives, the Dining Car China Exhibit, the Railway Post Office, and a number of freight cars.

Visitors have the opportunity to see how railroading of the past served both passengers and industry. Examine the equipment used to maintain the railroads, including hand propelled pump cars, track tools, a hyrail inspection car, and a steam-powered wrecker. Group opportunities for learning are available, but we recommend that you book in advance because space is limited.

SCHEDULES and FARES
The Lake Superior Railroad Museum is open year-round. The admission fee, which is generally under $10, is good for all museums connected to the Depot including the Duluth Children's Museum, the Duluth Art Institute, and the St. Louis County Historical Society. Rides are available through the North Shore Scenic Railroad. Please call or check website for current schedules and fares.

EQUIPMENT
Numerous steam locomotives, diesel locomotives, and cabooses
Mack Industrial Switcher Harvest States
SOO Line No. 700

CONTACT
Lake Superior Railroad Museum
506 W. Michigan Street
Duluth, MN 55802
218-733-7519
www.lsrm.org

LAKE SUPERIOR & MISSISSIPPI RAILROAD
Duluth, MN

The original Lake Superior and Mississippi Railroad was incorporated in 1863 and began building the first railroad linking the Twin Cities and Duluth. The line followed the St. Louis River through Fond du Lac, Morgan Park, and West Duluth, ending in downtown Duluth. The first passenger trains began operation in September 1870.

The Lake Superior and Mississippi Railroad existed until 1877, when it was purchased by the St. Paul and Duluth and later absorbed into the Northern Pacific System. The railroad was later relocated to eliminate a number of curves and ease the grade between West Duluth and Carlton. The new line split from the original route near the location of the present Lake Superior Zoo. However, the original line continued in service as the Northern Pacific Railroad provided commuter train service to Fond du Lac until the 1930s.

The present Lake Superior and Mississippi Railroad was incorporated in 1981 by a group of volunteers from the Lake Superior Transportation Club. The 90-minute trip follows the shoreline of the St. Louis River estuary, Spirit Lake, and Mud Lake. This historic route provides a chance to view wildlife in its natural environment, while enjoying the majestic beauty of the river and surrounding area.

SCHEDULES and FARES
The Lake Superior and Mississippi Railroad is open on weekends from June through October. It is also open on Labor Day. Adult fares are generally under $10. Please call or check website for current schedules and fares.

EQUIPMENT
General Electric center cab 50T type industrial switcher, 1946
Coach 29, built in 1912 by American Car and Foundry
Coach 85, built in 1912 by American Car
Safari Car, once a flatcar built in 1928 by Siems-Staubel Co.

CONTACT
Lake Superior & Mississippi Railroad
P.O. Box 16211
Duluth, MN 55816
218-624-7549
info@lsmrr.org
www.lsmrr.org

Photos: Lake Superior & Mississippi Railroad Museum

MINNESOTA TRANSPORTATION MUSEUM
Minneapolis, MN

If it rode on rails or was powered by steam, chances are it is part of the network of working exhibits and restored buildings that make up the Minnesota Transportation Museum.

Fans of steam railroading will want to take a ride on the Osceola & St. Croix Valley Railway. Although maintained by the Minnesota Transportation Museum, the train actually departs and returns to the Osceola Depot in Osceola, Wisconsin. The depot was built in 1916 to replace an earlier wooden structure. It was unusual for the builders, the Soo Line, to erect such a substantial brick depot in such a small town, but a local businessman persuaded the railroad to do so. Only three depots were built for the Soo Line using this floor plan. You can choose among several trips between Minnesota and Wisconsin, from hour-long excursions to guided tours to Sunday brunch and specialty-themed trains.

Fans of streetcars will want to hop aboard beautifully restored streetcars to take a scenic trolley trip on part of the original right-of-way that once stretched from

Stillwater to Lake Minnetonka. You can depart from a number of depots, including the Linden Hills Station (a replica of a turn-of-the-century depot built by the Twin City Rapid Transit and located on the shore of Lake Harriett in Minneapolis).

The Milwaukee Road Depot at Minnehaha Falls is nicknamed "The Princess" and is one of the oldest depots that museum visitors will encounter. It was built in 1875. There are plenty of docents and displays of interest. The museum also manages the Jackson Street Roundhouse (complete with restored turntable), the Excelsior Steamboat, the Excelsior Street Depot, and a number of other depots and building sites.

SCHEDULES and FARES
Operating schedules, admission fees, and fares vary according to the part of the museum complex you visit. Please call or check website for current schedules and fares.

EQUIPMENT
The museum features an extensive collection of rolling stock, including locomotives, rail cars, trolleys, interurbans, and related equipment.

CONTACT
Minnesota Transportation Museum, Inc.
4926 Minnehaha Avenue
Minneapolis, MN
651-228-0263
admin@mtmuseum.org
www.mtmuseum.org

Photos: Eric Hopp

NORTH SHORE SCENIC RAILROAD
Duluth, MN

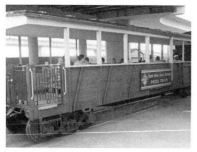

The North Shore Scenic Railroad operates excursions along the historic Lakefront Line, a 26-mile section of rail between Duluth and Two Harbors. This rail corridor served a vital link in the transportation system for over 100 years. Today the North Shore Scenic Railroad offers three different excursions:

The Lester River Excursion follows the shores of Lake Superior for 3.5 miles, then takes you 3.5 miles through wooded and residential areas, over two bridges, to the Lester River.

The Two Harbors Excursion travels for 3.5 miles along the shores of Lake Superior, through wooded and residential areas, and over seven scenic bridges to Two Harbors.

The Pizza Train Excursion includes half a pizza and soda as it travels for 3.5 miles along the shores of Lake Superior, through wooded and residential areas, and over five bridges to Palmer's Siding, just short of Knife River.

SCHEDULES and FARES
The three excursions offered by the North Shore Scenic Railroad are available from May through September. The Two Harbors Excursion is also available in October. Adult fares vary between $10 and $20. Please call or check website for current schedules and fares.

EQUIPMENT
Duluth, Missabe & Iron Range (DM&IR) No. 193
Soo Line No. 2500
Great Northern No. 192
BUDD CAR- referred to as an "RDC" or "rail diesel car"
Coaches A-13 & A-14
Duluth, Missabe & Iron Range (DM&IR) No. 33
Duluth, Missabe & Iron Range Railway Minnesota II
Open-air car
Baggage car No. 1000
Spokane, Portland and Seattle baggage car No. 66
Great Northern dining car No. 1250 "Lake of the Isles"
Northern Pacific No. 1311

CONTACT
North Shore Scenic Railroad
506 West Michigan Street
Duluth, MN 55802
218-722-1273
800-423-1273
www.northshorescenicrailroad.org

Photos: North Shore Scenic Railroad

Did You Know...

Mexican President General Antonia Lopez de Santa Anna owned stock in the Lackawanna Railroad, chartered in 1854 with plans to operate between Jessup and Nay Aug, Pennsylvania. Part of the route became a branch line of the Delaware, Lackawanna & Western Railroad.

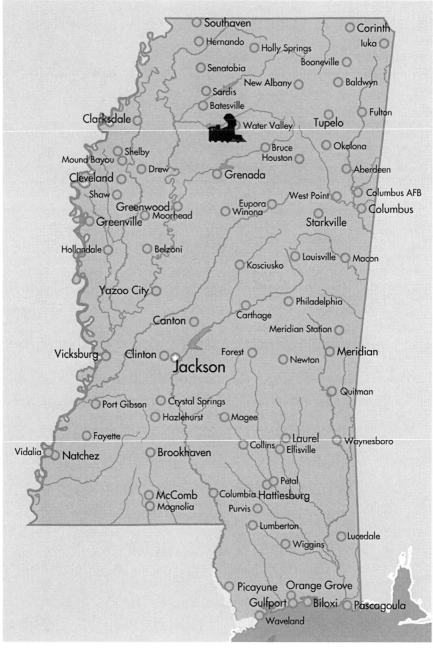

MISSISSIPPI

Southaven
Corinth
Hernando
Iuka
Holly Springs
Booneville
Senatobia
New Albany
Baldwyn
Sardis
Batesville
Fulton
Clarksdale
Water Valley
Tupelo
Bruce
Okolona
Shelby
Houston
Mound Bayou
Drew
Aberdeen
Cleveland
Grenada
Shaw
West Point
Columbus AFB
Greenwood
Eupora
Columbus
Moorhead
Winona
Greenville
Starkville
Hollandale
Belzoni
Louisville
Macon
Kosciusko
Yazoo City
Philadelphia
Canton
Carthage
Meridian Station
Vicksburg
Clinton
Forest
Meridian
Jackson
Newton
Quitman
Port Gibson
Crystal Springs
Hazlehurst
Magee
Fayette
Laurel
Waynesboro
Collins
Ellisville
Vidalia
Natchez
Brookhaven
Petal
McComb
Columbia
Hattiesburg
Magnolia
Purvis
Lumberton
Lucedale
Wiggins
Picayune
Orange Grove
Gulfport
Biloxi
Pascagoula
Waveland

WATER VALLEY CASEY JONES RAILWAY MUSEUM
Water Valley, MS

Many are fascinated by the life and times of Casey Jones and the crash in 1900 that took his life. The Water Valley Casey Jones Railway Museum, which contains Casey Jones stories and artifacts, is a living tribute to America's most famous train engineer. The museum is located very near the site in Vaughan where the wreck happened. Historians have worked over the years to separate fact from fiction. The Water Valley Lions Club is currently working on renovating the old depot that houses the museum.

Volunteers invite you to be a part of our annual Hobo Gathering in April following the Amory Railroad Festival at Amory, Mississippi, and preceding the gathering at the Casey Jones Museum in Jackson, Tennessee.

SCHEDULES and FARES
The museum and gift shop are open Thursday, Friday, and Saturday. You can also make an appointment. There is no entrance fee, but donations are welcome. Please call or check website for current schedules and fares.

CONTACT
Water Valley Casey Jones Railway Museum
105 Railroad Avenue
Water Valley, MS 38965
662-473-2849
662-473-1154
gurnerj@watervalley.net
www.watervalley.net/users/
caseyjones/home.htm

Photos: Water Valley Casey Jones Railway Museum

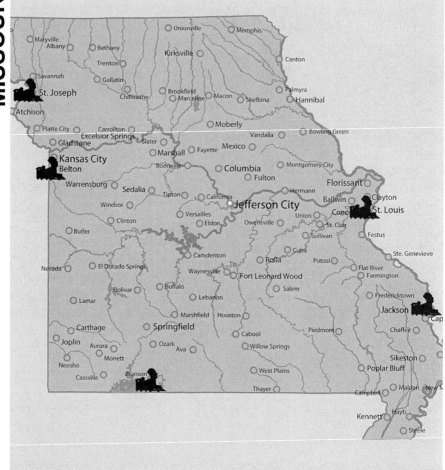

AMERICAN RAILWAY CABOOSE HISTORICAL EDUCATIONAL SOCIETY, INC.
St. Louis, MO

Want to buy or sell a caboose? Know the location of a long-forgotten caboose? Want to join people in more than 33 states and Canada who love the caboose as much as you do? Then become a member of the American Railway Caboose Historical Educational Society, Inc. The society has 30 "cabeese" stored at different locations in Missouri and Illinois. Some are on loan to other railroad museums.

Members of the society enjoy receiving the "Caboose News," and submitting items on the society's online members' bulletin board. The society also has published the definitive book on the caboose. *Captive Cabeese in America* is a reference to more than 5,000 caboose locations.

SCHEDULES and FARES
This is a membership organization. Please call or check website for current fares.

EQUIPMENT
The society owns over 30 cabeese

CONTACT
American Railway Caboose Historical
Educational Society
P.O. Box 2772
St. Louis, MO 63116-2255
314-752-3148
ed@arches.org
www.arches.org

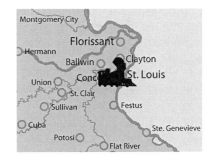

Photos: American Railway Caboose Historical Educational Society and Ed Mertes

BELTON, GRANDVIEW & KANSAS CITY RAILROAD CO.
Belton, MO

Come take a step back in time to the first half of the last century and ride a train like one that your grandparents may have ridden. Board a 1920s-era passenger coach or a open-air excursion car and take a ride behind a 1950s diesel locomotive through Old Towne Belton, Missouri, and the surrounding area. You could even ride in the caboose with the conductor or in the cab of the locomotive with the engineer.

The Belton, Grandview and Kansas City Railroad Co. is a short-line passenger railroad and demonstration museum. The BG&KC offers excursions on its line running south from Belton on a 5-mile, 45-minute round trip. The railroad is an all volunteer, not-for-profit organization dedicated to preserving rail travel and railroading.

While you are waiting for the train, walk around the yard and look at the display equipment, freight cars, club car, instruction car, maintenance-of-way equipment, and two static display steam locomotives. Visit the Baggage Car Gift Shop, talk to the train crew, and even visit the locomotive. Finish off your trip with a visit to the shops of Main Street Belton.

SCHEDULES and FARES
The BG&KC operates from June through October with regularly scheduled excursions. It offers locomotive and caboose rides along with an ice cream train. Schedules and fares vary. Note: Although the company does its best to accommodate all its guests, it is unable to accommodate persons in wheel chairs or those with very limited mobility. Please call or check website for current schedules and fares.

EQUIPMENT
B&O GP9 No. 102
Frisco 1918 Baldwin 2-10-0 No. 1632
Okmulgee No. 5
Alco 2-8-0
KCS observation lounge
MoPac 1972 wide-vision caboose
UP 1928 wood CA-1 caboose

CONTACT
Belton, Grandview & Kansas City Railroad Co.
502 E. Walnut Street
Belton, MO 64012
816-331-0630
info@beltonrailroad.org
www.beltonrailroad.org

Photos: Belton, Grandview & Kansas City Railroad Company

BRANSON SCENIC RAILWAY
Branson, MO

America's romance with the vintage passenger train lives on through excursions on the Branson Scenic Railway aboard a collection of unique passenger cars that travel through the foothills of the Ozark Mountains. This 1.75-hour trip takes passengers through tunnels, over trestles, and through the southwest Missouri or northwest Arkansas wilderness that is still home to much wildlife and to the ruins of long-ago communities now named only on railroad maps.

The train departs from the old depot heading either north or south. The northern route goes as far as Galena, Missouri, to the James River Valley; and the southern route extends into Arkansas to the Barren Fork Trestle. The railroad is known as the White River Route. The route crosses the White River in Branson, now Lake Taneycomo, and then runs alongside it after taking a fifty-mile "short cut" over the Ozark Mountains. Branson Scenic Railway explores territory inaccessible by automobile and offers views that are unattainable by any other means of transportation. A lively narration points out the landmarks, such as Crest Tunnel, Cricket Tunnel, Walnut Creek Trestle, Barren Fork Trestle, and Tharp's Grade. The extinct communities of Gretna,

Melva, and Ruth are described as they were in the early 20th century.

The comfort of the vintage passenger cars is quite a contrast to the harsh realities the railroad pioneers found when they undertook bringing rail service to the Ozarks. The railway was built in two sections: a northward line beginning at Batesville, Arkansas, and the other going south from Carthage, Missouri. Construction began in January 1902, and the final spike was driven on December 29, 1905, joining the northern and southern sections.

SCHEDULES and FARES
The Branson Scenic Railway runs its excursions from March through December. Special events and excursions are available. Fares vary according to excursion but generally range for adults from $20 to $50. Please call or check website for current schedules and fares.

EQUIPMENT
BSRX 98, locomotive, 1951 EMD F9PH, rebuilt 1981
BSRX 99, locomotive, 1962 EMD GP30M, rebuilt 1982
PPCX 800603, "Silver Eagle," 1949 Budd 60-seat coach
BSRX 3118, "Silver Lake," 1951 Budd buffet lounge
BSRX 9540, "Silver Island," 1947 Budd dome lounge
BSRX 8503, "Silver Chef," 1956 Budd 48-seat diner
PPCX 800287, "Silver Garden," 1952 Budd dome lounge coach
PPCX 800336, "Westport," 1939 Budd lounge observation car
BSRX 9320, "Silver Terrace," 1952 Budd dome observation car

CONTACT
Branson Scenic Railway
206 East Main Street
Branson, MO. 65615-0924
800-2TRAIN2
417-334-6110
417-336-3909 (fax)
reservations@bransontrain.com
www.bransontrain.com

Photos: Branson Scenic Railway

COLUMBIA STAR DINNER TRAIN
Columbia, MO

Treat your family, friends or business associates to a unique experience with a nostalgic dinning rail journey. The Columbia Star Dinner Train offers guests gourmet dining onboard a beautifully appointed vintage 1930s and 40s passenger cars pulled by 1950s streamlined passenger locomotives on a relaxing 2 1/2 to 3 hour journey.

Recapture the romance of a by-gone era while watching the Missouri landscape roll by your window. While on board our guests will be treated to delicious appetizers, drinks and a Chef-prepared elegant four course gourmet meal all prepared right on the train. Prestigious railroad dining is recreated on white linen and fine china by candlelight with exemplary service from their wait staff.

From a simple reception to a chartered car or train for a special day or evening trip, guests will be pampered by the impeccably trained service staff. From hors d'oeuvres to a full gourmet dinner & music, they can customize the details.

SCHEDULES and FARES:
The Columbia Star Dinner Train runs year round on Saturdays and Sundays. Fares are between $60 and $80. The train travels on a two and a half to three hour long trip covering 30 miles. All reservations must be taken over the phone. Dates and other information is available at www.dinnertrain.com

EQUIPMENT:
The locomotives are a1950 and 1950 F-Unit built by the Electro-Motive Division of General Motors. Our dining cars were built by the Pullman Car Company in 1938 for the Southern Pacific Railroad as coach cars and were later converted to dining cars. They are unique in that they are articulated, meaning that they share a set of trucks between two car bodies. The kitchen is a former Chicago Burlington and Quincy Baggage car that has been converted to a full kitchen.

CONTACT:
Columbia Star Dinner Train
6501 North Brown Station Road
Columbia, MO 65202-9324
(573)-474-2223
877-236-8511
www.dinnertrain.com

MUSEUM OF TRANSPORTATION
St. Louis, MO

The Museum of Transportation houses "one of the largest and best collections of transportation vehicles in the world," according to John H. White, Jr., Curator Emeritus of the Smithsonian Institution. The museum is located on 150 acres west of the city of St. Louis, on the site of the first manmade railroad tunnels west of the Mississippi River. It features over four miles of exhibit and switching track, parts of which are covered by two large train sheds.

The museum can be easily visited on hardsurfaced paths throughout the grounds. Excellent signs describe the items on exhibit and make self-guided visits easy, fun, and informative. Visitors will find cabooses, rail cars, and locomotive cabs open, with special stairs and signs to allow anyone to be the engineer. The "Big Boy" cab is normally open, and in another steam locomotive you can ring the bell. You can also walk the deck of the "H. T. Pott," a Missouri River towboat, and see our WWII C-47 transport airplane.

SCHEDULES and FARES
The museum is open year-round. It is closed on most national holidays. The museum's hours of operation vary with the season. Adult admission is generally under $5. Please call or check website for current schedules and fares.

EQUIPMENT
The rail collection contains more than 140 pieces, including 33 steam locomotives, the largest in North America.

CONTACT
Museum of Transportation
3015 Barrett Station Road
St. Louis, MO 63122
314-965-7998
www.museumoftransport.org

Photo: **Museum of Transportation**

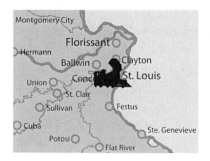

PATEE HOUSE MUSEUM
St. Joseph, MO

Visitors to Patee House may sip a sarsaparilla while listening to the nickelodeon in the 1854 Buffalo Saloon. There's a large operating model railroad, a Japanese Tea House ice cream parlor, and right next door is the Jesse James Home Museum where the outlaw was killed. Inside Patee House Museum is the last Hannibal & St. Joseph Railroad steam locomotive and railway mail car. This static exhibit sits beside the 1878 railroad depot in an authentic setting.

The Hannibal & St. Joseph Railroad stretched from Hannibal, Missouri, on the Mississippi River to St. Joseph on the Missouri River, a distance of 196 miles across northern Missouri. When the line was completed on February 14, 1859, it made St. Joseph the western terminus of railroads in the United States until after the Civil War.

The Patee House fills a square block and houses a museum of transportation and communication. It is now a National Historical Landmark for being the headquarters of the Pony Express.

SCHEDULES and FARES
The Patee House Museum is open from April through October. Admission for adults is generally under $5. Please call or check website for current schedules and fares.

EQUIPMENT
Baldwin 4-4-0, 1880
Tender for the wood-burning locomotive
One of the first railway mail cars, invented by a St. Joseph postmaster

CONTACT
Patee House Museum
1202 Penn Street.
Saint Joseph, MO 64503
816-232-8206
816-232-3717 (fax)
www.stjoseph.net/ponyexpress/

Photos: Patee House Museum

ST. LOUIS IRON MOUNTAIN & SOUTHERN RAILWAY
Jackson, MO

Whether you have an hour or a day to spend, you will not want to miss the chance to take a ride back in time on the St. Louis Iron Mountain & Southern Railway. Sit back and relax as you take a trip on the historic Iron Mountain line. Enjoy the stories of Jesse James, Civil War battles, and the pioneering spirit that made the Iron Mountain one of America's great railroads. Your trip takes you to Gordonville, a 10-mile, 1.5-hour excursion.

Dinner trains are available from May through October. Enjoy scrumptious food while you travel a leisurely two-hour trip on 16 miles of rail. Special Murder Mystery trains are scheduled throughout the year. Be a hero by solving the mystery of the Iron Mountain "killer," all the while enjoying a fine meal and an entertaining train ride. Other special weekends include sightseeing excursions and the James Gang Weekend.

SCHEDULES and FARES
The St. Louis Iron Mountain & Southern Railway offers numerous excursions from May through October. It also offers a winter schedule. Fares vary according to the trip. Please call or check website for current schedules and fares.

EQUIPMENT
E8 No. 5898

CONTACT
St. Louis Iron Mountain & Southern Railway
Intersection of Highways 61, 72, and 25
Jackson, MO
800-455-RAIL (7245)
573-243-1688
www.rosecity.net/trains

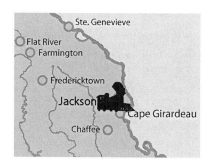

Photos: St. Louis Iron Mountain & Southern Railway

AMERICAN ASSOCIATION OF RAILROADERS, INC.
St. Louis, MO

The American Association of Railroaders, Inc., is one of the most active rail interest groups in the country, sponsoring more than 40 events a year. Events range from local rail industry visits to one-day excursions and extended rail tours. An annual meeting held during the first weekend of March reviews the events of the previous year and plans for the months ahead. A slide show program with vignettes from the last 40 years is a favorite feature.

The organization has over 700 members mainly from the Missouri-Illinois region, but our activities have drawn participants from 25 states and several foreign countries. The association provides a monthly newsletter listing upcoming events. In addition to the rail tours, the group is Amtrak's best customer in Missouri and a strong supporter of public transportation. In 2007 the nonprofit organization celebrated 40 years of railroading.

SCHEDULES and FARES
Anyone can become a member. Dues are $15 annully. Part of your membership includes a subscription to the AAR newsletter that goes out every 4 to 6 weeks. Special excursions are planned throughout the year. Please call or check website for current schedules and fares.

EQUIPMENT
1958 Trailways bus used for members and local excursions.

CONTACT
American Association of Railroaders, Inc.
4351 Holly Hills Boulevard
St. Louis, MO 63116-2255
314-752-3148
www.aar-therailroaders.org

Photo: Ed Mertes

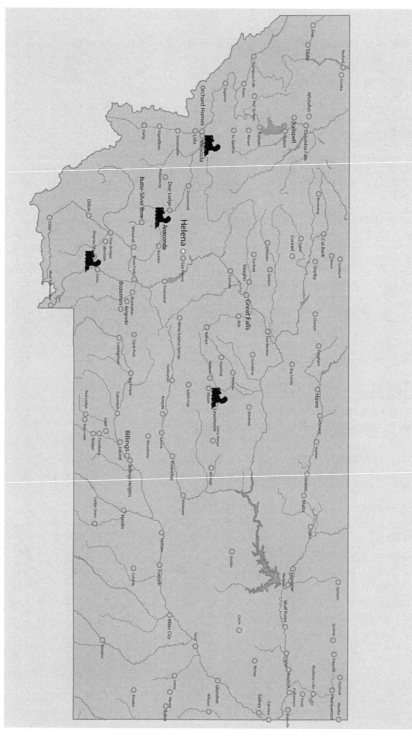

MONTANA

ALDER GULCH SHORT LINE RAILROAD
Virginia City, MT

A century ago, the coming of the railroad was the biggest news for many Montana communities but the main-line rails never reached Virginia City during the great era of railroad building. In May of 1902, the railroad did reach Alder, about ten miles away. It was not until 1964 that things changed for Virginia City. Charlie Bovey bought and opened the 30-inch gauge "Alder Gulch Short Line Railroad". The 1.5-mile line now connects Virginia City to Nevada City following the Alder Creek.

The Virginia City Depot, originally built by the Northern Pacific at Harrison, Montana, about 1895, arrived a few weeks later, prompting a Virginia City citizen to remark, "I have often gone down to the depot to see the train pull in, but this is the first time I ever went down to the train to watch the depot pull in."

SCHEDULES and FARES
The Adler Gulch Short Line Railroad runs excursions daily from late May to early September. New schedules and rates are posted annually. Special excursions are available. Please call or check website for current schedules and fares.

EQUIPMENT
No. 12, 1910 Baldwin steam locomotive
Plymouth passenger coaches, 191 (50-60 passengers)
No. 8, gasoline powered engine, 1992
4 passenger cars (32 passengers)

CONTACT
Montana Heritage Commission
P.O. Box 338
Virginia City, MT 59755
406-843-5247
406-843-5468 (fax)
www.virginiacitymt.com
(click on Alder Gulch Short Line Railroad)

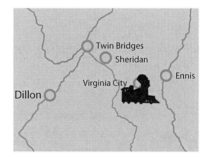

CHARLIE RUSSELL CHEW-CHOO
Lewistown, MT

As you ride the Charlie Russell Chew-Choo from Kingston Junction to Denton, you will pass though some of the most scenic country in Central Montana. The route follows the old Milwaukee Railroad line through the landscape that inspired much of the art done by turn-of-the-century Western artist Charlie Russell. The 3.5-hour ride also offers dinner on board 1950s vintage train cars.

You will travel 28 miles to Denton, crossing three trestles, passing through a tunnel, enjoying a prime rib dinner catered by the Yogo Inn of Lewistown, and perhaps encountering a surprise or two along the way. This is wonderful "watchable wildlife" country, particularly around dusk, so keep an eye out for pronghorn, deer, coyotes, hawks, and eagles, and many other species as we travel.

SCHEDULES and FARES
The train, now owned by the YOGO Inn, operates from June through September on Saturdays. Special events happen throughout the year. Please call or check website for current schedules and fares.

EQUIPMENT
5 Budd RDC cars

CONTACT
Charlie Russell Chew-Choo
211 East Main
Lewistown, MT 59457
800-860-9646
406-538-2527
www.yogoinn.com

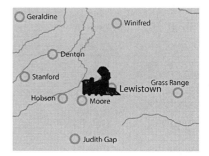

Photos: Charlie Russell Chew-Choo

COPPER KING EXPRESS
Anaconda, MT

A ride on the Copper King Express will put you on refurbished passenger cars to hear an historical narrative about this part of Montana. It is a 52-mile round trip through Durant Canyon that takes approximately 3-4 hours.

Marcus Daley was the Copper King. His mine and smelting facilities were 30 miles apart, and he built and incorporated the Butte, Anaconda and Pacific Railroad in the late 1800s to save money in moving his freight.

In 1912 the B.A.&P. was the first railroad in the nation to electrify at 2400 volts. At this time electrification was big news in the railroad industry, and it led to the steam engines becoming obsolete in the railroad industry.

In 1985 the railroad was privatized, and in 2006 the new owners, Rarus, launched the inaugural season of the Copper King Express.

SCHEDULES and FARES
The Copper King Express season runs from June through September with scheduled Friday and Saturday departures. Special-events trains are available at any time. Reservations are strongly suggested. Please call or check website for current schedules and fares.

EQUIPMENT
The City of Anaconda, first refurbished passenger car, unveiled in 2005 (all of the passenger cars are equipped with video monitors)

CONTACT
Rarus Railway Company
Operator of the "Copper King Express"
300 West Commercial Avenue
Anaconda, MT 59711
406-563-5458
rarusrailway@yahoo.com
www.copperkingexpress.com

Photos: Copper King Express

HISTORICAL MUSEUM AT FORT MISSOULA
Missoula, MT

The city of Missoula's success was shaped in great part by the arrival of the Northern Pacific Railroad in 1883, the year that the city was incorporated. Today, you can visit the Historical Museum at Fort Missoula to see the role that the railroad played in the city's history.

Located on 32 acres, the complex includes five of the original fort structures and a variety of other structures, including the Drummond Depot, built in 1910. Constructed by the Chicago, Milwaukee, St. Paul and Pacific Railroad Company, the depot served the town of Drummond, about 30 miles east of Missoula.

Today the depot features the exhibit "Rails through Missoula," which interprets the history of railroad transportation in western Montana. You'll also see the importance of railroading at the Forestry Interpretive Area, which includes a re-created railroad logging spur, a Shay-type engine, logging flatcars, a log-loading slide jammer, and shuttle cars.

SCHEDULES and FARES
The Historical Museum of Fort Missoula is open year-round. Please call or check website for current schedules and fares.

EQUIPMENT
The museum houses a variety of rail equipment relating to the timber and mining industries.

CONTACT
Historical Museum at Fort Missoula
Bldg. 322
Fort Missoula, MT 59804
406-728-3476
406-543-6277 (fax)
www.fortmissoulamuseum.org.

Photos: The Historical Museum at Fort Missoula

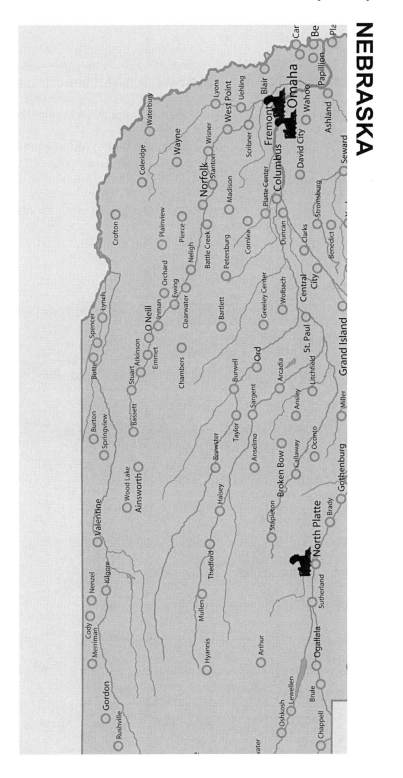

NEBRASKA

DURHAM WESTERN HERITAGE MUSEUM
Omaha, NE

Beautiful architecture blends with memories of a time gone by at the historic Durham Western Heritage Museum. Opened in 1931, Union Station was built by the Union Pacific Railroad as a showpiece in the city of its headquarters. The renovated art deco building offers an exquisite look at Omaha's history.

The Durham Western Heritage Museum offers unique, hands-on learning for people of all ages. Explore Omaha's history, discover something new in our temporary exhibits, and remember the past through our special collections. Explore Omaha of years past as you learn through today's technology.

SCHEDULES and FARES
The Durham Western Heritage Museum is open year-round. It is closed on Mondays and major holidays. Adult admission is generally under $10. Group rates and special events are available. Please call or check website for current schedules and fares.

EQUIPMENT
Union Pacific 1243 steam locomotive (c.1890)
Union Pacific 25559 caboose (1962)
Union Pacific 1202 Pullman National Command sleeper (1956)
Southern Pacific 2986 lounge car (1949)
Pullman Cornhusker car (1924)
No. 1014 streetcar

CONTACT
Durham Western Heritage Museum
801 South 10th Street
Omaha, NE 68108
402-444-5071
402-444-397 (fax)
info@dwhm.org.
www.dwhm.org

Photos: Durham Western Heritage Museum

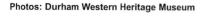

FREMONT & ELKHORN VALLEY RAILROAD
Fremont, NE

The Fremont & Elkhorn Valley Railroad (FEVR) is Nebraska's longest and largest tourist railroad. You'll enjoy a ride in railcars dating from the 1920s on track that was laid out in 1869. Until the mid-1980s the track served as the gateway route for the Chicago and Northwestern Railroad to northern Nebraska, Wyoming, and South Dakota. The route to Wyoming was known as the "Cowboy Line" and is being converted to a trail.

The trip is 17 miles from Fremont to Hooper. You'll cross the historic Indian Road, the route of Major Stephen Long's 1820s western military expedition, and the 1840s Mormon Trail. Once in Hooper, you can explore the town's Main Street, designated as an historic district on the National Register of Historic Places.

SCHEDULES and FARES
The trains run from May through October. Special holiday runs are available on Memorial Day, July 4th, and Labor Day. Santa Claus runs are available around Christmas time. Adult fares are generally under $15, depending on seating choice. Please call or check website for current schedules and fares.

EQUIPMENT
No. 1481,EMD SW1200, Davenport 44-ton
"Lake Bluff" passenger car
"Fort Andrew" passenger car built in 1927
BN wide-vision caboose

CONTACT
Fremont & Elkhorn Valley Railroad
1835 North Somers Avenue
Fremont, NE 68025
402-727-0615
402-727-8321 (dinner train)
fevr@radiks.net
www.fremontrailroad.com

Photos: Fremont & Elkhorn Valley Railroad

GOLDEN SPIKE TOWER
North Platte, NE

The Golden Spike Tower in North Platte, Nebraska, rises 8-stories above Union Pacific's Bailey Yard—the world's largest train yard. Visitors enjoy a 360-degree panoramic view from the enclosed 8th floor viewing area, while the sights and sounds of the railroad below can be enjoyed from the 7th floor open-air platform. It's a one-of-a-kind experience for railroad lovers of all ages.

The Golden Spike location is where east meets west on the Union Pacific line, and where 10,000 cars are handled each day on 2,850 acres of land stretching out eight miles.

Of the 10,000 rail cars, 3,000 are sorted daily in the eastward and westward yards. These yards are nicknamed "hump yards" because they utilize a mound (hump) ranging in height from 20-34 feet. An average of four cars per minute are sent gently down the humps where they're united with trains going to one of dozens of destinations.

Locomotive repair is also handled at Bailey Yard. Encompassing the same area as three football fields, mechanics handle everything from major engine repair to the smoothing of wheels. The shop crew can handle 300 loco-motives each day, processing more than 8,500 engines per month.

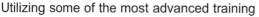

Utilizing some of the most advanced training available workers in the "One Spot" car shop services 50 rail cars per day and replaces 10,000 pairs of wheels annually. The shop can repair up to 20 cars per hour, 24 hours a day.

All told, 14 million gallons of fuel are pumped each month at Bailey Yard to keep the trains moving the products that touch our lives in every way, every day.

The Golden Spike Tower and Visitor Center also features a courtyard proudly flying the 23 flags representing each state Union Pacific Railroad serves. The Memorial Brick Pavilion honors members of the North Platte community, employees of Union Pacific and others with commemorative bricks embossed with the name of the person for which the brick was purchased.

On the grounds of the Golden Spike Tower and Visitor Center is a vintage dining car currently being renovated. When completed, the car will take you back to the romance of passenger trains with both the look and feel of a real railroad dining car with all the amenities.

The Golden Spike Tower and Visitor Center in North Platte, Nebraska is truly a once in a lifetime experience. The Golden Spike Tower and Visitor Center—more trains than you can keep track of!

SCHEDULES AND FARES
Admission: $7.00 Adults
$6.00 Seniors
$5.00 Students Ages 6-16
Children under 6 are admitted free

EQUIPMENT
10,000 rail cars per day move through Bailey Yard in North Platte, Nebraska. Visitors will see manifest trains, made up of mixed railcars from boxcars, tank and piggyback cars. You'll see coal trains, intermodal trains that haul truck and ship containers across the U.S., bulk trains that carry grain, pot ash and ore and run through trains that don't have any rail cars to pick up or to leave off at Bailey Yard.

CONTACT
Golden Spike Tower and Visitor Center
1249 North Homestead Road
North Platte, Nebraska 69101
308.532.9920
www.GoldenSpikeTower.com

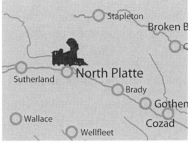

ROCK ISLAND DEPOT RAILROAD MUSEUM
Fairbury, NE

Located in one of the state's two intact Rock Island depots, the Rock Island Depot Railroad Museum gives visitors a look at life when trains were the fastest and classiest way to go anywhere--from billowing steam engines to the 1950s streamlined Rock Island Rocket.

The main floor of the depot has been restored and is used as the museum portion, including the baggage room, which looks just as it did when the Rock Island closed the depot's doors in 1980--complete with baggage carts. On the second floor you'll find a model railroad display and the museum's historical library and archives.

Outside, the original freight house still stands; and across the tracks, now used by Union Pacific, you can see the old diesel shop. The garden, a true showplace in the 1920s and 1930s, is being restored and is home to the brick Memory Wall honoring the men and women who made train transportation an important part of Fairbury's history. In the 1920s Rock Island employed 1,290 people in Fairbury alone.

Another feature is The Little Blue Railroad, a 7.25-inch scale railroad, that visitors can ride during the summer months and on special occasions. And the Rock Island Motor Car 9407 is a doodlebug acquired through a local donation and moved about 30 miles to the depot.

SCHEDULES and FARES
The museum is open on Wednesdays, Thursdays, Saturdays, and Sundays. You may also schedule an appointment at other times. Visitors can ride the Little Blue Railroad during the summer months on Sunday afternoons. There is no admission charge, but donations are appreciated. Please call or check website for current schedules and fares.

EQUIPMENT
Rock Island Rocket
Little Blue Railroad
Rock Island motor car 9407

CONTACT
Rock Island Railroad Museum
910 Second Street
Fairbury, NE 68352
402-729-5131
fairburyridepot@alltel.net
www.jeffersoncountyhistory.com

Photos: Rock Island Depot Railroad Museum

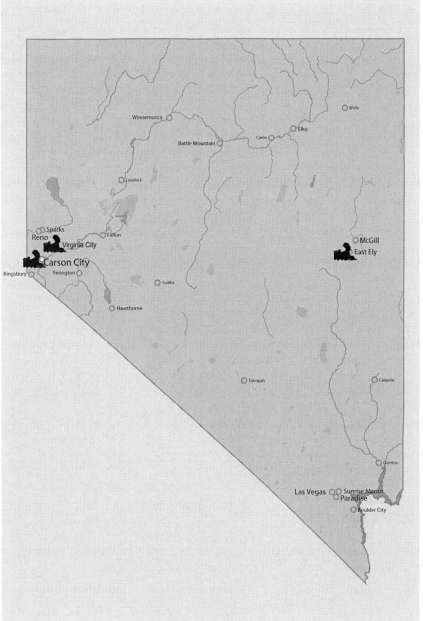

NEVADA

Wells

Winnemucca

Elko

Battle Mountain Carlin

Lovelock

Sparks
Reno Fallon
Virginia City McGill
East Ely
Carson City
Kingsbury Yerington
Gabbs

Hawthorne

Tonopah Caliente

Overton

Las Vegas Sunrise Manor
Paradise
Boulder City

NEVADA NORTHERN RAILWAY MUSEUM
East Ely, NV

This historical operating railway museum offers you the chance to explore the East Ely Shops and Yard National Historic Landmark District, home to the Nevada Northern locomotive and railcar collection. Built in the early 1900s to move the copper being mined in Ely, the Nevada Northern Railway ended passenger service in 1941 and freight service in 1983. But in 1983 the White Pine Historical Railroad Foundation was organized to develop an operating railroad museum, and Kennecott (successor to the Nevada Consolidated Copper Company) made substantial donations including 32 miles of track, the East Ely Complex of machine shops, roundhouse, yards, rolling stock and McGill Depot. In 1986, Engine No. 40 was steamed up for the first time in more than 20 years and a new era was born. The "Ghost Train of Old Ely" began chugging along familiar rails once again, to delight generations for years to come.

You can choose a Keystone steam excursion for a 1.75-hour trip to the historic Robison Copper Canyon Mining District, or climb aboard the Adverse diesel excursion, which consistently climbs a 1/4-percent grade on the old high line to McGill. On selected Saturdays, during the operating season, you can choose either the Wine Train, an excursion that offers you the opportunity to sip fine wines and sample hors d'oeuvres while enjoying a classic railroad experience; the Chocolate Train, a chocolate lovers delight, the BBQ Train, authentic western BBQ or the Steptoe Valley Flyer, our heritage train consisting of the original passenger cars.

SCHEDULES and FARES
The museum is open daily from Memorial Day through Labor Day. Fares vary according to excursion. Excursions begin in April and run through December. Please call or check website for current schedules and fares.

EQUIPMENT
3 steam locomotives, built between 1909 and 1917, including No. 40, "The Ghost Train"
9 diesel locomotives, built between 1942 and 1956
2 electric locomotives
No. 80, 75-ton GE, built in 1937
No. 81 85-ton GE, built in 1941
7 passenger cars, including the No. 6, Pullman coach, built in 1872

CONTACT
Nevada Northern Railway Museum
1100 Avenue A
East Ely, NV 89315
866-40STEAM
775-289-2085
info@nnry.com
www.nnry.com

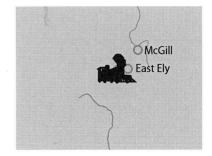

Photos: Rock Island Depot Railroad Museum

NEVADA STATE RAILROAD MUSEUM
Carson City, NV

The Nevada State Railroad Museum houses over 60 pieces of railroad equipment from Nevada's past. It is the official home of the Virginia & Truckee Railroad Collection of Cars and Locomotives, America's richest and most famous short line. The museum is considered one of the finest regional railroad museums in the country. Included in the museum's collection is the Inyo, built in 1875, the oldest operating locomotive in the country.

Museum activities include the operation of historic railroad equipment, lectures, an annual railroad history symposium, and a variety of exhibits and special events. As part of your visit, you may take a steam train or motorcar ride on the museum's 1-mile loop.

SCHEDULES and FARES
The museum is open daily except for New Year's, Thanksgiving, and Christmas days. The train and motorcar operate on selected weekends and holidays from May through September. Several themed train rides are held throughout the year. Please call or check website for current schedules and fares.

EQUIPMENT
No. 1, "Glenbrook," 2-6-0 narrow gauge locomotive, built in 1875
No. 3, baggage-mail-express car, narrow gauge, built in 1881
No. 303, narrow gauge boxcar, LaMothe patent "pipe boxcar", built in 1881
No. 22, "Inyo," 4-4-0 standard gauge locomotive, built in 1875
No. 401, "Washoe Zephyr" motorcar, built in 1926
Southern Pacific-style gallows turntable
Lifeboat from the steamer "Tahoe"
Total collection of more than 50 pieces

CONTACT
Nevada State Railroad Museum
2180 S. Carson Street
Carson City, NV 89701
775-687-6953
www.nsrm-friends.org/nsrm

Photos: Nevada State Railroad Museum

VIRGINIA & TRUCKEE RAILROAD
Virginia City, NV

The mining boom turned Virginia City into one of the most important cities inn the West. It made instant millionaires out of the crusty prospectors, who soon replaced tents with mansions and pine chairs with imported furniture. It even helped finance the Civil War and then went on to build empires.

An important element in this success was the

railroad. It was a way to guarantee the delivery of silver ore for a fraction of the previous cost. So a group of private investors developed a railroad to connect the silver mines in Virginia City to the mills in Carson City. Constructed in 1869, the first Virginia & Truckee Railroad cost $1.5 million to build, required seven tunnels to be drilled, depended on equipment brought by horse teams from Reno, and employed 1,500 workmen.

You can see the past reflected in the present with a trip on the "new" Virginia & Truckee Railroad, which began tourist operations in 1976. You'll take a 35-minute steam train ride to Gold Hill and then through the heart of the historic Comstock mining region. But the whistle of the 1916 Baldwin locomotive may do more than just attract riders from the valley, it tends to bring "robbers" who "rob" the passengers for contributions to restore the Gold Hill Depot.

SCHEDULES AND FARES:
The Virginia & Truckee Railroad operates from May through October. Please call or check website for current schedules and fares.

EQUIPMENT:
No 29, 1916 Baldwin 2-8-0, Ex Longview Portland Northern 680
No 30, 1916 S.P. 0-6-0, Southern Pacific
No D-1, 1953 GE 80 on
1907 Private car, ex Bangor and Aroostock 100
1914 Pullman coach, Gold Hill, ex D L & W, 583
1914 Pullman coach, Silver City, ex D L & W, 573
No 54, tunnel car, ex 1916 WP
No 50 open air car, ex 1916, WP caboose 680
Unrestored coaches, 1888 NP combine and a 1920's freight train set

CONTACT:
Virginia & Truckee Railroad
P.O. Box 467
Virginia City, NV 89440

Photos: Virginia & Truckee Railroad

NEW HAMPSHIRE

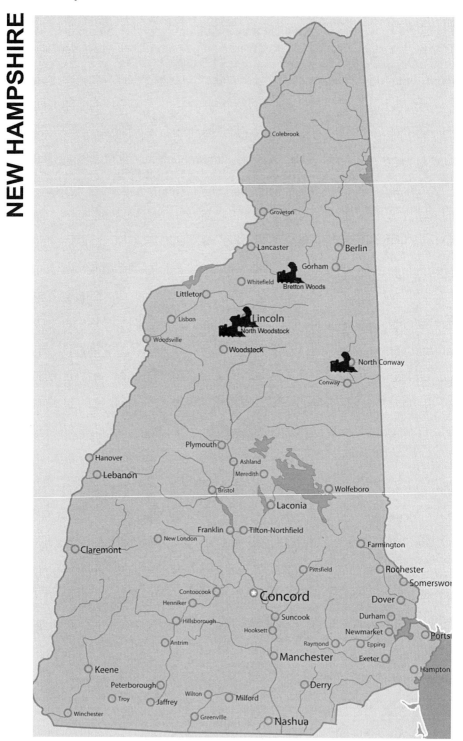

Colebrook

Groveton

Lancaster   Berlin

Gorham

Whitefield   Bretton Woods

Littleton

Lisbon   Lincoln

North Woodstock

Woodsville

Woodstock   North Conway

Conway

Plymouth

Hanover   Ashland

Lebanon   Meredith

Bristol   Wolfeboro

Laconia

Franklin   Tilton-Northfield

New London   Farmington

Claremont

Pittsfield   Rochester

Somerswo

Contoocook   Dover

Henniker   Concord

Hillsborough   Suncook   Durham

Hooksett   Newmarket   Ports

Antrim   Raymond   Epping

Manchester   Exeter

Keene   Hampton

Peterborough   Derry

Troy   Jaffrey   Wilton   Milford

Winchester   Greenville   Nashua

THE CAFÉ LAFAYETTE DINNER TRAIN
North Woodstock, NH

The Café Lafayette Dinner Train has been in operation since 1989. It is one of only some 20 moving dinner trains in all of North America. You are invited to escape the ordinary and relive the romance of dining on the rails. While riding in one of three beautifully restored Pullman dining cars, enjoy five courses of fine food and spirits served to you in the grand European manner.

With magnificent mountain vistas and lush New England forests surrounding the train, you are assured of having the best seat in the house, all evening long. After dinner, with the compartment lights down low and the dramatic sunset outside your window, you may allow yourself a wistful romantic journey back in time, and you might wish the evening would never end.

From the moment you arrive, you will be swept into an era of the past, experiencing new excitement or reliving childhood memories. This two-hour, 20 mile round trip will take you on a tour of the historic Boston and Maine Railroad built in the late 1800s to serve the historic "grand" hotels of the region.

SCHEDULES and FARES
The Café Lafayette Dinner Train runs from May through October. Fares run between $60 and $80. Note: For all reservations, you must call direct. Reservations will not be honored via e-mail or regular mail. Please call or check website for current schedules and fares.

EQUIPMENT
No. 221, Indian Waters, restored 1924 Pullman dining car originally built for the New York Central
No. 2211, Granite Eagle, originally built for the Missouri-Pacific Railroad, operating from St. Louis, Missouri, to San Antonio, Texas, in the mid 1950's
No. 3207, Algonquin, a 1953 X-CNR café coach was purchased in 1995 from the Canadian government

CONTACT
Café Lafayette Dinner Train
P.O. Box 8
North Woodstock, NH 03262
800-699-3501 (outside NH)
603-745-3500 (inside NH)
www.cafelafayette.com

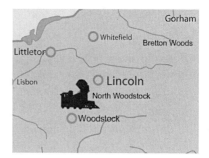

Photos: Cafe Lafayette Dinner Train

CONWAY SCENIC RAILROAD
North Conway, NH

Enjoy an old-fashioned rail-roading experience on vintage trains, all departing from the 1874 Victorian Station in North Conway. Passengers may choose one of the Valley routes: the 55-minute, (11 miles) round trip to Conway or the 1-_ hour (21 miles) round trip to Bartlett; or the legendary Crawford Notch excursion, the 5 hour (50+ miles) round trip through some of the finest natural scenery in the Northeast. All trains run rain or shine from mid-April through December.

On the "Valley Train, passengers journey on historic rail routes as they travel to Conway or Bartlett. Coach and First Class seats are available on all departures. Passengers in First Class travel aboard a beautifully-restored 1898 Pullman Parlor Observation Car, the Gertrude Emma." From early-June to late-October, daily luncheon service is available aboard the elegant dining car, Chocorua, and dinner is served on selected nights of the week.

The Notch Train travels on what was once the Maine Central Railroad's famed Mountain Division line, on tracks that were laid down in the 1870s. Some of the most dramatic natural scenery in the Northeast is enjoyed as the train travels through spectacular Crawford Notch – past sheer bluffs, steep ravines, cascading brooks and streams, panoramic mountain vistas, across Frankenstein Trestle and Willey Brook Bridge – enroute to Crawford or Fabyan stations. As the train travels through this rugged terrain, passengers can begin to appreciate what a remarkable engineering achievement constructing this railroad was 140 years ago. Live commentary onboard includes history and folklore of the railroad and area, as well as points of interest.

All trains are powered by diesel electric locomotives, except during the busy Fall Foliage season, when the popular steam locomotive #7470 provides the motive power for the North Conway to Conway excursion.

In the 1800s, carpenter crews of the PGF&C Railroad had already built several Victorian-style stations along the line prior to reaching North Conway, but the North Conway station was truly a showcase for their craft. The station merited their finest efforts because the town, a prestigious summer resort, served as the northern terminus of the Conway Branch of the railroad. Now a National Historic Landmark, the station still reflects its original character and remains an iconic, stately presence in the center of North Conway Village.

SCHEDULES & FARES
The Conway Scenic Railroad is in operation from mid-April through December. Schedules and fares vary according to each excursion. Please call or check website for current schedules and fares.

EQUIPMENT
Steam Locomotives:
No. 7470, 0-6-6 coal burner
No. 501, Alco 2-8-0 coal burner (owned by 470 Club, display)
Diesel Electric Locomotives
No. 216, Model GP-35, 2,500-hp, GM
No. 252, Model GP-38, 2,000-hp, GM
No. 573, Model GP-7, 1,500-hp, GM
No. 4266, Model F-7, 1,500-hp, GM

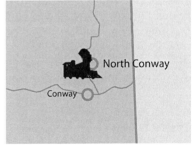

CONTACT
Conway Scenic Railroad
Route 16
North Conway, NH 03860
800-232-5251
603-356-5251
info@conwayscenic.com
ConwayScenic.com

Photos: Conway Scenic Railroad

HOBO RAILROAD AND WINNIPESAUKEE RAILROAD
Lincoln, NH

You won't have to try to jump on a moving railcar to take a hobo ride on the Hobo Railroad. Instead, you can board at the Hobo Junction Train Station in Lincoln, New Hampshire. You'll head for the Jack O'Lantern Golf Resort, where the Hobo tracks travel directly down the middle of this famed golf course. While there, you can see a small covered bridge and a sizable part of the golf course.

Then you can enjoy a delightful Hobo lunch (complete with your souvenir Hobo bindle stick) on your way back to Lincoln. You cross a river and several trestles and follow the "East Branch" back to Hobo Junction for a delightful scenic 1-hour, 20-minute ride.

The Winnipesaukee train runs from Meredith, New Hampshire, along Meredith Bay and arrives at Weirs Beach. After a brief stop to pick up passengers, the excursion continues to Lakeport along Paugus Bay. A brief stop at Lakeport lets you view the boats and enjoy the beach breezes. The engine disconnects from the coaches and runs up the side track to get to the other end. After hitching again, the train heads back to Weirs Beach and then on to Meredith. The excursion lasts about 2 hours.

Both trains offer an extensive variety of themed excursions, including holiday themed train rides, supper trains, and more.

SCHEDULES and FARES
The Hobo and Winnipesaukee trains operate from May to December. Fares vary according to the excursion. Please call or check website for current schedules and fares.

EQUIPMENT
EMD GP7 No. 302, former NEGS and Rock Island locomotive
Alco S-1 No. 1186, former Wolfboro No. 1186 and B&M No. 1186
Alco S-1 No. 959, former Northern Stratford RR, former Maine Central No. 959
Alco S-1 No. 1008, former Portland Terminal Co. No. 1008

CONTACT
Hobo Railroad
Main Street
P.O. Box 9
Lincoln, NH 03251
603-745-2135

Winnipesaukee Railroad
Main Street
P.O. Box 9
Lincoln, NH 03251
603 279-5253
ride@hoborr.com
www.hoborr.com

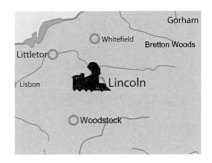

Photos: Hobo Railroad and Winnipesaukee Railroad

MOUNT WASHINGTON COG RAILWAY
Bretton Woods, NH

His dream began in 1852 when, after becoming lost near the summit of Mount Washington, Sylvester Marsh knew that there had to be a better way for people to reach the highest mountain peak in the Northeast. Upon his return home, he immediately started working on a plan to build the world's first mountain-climbing cog railway.

Marsh, a native of Campton, New Hampshire, had made his fortune in Chicago's meat-packing industry and was considered by his contemporaries to be a creative and innovative thinker. However, when he first presented his idea to members of the New Hampshire Legislature, they laughed at him and said that he "might as well build a railway to the Moon." Marsh was undaunted, and by July 3, 1869, the first cog-driven train climbed 6,288 feet to the top of Mount Washington.

Today you can still get to the top of the summit of Mount Washington and see a span of four different states, Quebec, and the Atlantic Ocean. Your view is limited only by the curvature of the Earth. And some days you have to literally climb above the clouds. It's all an unforgettable 3-hour journey.

SCHEDULES and FARES

The Mount Washington Cog Railway is open year-round. Dress in layers. Reservations are strongly recommended. Adult fares are generally under $60. Please call or check website for current schedules and fares.

EQUIPMENT

0-2-2-0 COG steam locomotives (7)
1870-style replica coaches

CONTACT

Mount Washington Cog Railway
Base Road
Mount Washington, NH 03589
800-922-8825
603-278-5404 (in New Hampshire)
603-278-5830 (fax)
www.thecog.com

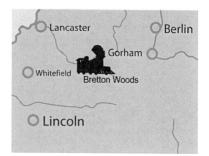

Photos: Mount Washington Cog Railway

WHITE MOUNTAIN CENTRAL RAILROAD
Lincoln, NH

Join us for this 2.5-mile, 30-minute excursion on the classic White Mountain Central Railroad. Steam across the scenic Pemigewasset River, through rustic woods and into the past. The tour takes you on one of only three wood-burning steam Climax locomotives still running in the world and crosses over the only standing Howe-Truss covered bridge still in use today.

The railroad covered bridge located in East Montpelier, Vermont, was dismantled, transported, and reassembled spanning the Pemigewasset River on the White Mountain Central creating a scenic extension to the Railroad and a monumental accomplishment.

The railroad has been running for over 40 years. The dream started some 50 years ago when the Clark brothers began to rescue steam locomotives from the cutting torch. They soon created "green pastures for iron horses" at the Trading Post. This promises to be a fun ride with beautiful vistas and some surprises along the way. Note: this trip may not be suitable for preschoolers.

SCHEDULES and FARES
The White Mountain Central Railroad is open from June through mid-October. Fares are generally under $15. Please call or check website for current schedules and fares.

EQUIPMENT
The White Mountain Central Railroad is home to the Climax, Heisler, Shay and Porter locomotives

CONTACT
White Mountain Central Railroad
P.O. Box 1
Lincoln, NH 03251
603-745-8913
info@clarkstradingpost.com
www.clarkstradingpost.com

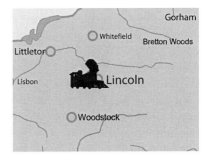

Photos: White Mountain Central Railroad

Did You Know...

Turntables give locomotives access to the roundhouse and allow them to turn around.

Fact by: Steamtown Historic National Site

NEW JERSEY

Sussex
Highland Lakes
Crandon Lakes
Branchville
Franklin
Newton
Ramsey
Andover
Pompton Lakes
Ridgewood
Hopatcong
Boonton
Paterson
Budd Lake
Dover
Hackensack
Whippany
Clifton
Passaic
Belvidere
Verona
Washington
Livingston
Union City
Mendham
Madison
Newark
New Providence
Jersey City
Madison
High Bridge
Phillipsburg
Alpha
Elizabeth
Bayonne
Milford
Rahway
Carteret
Frenchtown
Somerville
Edison
Flemington
Somerset
Perth Amboy
Stockton
New Brunswick
Ringoes
East Brunswick
Hazlet
Keansburg
Lambertville
Middletown
Princeton
Jamesburg
Old Bridge
Rumson
Princeton Junction
Cranbury
Red Bank
Monmouth Beach
Hightstown
Eatontown
Long Branch
Freehold
Interlaken
Asbury Park
Trenton
Allentown
Neptune City
Belmar
Allaire
Spring Lake
Bordentown
Lakewood
Brielle
Manasquan
Burlington
McGuire AFB
Point Pleasant
Point Pleasant Beach
Riverside
Mantoloking
Riverton
Lakehurst
Silverton
Mount Holly
Brown Mills
Toms River
Lavallette
Camden
Beachwood
Gilford Park
Gloucester City
Leisuretowne
Seaside Park
Cherry Hill
Woodbury
Blackwood
Lindenwold
Waretown
Barnegat
Mullica Hill
Chesilhurst
Ocean Acres
Barnegat Light
Glassboro
Manahawkin
Harvey Cedars
Clayton
Beach Haven West
Surf City
Pennsville
Hammonton
Ship Bottom
Salem
Collings Lakes
Tuckerton
Beach Haven
Elmer
Alloway
Newfield
Elwood-Magnolia
Buena
Egg Harbor City
Port Republic
Vineland
Pomona
Shiloh
Corbin City
Absecon
Bridgeton
Millville
Pleasantville
Brigantine
Fairton
Atlantic City
Somers Point
Ventnor City
Port Norris
Woodbine
Longport
Ocean City
Sea Isle City
Cape May Court House
Avalon
Villas
Stone Harbor
North Cape May
Rio Grande
Cape May Point
Wildwood
Cape May

BLACK RIVER & WESTERN RAILROAD
Ringoes, NJ

Climb aboard the Black River & Western Railroad for a scenic one-hour excursion between Flemington and Ringoes. There's something soothing about sitting back and relaxing while the coach gently rocks back and forth and the whistle echoes through a valley.

The members of the Black River Railroad Historical Trust (BRRHT) run trains that speed passengers back in time. From the conductor dressed in traditional railroad uniform to the antique passenger coaches from the 1920s, everything you will encounter during your visit plays its part in telling the story of small-town railroading as it was many years ago. You can also enjoy a winter ride.The Jack Frost made its inaugural run in 2003, offering the first winter service of the railroad in 38 years. The railroad also offers freight service in New Jersey and Pennsylvania.

SCHEDULES and FARES
Please call or check website for current schedules and fares.

EQUIPMENT
No. 60, Alco 2-8-0, built in 1937
No. 752, 1750-hp EMD GP-9, built in 1956
No. 780, 1500-hp EMD GP-7, built in 1950
No. 820, 1200-hp EMD NW-2, built in 1949
No. 1848, 1750-hp EMD GP-9, built in 1954
No. 1854, 1600-hp EMD GP-8, built in 1953

CONTACT
Black River & Western Railroad
P.O. Box 200
Ringoes, NJ 08551
908-782-9600
908-782-8251 (fax)
info@brwrr.com
www.brwrr.com

Photos: Black River & Western Railroad

CAPE MAY SEASHORE LINES
Cape May, NJ

Take a ride on the Cape May Seashore Lines for a comfortable, relaxing trip back in time. Workers want you to remember when a train trip to the shore was an exciting and memorable experience. You will ride on the original equipment operated in South Jersey by the Pennsylvania-Reading Seashore Lines, the Reading Company, and the Pennsylvania Railroad.

Cape May Seashore offers two different excursions. The first is a 30-mile round trip between Richland and Tucahoe. The second is a 22-mile round trip between Cape May Court House, Cold Spring Village, and Cape May City. Both run on the former Reading Company's steel speedway to the shore and offer breathtaking vistas of the Atlantic ocean.

SCHEDULES AND FARES
Please call or check website for current schedules and fares.

EQUIPMENT
8 Budd RDC1s
2 RDC9s
EMD RS2
EMD GP9
5 P-RSL P70 coaches
CNJ GP7 1523

CONTACT
Cape May Seashore Line
P.O. Box 152
Tucahoe, NJ 08250
609-884-5300
info@capemayseashorelines.org
www.capemayseashorelines.org

Photos: Cape May Seashore Lines

NEW JERSEY MUSEUM OF TRANSPORTATION/PINE CREEK RAILROAD
Allaire, NJ

The Pine Creek Railroad was founded in 1952 as a club, when three men purchased a small steam locomotive and installed rail at their first location on U.S. Route 9 in Marlboro, New Jersey. This narrow gauge operating steam preservation railroad was second after Edaville in Massachusetts (est. 1948), and the first such railroad to utilize volunteers to run every aspect of the operation. In 1963, the railroad was reorganized as the New Jersey Museum of Transportation, Inc. The group outgrew the space on Route 9 and signed a contract with the New Jersey State Park Service.

The members then proceeded to move the entire railroad one piece at a time, using flatbed tractor trailers, to Allaire State Park in Wall Township, New Jersey. The railroad was built, shop facilities established, and more equipment acquired. Many historic pieces were restored, and can be found in operation at various times of the year. The Pine Creek Railroad exhibit has been in operation for more than 50 years. It is currently the oldest all-volunteer railroad in the country.

SCHEDULES and FARES
The New Jersey Museum of Transportation/Pine Creek Railroad is open year-round. The train operates on weekends from April through December. The trains also run daily in July and August. Fares vary depending on your excursion. Please call or check website for current schedules and fares.

EQUIPMENT
In the museum's restoration shop you will see how volunteers are trying to bring a number of vintage trains back to life and are taking part in what is called the Dignity Project. The idea is to make trains accessible to everyone, including patrons in wheelchairs.

CONTACT
New Jersey Museum of Transportation, Inc.
Route 524
Wall Township, NJ
732-938-5524
info@njmt.org
www.njmt.org

Photos: New Jersey Museum of Transportation

WHIPPANY RAILWAY MUSEUM
Whippany, NJ

Headquartered in the restored 1904 freight house of the Morristown & Erie Railroad, the Whippany Railway Museum has an outstanding collection of railroad artifacts and memorabilia. Preservation efforts trace back to 1965, when several employees and volunteers of the Morris County Central began displaying a small collection of railroad memorabilia in the Morristown & Erie Freight House. The railroad yard includes the elegant Whippany passenger depot, coal yard, wooden water tank, and historic rail equipment.

The railroad itself dates back to the late 1800's which explains why the museum is constantly expanding, with several restoration projects underway at any one time. Families and groups alike will enjoy the visit, as well as a number of special activities and events throughout the year, including special excursion rides. You can also enjoy operating model train layouts and a display of ocean liner artifacts. Top off your trip with a 10-mile, 45-minute round trip excursion.

SCHEDULES and FARES

The Whippany Railway Museum is open from April through October. Throughout each season, special excursion trains operate for various holidays and events. During the summer months, a series of special Caboose Train Rides operate on select Sundays. Please call or check website for current schedules and fares.

EQUIPMENT

Railbus No. 10
D&H Caboose No. 35886
"Jersey Coast" CRRNJ commuter club car
Morristown & Erie caboose No. 1
Steam locomotive No. 4039
NYS&W Whitcomb switcher No. 150
PRR cabin car No. 477823
Rahway Valley RR Nos. 16 and 17

CONTACT

Whippany Railway Museum
1 Railway Plaza
Whippany, NJ 07981
973-887-8777
wrym-web@comcast.net
www.whippanyrailwaymuseum.org

Photos: Whippany Railway Museum

Did You Know...

The U.S. has some of the longest freight trains in the world. U.S. freight trains have been known to stretch for miles.

NEW MEXICO

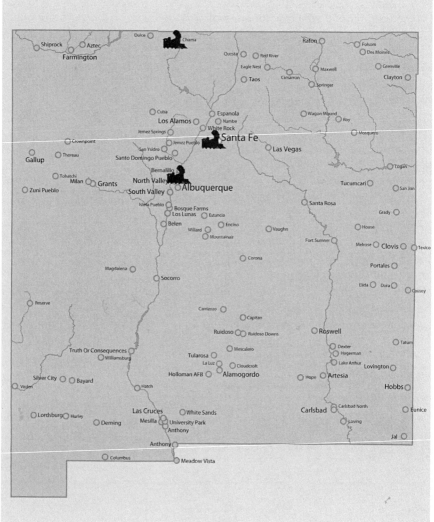

CUMBRES & TOLTEC SCENIC RAILROAD
Chama, NM

Owned by the states of Colorado and New Mexico, the Cumbres & Toltec Scenic Railroad is the best preserved steam era railroad in North America. Built in 1880 and little changed since, the C&TS is a 64-mile portion of the former Denver & Rio Grande Western Railroad's three-foot narrow gauge system that once extended from Denver to Santa Fe and Silverton.

The railroad runs through two National Forests and areas of little habitation. It is the longest narrow gauge railroad in North America, and with a peak elevation of 10,015 feet, it is also the highest. Passengers experience the spectacular scenery as if they were travelers of a bygone era. Trains are pulled by authentic Rio Grande steam locomotives affording tourists magnificent views of the San Juan Mountains, Toltec Gorge, and the Rio Grande Valley.

The entire railroad is a designated National Historic Site. It has well over 140 historic freight and maintenance-of-way cars, some dating to the nineteenth century. Four historic sites are preserved along its right-of-way: the Chama yard with many historic structures; the section village and snowshed at Cumbres Pass, Colorado; the station and section village at Osier, Colorado, where passengers stop for lunch; and the section village of Sublette, New Mexico. Buildings at each of these sites date to the era of original construction.

In the late 1960s, this class of railroad engineering was rescued from extinction by the combined efforts of a group of citizens and the governments of the states of New Mexico and Colorado through which it runs. The states established a joint commission to oversee the railroad and to contract with a private company to operate it.

SCHEDULES and FARES
The Cumbres & Toltec Scenic Railroad operates Late-May to Mid-October annually. Adult fares range in price from $75 to $165. The Railroad is celebrating forty historic years as a New Mexico and Colorado owned and operated tourist railroad August 27-29th, 2010. Please call 1-888-CUMBRES or visit CUMBRESTOLTEC.COM for current schedules and fares.

EQUIPMENT
Steam Locomotives
No. 463, 2-8-2 type, K-27 class, 1903
No. 484, 2-8-2 type, K-36 class, 1925
No. 487, 2-8-2 type, K-36 class, 1925
No. 488, 2-8-2 type, K-36 class, 1925
No. 489, 2-8-2 type, K-36 class, 1925
No. 497, 2-8-2 type, K-37 class, 1902/1928-30
Diesel Locomotive
No. 19, B+B type, 1943
39 coaches
5 boxcars
20 high side gondolas
6 drop bottom gondolas

CONTACT
Cumbres & Toltec Scenic Railroad
P.O. Box 789
Chama, NM 87520
505-756-2151
888-CUMBRES
www.cumbrestoltec.com

Photos: Cumbres & Toltec Scenic Railroad

FRIENDS OF THE CUMBRES & TOLTEC SCENIC RAILROAD
Chama, NM

Have you ever wanted to become part of a highly praised effort to pass on something of value for the generations to come? Does the notion of working on projects in stunning western high country locations with a dedicated team of interesting people stir your passions? If the answer is "yes," then we invite you to join the Friends of the Cumbres & Toltec Scenic Railroad, Inc.

The Friends of the Cumbres & Toltec Scenic Railroad is the museum arm of the 64-mile long Cumbres & Toltec Scenic Railroad. The Friends have approximately 2,200 members world wide and have been in existence since 1988. The Friends mission is to preserve and interpret the history of the Cumbres & Toltec Scenic

Railroad and the narrow gauge system of its predecessor, the Denver & Rio Grande Western.

For over 21 years the Friends, non-profit organization, has worked to preserve this national treasure. We are a diverse group of highly committed men and women from many walks of life, all with a shared vision and the tenacity to fulfill it. The goal is simple but challenging and that is to preserve the Cumbres & Toltec as a dynamic, living museum for those who follow.

Some of our members are rail enthusiasts, some are history buffs and others are people who have fallen in love with the jewel that is this railroad. While many members participate directly in our activities, most simply support our work through the crucial financial investment that their membership provides.

As a member, you'll help to preserve this piece of the American heritage and know the honor and fulfillment of sharing in that legacy. Some of our membership benefits include; receiving our quarterly newsletter The C&TS Dispatch, provided the opportunity to participate in seasonal work sessions and receiving a 10% discount on Cumbres & Toltec train tickets.

Basic memberships begin at $30 in the U.S. and $40 for those outside the United States.

WORK SESSION SCHEDULES:
Two weeks are scheduled in May, two weeks in June and four weeks in August.

During these sessions volunteers work on a variety of restoration projects involving historic rolling stock equipment (boxcars, reefers, tank cars, stock cars) in the C&TS fleet. Other preservation projects entail work on historic structures along the railroad. Some crews are also involved in work on the mileposts and whistleposts along the right-of-way while others help the railroad with brush cutting and tree trimming efforts along the route.

The first six weeks of sessions take place along the Cumbres & Toltec while the last two weeks in August are conducted on the Alder Gulch Railroad in Nevada City, MT as part of a cooperative agreement and partnership with the Montana Heritage Commission.

Weekend work sessions are also conducted on a monthly basis at a Friends work site in Colorado Springs Colorado.

EQUIPMENT:
The Friends, through a General Operating Agreement with the C&TS Railroad Commission oversee stewardship of all historic assets on the Cumbres & Toltec

Scenic Railroad. This includes approximately 150 pieces of historic narrow gauge freight rolling stock which includes; boxcars, stockcars, gondolas, tank cars, flats cars and MOW equipment.

CONTACT:
Friends of the Cumbres & Toltec
Scenic Railroad, Inc.
4421 McLeod Road NE, Suite F
Albuquerque, NM 87109
505-880-1311
www.cumbrestoltec.org

SANTA FE SOUTHERN RAILWAY
Santa Fe, NM

Most people know it as "the Santa Fe" and it first arrived in 1880. The 120-year-old spur from Lamy to Santa Fe, the vintage railcars, and the charming California mission-style depot combine to make a charming slice of history. Every year, tens of thousands of visitors come to see, photograph, and paint the old Santa Fe Depot and ride the train along the original high-desert route that carried early tourist adventurers, settlers, artists, and scientists into the city.

For many visitors, the railway is the only thing they know about Santa Fe before they come here: they hum the 40's swing song "The Atchison, Topeka & Santa Fe," and they point excitedly to the familiar Santa Fe herald, the blue cross in the circle.

Since 1992, this rail line continues as the Santa Fe Southern Railway, a piece of living history still carrying passengers through the high-desert beauty, and still carrying freight to serve the community. When you come to ride the Santa Fe Southern, you'll enjoy visiting the historic depot and gift shop where you'll find many books about the railroad and its history.

SCHEDULES and FARES
Santa Fe excursions are available year round. Reservations are required for all trains leaving the Santa Fe Depot. Coach, Silver and Dome Class seats are available. Please call or check website for current schedules and fares.

EQUIPMENT
GP7s Nos. 92 & 93
New Jersey Central coach No. 1158
Santa Fe Pleasure Dome "Plaza Lam"
New Jersey Central coach No. 1195
New Jersey Central combine No. 300

CONTACT
Santa Fe Southern Railway
410 S. Guadalupe Street
Santa Fe, NM 87501
888-989-8600
505-989-8600
depot@sfsr.com
www.santafesouthernrailway.com

Photos: Santa Fe Southern Railway

Did You Know...

When boiled, a cup of water creates about 1,600 cups of steam! When the resulting steam is contained in a vessel such as a steam locomotive boiler, it can create up to 300 pounds per square inch of pressure.

NEW YORK

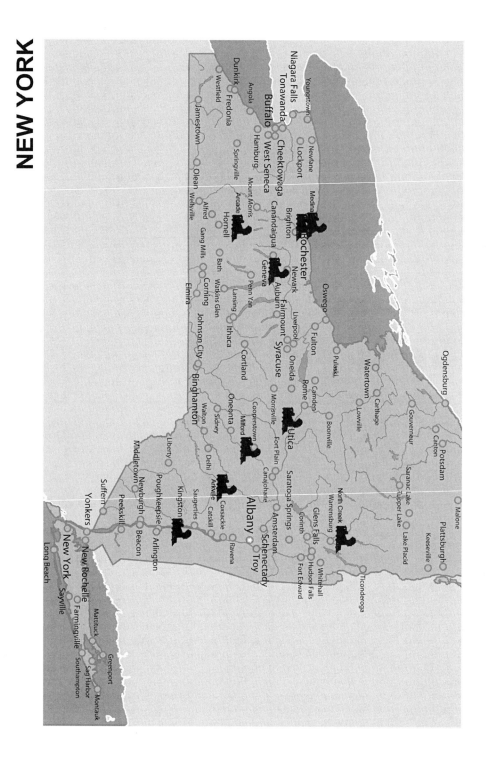

ADIRONDACK SCENIC RAILROAD
Utica, NY

Once known as the Golden Chariot Route, today this magnificent stretch of New York Mountain main line is the spectacular Adirondack Scenic Railroad.

The railroad gives visitors an opportunity to explore the beautiful Adirondack Mountains from either air-conditioned coaches or open-air railcars on any of several train ride adventures. The railroad offers three unique ways to experience the old line that for most of the 1900s was part of the New York Central System.

Utica-Old Forge Wilderness Adventure: This excursion includes a 2-1/4-hour train ride each way and either a 4-3/4-hour layover at Thendara or a 3-hour layover at Carter Station.
Old Forge Moose River Locals Adventure: Ride from Thendara Station to Otter Lake and return after an exciting 20-mile, 1-1/4-hour ride along the Moose River.
Adirondack High Peaks Wilderness Train Adventures: The train takes 45-minutes running from Lake Placid to Sarnac Lake where riders have a half-hour layover for a walk through Sarnac village.

Dr. William Seward Webb figured that the best way to get to Nehasane Park, his large hunting preserve to the north, was by train. In 1890, he financed a railroad into the Adirondack wilderness. The first train ran from Herkimer to Thendara on July 1, 1892, and the first through train ran from New York City to Montreal on October 24, 1892. The railroad later became part of the New York Central System. The railroad carried the Webb, Morgan, Vanderbilt, Whitney, and Roosevelt families along with other not so famous families to their Great Camps in the Adirondack Mountains.

The line was returned to service in 1977 when the Adirondack Railway Corporation contracted with the state to run passenger service from Utica to Lake Placid for the 1980 Winter Olympic Games in Lake Placid. In February of 1981, however, the railroad was abandoned.

In 1992 a group of devoted rail enthusiasts banded together and proposed to operate a short section of the line from Thendara south to Minnehaha. By the year 2000 the railroad had restored the line all the way south to Snow Junction. At that point it connects with a freight railroad, the Mohawk, Adirondack and Northern and continues on to Union Station in Utica, 6 miles north from Thendara Station to Carter Station and between Saranac Lake and Lake Placid.

SCHEDULES and FARES
The Adirondack Scenic Railroad is open from Memorial Day through mid-October. Fares vary according to excursion. Please call or check website for current schedules and fares.

EQUIPMENT
1941 EMD diesel switcher
1942 GE diesel switcher
1950 Alco road/switcher
2-1952 EMD diesel locomotives
2-1964 Alco diesel locomotives
16 coaches
1 cafe/lounge car
2 baggage cars

CONTACT
Union Station
Thendara Home Office
P.O. Box 84
Thendara, NY 13472
877-508-6728
315-369-2479 (fax)
train@telenet.net
www.adirondackrr.com

Photos: Adirondack Scenic Railroad

Did You Know...

As early as 1556, Georgius Agricola, in his book on minerals, De Re Metallica, mentioned a mining railway running on wooden poles.

ARCADE & ATTICA RAILROAD
Arcade, NY

Your journey aboard this railway in Western New York begins with a tour of the historic station. View the history of railroading through a variety of exhibits. You'll see everything from antique railroad lanterns to switch locks and even an old switch stand. The train room includes a scale model railroad, and then you go through the authentic ticket office to purchase your tickets for the train ride.

Your 90-minute train ride takes you through beautiful countryside and farmlands that have remained virtually unchanged since the original track line was laid in the 1880s. You'll journey to Curriers Depot where you can take photos, talk to the crew, and examine the train as it is prepared for its return journey. It's a delightful, relaxing trip that you will not want to miss.

SCHEDULES and FARES
There are regular excursions year-round and seasonal excursions from Memorial Day weekend until the last full weekend in September. There are also special excursions throughout the year. Departure times vary. Please call or check website for current schedules and fares.

EQUIPMENT
1920 American steam locomotive
1915 DL&W coaches

CONTACT
Arcade & Attica Railroad
278 Main Street
Arcade, NY 14009
585-492-3100
585-496-9877
www.anarr.com

Photos: Arcade & Attica Railroad

COOPERSTOWN & CHARLOTTE VALLEY RAILROAD
Milford, NY

Built in 1869, the Cooperstown & Charlotte Valley Railroad gives visitors to our area the chance to experience what was once the primary form of transportation throughout the country--riding the rails. In an area rich with railroad history, the Cooperstown & Charlotte Valley Railroad takes visitors back in time with vintage railcars and locomotives through the scenic wilderness of the Upper Susquehanna River Valley. The railroad crosses the river twice over two steel-truss bridges, and travels through a variety of landscapes, including forests, wetlands, and agricultural land.

In the beautifully restored depot in Milford, New York, also built in 1869, visitors can view a variety of exhibits and displays. In 2001 the Cooperstown & Charlotte Valley Railroad added an open-air car to its fleet, so that passengers could enjoy the railroad's beautiful scenery without having to look through a window.

SCHEDULES and FARES
The Cooperstown & Charlotte Valley Railroad operates from June through October with several hourly runs daily from Cooperstown. Please call or check website for current schedules and fares.

EQUIPMENT
2 MLW Alcos, 1950's
Locomotives
PRR GG1 electric locomotive No. 4917* (ex-Amtrak No. 4934)
PRR GG1 electric locomotive No. 4909 (ex-Amtrak No. 4932)
Two FL 9s
Cabooses
D&H wide-vision caboose No. 35794*
D&H bay window caboose No. 35723* (Ed Nebauer & John Dunne)
D&H wooden caboose No. 35707R* (Jim, Judy & Philip Mitchell)
Erie-Lackawanna bay window caboose No. 316
* Leased from Leatherstocking Railroad Historical Society by the Cooperstown & Charlotte Valley Railroad

CONTACT
Cooperstown & Charlotte Valley Railroad
E. Main Street (New York Rt. 166)
Milford, NY 13280
607-432-2429
www.lrhs.com
wendy@lrhs.com

Photos: Cooperstown & Charlotte Valley Railroad

DELAWARE & ULSTER RAILROAD
Arkville, NY

Enjoy a nostalgic ride through the legendary Catskill Mountains on the Delaware & Ulster Railroad. Your trip, which lasts just about two hours, takes you along the East Branch of the Delaware River Valley. All trains depart from Arkville, where you can enjoy train-themed exhibits and an enchanting gift shop.

Specially scheduled moonlight excursions with live music are featured. Streamliner trains operate on a special scheduled with white linen meal service. Check website for available trips on The Rip Van Winkle Flyer.

SCHEDULES AND FARES
The Delaware & Ulster Railroad operates weekend runs from Memorial Day weekend through October. From July through September there are also Thursday and Friday rides. Schedules and fares vary according to the excursion you choose. Please call or check website for current schedules and fares.

EQUIPMENT
No. 5017, RS36 Alco
No. 5106, Alco S-4, Former Chesapeake & Ohio, built in 1953
No. 1012, Alco S-4, former Ford Motor Co, built in 1954
M-405 J.G. Brill Co. diesel-electric rail car built in 1928, former New York Central
NYC 61 – Budd round end observation, 1949
Locus Grove – Former IC Budd vista dome, 1949
East Branch – Former AC Budd diner, 1950
Olive Branch – Former South American Orient Express tavern, Budd 1949

Two slat cars with benches, former PRR
Two boxcars, former NYC

CONTACT
Delaware & Ulster Railroad
Route 28
Arkville, NY
Or
PO Box 310
Stamford, NY 12167
800-225-4132
607-652-2821
fun@durr.org
www.durr.org

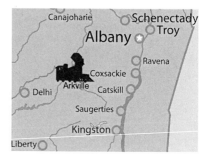

Photos: Delaware & Ulster Railroad Historical Soceity

FINGER LAKES SCENIC RAILWAY
Geneva, NY

Although the Finger Lakes Railway Corporation began operation on July 23, 1995, it operates on track that dates back to 1835. The railway has 118 miles of track, once known as the Geneva Cluster from Syracuse to Canandaigua.

With the breakup of Conrail, Finger Lakes Railway now has connections with three Class I Railroads: CSX, Norfolk Southern, and CP Rail, a benefit to all its customers.

What is known as Finger Lakes Railway is just one part of the company. The nostalgic experience of rail travel has spurred the latest resurrection, since 2000, of passenger excursion service throughout Central New York State. Finger Lakes Scenic railway is helping stimulate tourism in the region. The rail excursions take passengers through beautiful countryside, into areas not seen from the common roadway.

SCHEDULES AND FARES
Finger Lake offers year-round excursions as well as private charters and special events. Schedules and fares vary according to the excursion. Please call or check website for current schedules and fares.

CONTACT
Finger Lake Scenic Railway
68 Border City Road
Geneva, NY 14456
315-781-1234
events@fingerlakesscenicrailway.com
www.fingerlakesscenicrailway.com

Photos: Finger Lakes Scenic Railway

MEDINA RAILROAD MUSEUM
Medina, NY

Located in the old New York Central freight depot, the Medina Railroad Museum is believed the largest freight depot museum in the country. The building was built in 1905, and is one of the largest and last surviving wooden freight depots in the United States.

The museum's ever-growing number of exhibits and interactive displays show how the railroad influenced our culture, industry, and history. The refinished freight depot office area now serves as the lobby to the museum. The desk and two typewriters are those used in this office during New York Central times.

Currently, workers are building what will become one of the largest prototypical HO-scale layouts in the nation. When finished, it will be 204 feet long by 14 feet wide.

Not all of the fun is in the museum. Relax and enjoy a leisurely 2-hour, 34-mile round trip ride through the scenic Erie Canal Heritage Corridor aboard comfortable vintage 1947 Budd passenger coaches.

SCHEDULES and FARES

The Medina Railroad Museum is open year-round, Tuesday to Sunday. Train excursions are available from May through October, with special excursions offered at other times during the year. Trains board in both Medina and Lockport. Adult fares are generally under $20. Please call or check website for current schedules and fares.

EQUIPMENT

1947 Budd passenger coaches
NYC 999 locomotive
The Empire State Express
The Twentieth Century Limited

CONTACT

Medina Railroad Museum
530 West Avenue
Medina, NY 14103
585-798-6106
office@railroadmuseum.net
www.railroadmuseum.net

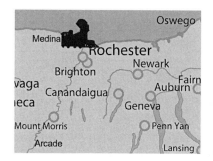

Photos: Medina Railroad Museum

ROCHESTER & GENESEE VALLEY RAILROAD MUSEUM
Rochester, NY

The Rochester & Genesee Valley Railroad Museum is a project of the Rochester Chapter of the National Railway Historical Society, Inc. Volunteers work hard to make sure visitors get a unique museum experience.

The R&GV Railroad Museum was founded in 1971, when the Rochester Chapter purchased the Erie Railroad's Industry, New York depot from the then Erie-Lackawanna Railroad for $1.00. Over the years, museum volunteers have carefully restored the Industry depot to its 1930s appearance.

Beyond the depot, the museum's volunteers have built a five-track yard around the depot for displaying equipment. In 1995, volunteers drove the golden spike on a two mile, standard gauge demonstration railroad that joins the R&GV Railroad Museum to the New York Museum of Transportation. The following year joint public museum operations began offering track-car rides between the two museums for visitors.

In 1998, the museum also constructed a 60-foot-by-140-foot, two-track restoration facility. Voluneers are still working to install the permanent track to the building and complete the interior of the building, which will include a locomotive inspection pit and a concrete floor.

SCHEDULES and FARES
The Rochester & Genesee Valley Railroad Museum is open from late May through late October on Sundays. Adult admission is generally under $10. Please call or check website for current schedules and fares.

EQUIPMENT
The R&GV Railroad Museum currently rosters over 40 pieces of railroad rolling stock, including seven serviceable diesel-electric locomotives: two steam locomotives, which are currently under restoration to operating condition; six cabooses; seven freight cars; and several passenger cars. The museum also owns the last remaining Rochester Subway Car No. 60, which is currently undergoing a multiyear restoration to operating condition.

CONTACT
Rochester Chapter NRHS
P.O. Box 23326
Rochester, NY 14692-3326
585-533-1431
info@rgvrrm.org
www.rgvrrm.org

Photos: Rochester & Genesee Valley Railroad Museum

SARATOGA AND NORTH CREEK RAILROAD
North Creek, NY

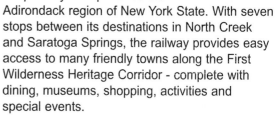

The Saratoga & North Creek Railway offers visitors a unique way to experience the Adirondack region of New York State. With seven stops between its destinations in North Creek and Saratoga Springs, the railway provides easy access to many friendly towns along the First Wilderness Heritage Corridor - complete with dining, museums, shopping, activities and special events.

The train offers a choice of either vintage coach car or dome car seating. The coach cars are roomy and comfortable, ideal for family traveling, while the dome cars offer uninterrupted views of the Adirondacks landscape through large dome windows that wrap overhead. Dining and beverage service s also available along the train's route.

Passengers traveling to North Creek will find a number of activities at their disposal, including direct access to the great outdoors at Gore Mountain and small town pleasures along Main Street. The railway's southern depot in Saratoga Springs brings visitors to the heart of the historic Spa City - home to world-class thoroughbred racing at Saratoga Race Course and the charms of downtown.

The Saratoga & North Creek Railway also hosts a number of on-board special events and activities throughout the summer season. A full schedule is available on the railway's website.

SCHEDULES and FARES
The Saratoga North Creek Railway operates from Memorial Day through October 31st. The popular Polar Express operates in November and December. The winter "Snow Train" operates late December through mid-March

EQUIPMENT
The two depots at Saratoga Springs and North Creek welcome diesel locomotives, full length dome cars and vintage restored coach cars for the year round passenger service provided by the railroad.

CONTACT
Saratoga and North Creek Railroad

North Creek Depot
3 Railroad Place
North Creek, NY 12853

Saratoga Springs Depot
26 Station Lane
Saratoga Springs, NY 12866
877-726-7245
www.sncrr.com
info@sncrr.com

Photos: Greg Klinger

TROLLEY MUSEUM OF NEW YORK
Kingston, NY

The Trolley Museum of New York is a nonprofit educational museum founded in 1955. The goals of the museum are to offer a ride to the public and, through exhibits and educational programs to share the rich history of rail transportation and the role it played in the Hudson Valley region. In addition to static displays of trolley, subway, and rapid transit cars from the United States and Europe, an excursion ride runs 1.5 miles from the foot of Broadway in downtown Kingston, New York, to picnic grounds on the shore of the Hudson River. Picnic tables are available at the Hudson River and the West Strand Park (Rondout Creek) trolley stops. Along the way, we stop at the museum grounds.

The museum is on the original site of the Ulster and Delaware Railroad yards at Milepost 1. The main building is built on the foundation of the engine house which existed at the turn of the century. The upper level includes a Visitors Center featuring seasonal and permanent displays, a video-viewing area, and large windows overlooking the restoration shop. Visitors can see up to eight trolley cars being housed and restored below.

SCHEDULES and FARES

The Trolley Museum of New York is open from Memorial Day Weekend through Columbus Day, Saturdays, Sundays, and holidays from 12 noon to 5:00 p.m. Your fee covers admission to the gallery, shops, and trolley excursion. Adult fares are generally under $5. Please call or check website for current schedules and fares.

EQUIPMENT

Trolley Cars:
No. 1504 Belgian car, 1910
No. 79 Swedish car, 1912
No. 250 Atlantic City car, 1917
No. 8361 Brooklyn Peter Witt, 1925
No. 358 Johnstown car, 1925
No. 601 Queensborough Bridge, 1930
No. 1000 Brooklyn PCC, 1936
No. 3204 Boston MBTA PCC, 1946

Equipment cont.

No. 3214 Boston MBTA PCC, 1946
No. 3216 Boston MBTA PCC, 1946
No. 3584 Hamburg car, 1952
Rapid Transit cars:
No. 1602A BMT Q car, 1907
No. 5600 Lo-V, 1925
No. 127 SEPTA N. Broad Street, 1927
No. 510 H&M Black car, 1928
No. 513 H&M Black car, 1928
No. 825 R-4 car, 1932
No. 175 SEPTA S. Broad Street, 1938
No. 6398 BMT R-16, 1955
Railroad:
No. 120 Model 55 car, 1929
No. 9 diesel locomotive, 1943

CONTACT

Trolley Museum of New York
89 East Strand
Kingston, NY 12402
845-331-3399
www.tmny.org

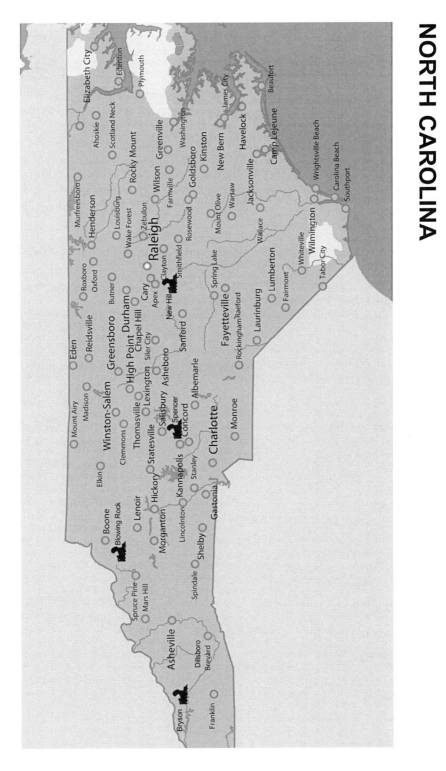

NORTH CAROLINA

GREAT SMOKY MOUNTAINS RAILROAD
Bryson City, NC

With the romance and mystique of an era gone by, the Great Smoky Mountains Railroad takes you through a remote corner of Western North Carolina into river gorges, across fertile valleys and through tunnels carved out of mountains. You may choose from a variety of excursions departing from the Bryson City, NC depot; including a Raft & Rail combination, Special Event Dinner Trains or one of many Premier Special Events.

Enjoy the warm summer breezes and crisp fall air while you take in the panoramic views from your open car featuring long padded outward facing seats, relax in restored Deluxe Class coaches dating from 1925 or travel Presidential Class and dine on lunch served by the car's private attendant. No matter your seating preference, you will enjoy the beautiful scenery Western North Carolina Mountains offer – the very elements that create a happy group and memories of a great trip.

FARES and SCHEDULES
The Great Smoky Mountains Railroad offers excursions year round. Schedules and fares vary based on season and excursion. Call 800-872-4681 or visit www.gsmr.com for the most current information.

EQUIPMENT
Locomotives:
Steam No. 1702 2-8-0 Baldwin, 1942
Diesel No. 711 EMD GP-7, 1954
Diesel No. 777 EMD GP-7, 1954
Diesel No. 1751 EMD GP-9, 1955
Diesel No. 1755 EMD GP-9, 1956
Passenger cars and cabooses:
10 Open-air "Kodak" cars, built from flatbed or Amtrak baggage cars
6 Standard coaches, built 1921-1952
4 Deluxe coaches, built 1926
2 Presidential cars, built 1940's-1956
4 dining cars, built 1949-1956
4 cabooses, built 1944-1971

CONTACT
Great Smoky Mountains Railroad
P.O. Box 1490
Bryson, NC 28713
800-872-4681
www.gsmr.com

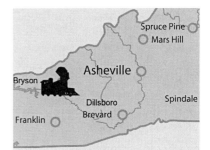

Photos: Great Smoky Mountains Railroad

NEW HOPE VALLEY RAILWAY
New Hill, NC

The New Hope Valley Railway at the North Carolina Railroad Museum has monthly ride days with activities, themes, and events for visitors of all ages to enjoy. It is a 9-mile round trip along the original Norfolk Southern Railway's Durham branch with open cars and cabooses. It's a leisurely one-hour ride. There is also an opportunity for you to take charge by signing up for the museum's Operate-A-Loco program. The museum has equipment on display that showcases North Carolina's role in rail history.

The New Hope Valley Railroad (NHV) was originally organized in 1904. The New Hope Valley Railway of today began in 1982 when the East Carolina Chapter of the National Railway Historical Society purchased the tracks and right-of-way in Bonsal and New Hill from the Southern Railway. The first public-ride operations were held in April of 1984, and it has been operated as a living railroad museum ever since.

SCHEDULES and FARES
The museum is open on Saturdays and Sundays throughout the year. Trains run on the first Sunday of the month from May through December. There are month-

ly Work Days and Group Ride Days. Tickets are generally under $10. Please call or check website for current schedules and fares.

EQUIPMENT
Diesel locomotives:
NHV No. 71 built in 1945
NHV No. 67, built in 1942
NHV No. 70, built in 1941
Beaufort & Morehead No. 75, built in 1947
Steam locomotive:
West Virginia Northern No. 17, built in 1941
Wood-sided caboose
Seaboard Air Line No. 5228
Aberdeen and Rockfish No. 308

CONTACT
New Hope Valley Railway
P.O. Box 40
New Hill, NC 27562
919-362-5416
nhvry@mindspring.com
www.nhvry.org

*Photos: Timothy Telkamp

Did You Know...

There are about 1,950 steam locomotives in the United States. About 250 of these are capable of running. At any given time, fewer than 100 can operate.

Fact by: Steamtown National Historic Site

NORTH CAROLINA TRANSPORTATION MUSEUM
Spencer, NC

The North Carolina Transportation Museum operates a 25 minute on-site narrated train ride across the 57 acre historic Spencer Shops, once the Southern Railway Company's largest steam locomotive repair facility. Departing from Barber Junction, the ride provides views of the town of Spencer, the Master Mechanic's Office, Roundhouse and Back Shop. The train ride began in 1986, when several ex-Southern Railway Spencer Shops employees worked to restore their two commuter coaches. Over time, four diesel locomotives were placed in service to pull the train. Passenger cars have been leased from the Roanoke Chapter of the National Railway Historical Society. The Norfolk and Western Combine 1506 provides us with a handicap accessible passenger car, making the train ride available to those with limited mobility. Private cars, like the Pine Tree State, and the Doris are used for members during special events.

SCHEDULES and FARES:

The museum is open year-round with seasonal train and turntable rides offered. Ticket prices for the train are under $10 for adults. Group rates are available. Turntable rides are $1. Please call 704-636-2889 or visit www.nctrans.org for current schedules and fares.

EQUIPMENT:
Diesel Locomotives:
Southern FP-7 6133
Southern GP-30 2601
N&W GP-9 620
Beaufort and Morehead #1860
Coaches:
Roanoke NRHS Chapter Pullman Standard Passenger Cars - #512, #537, #1827
Norfolk and Western Combine # 1506
#1292 - "Jack Vail"

CONTACT:
North Carolina Transportation Museum
411 S. Salisbury Avenue
Spencer, NC 28159
704-636-2889
www.nctrans.org

Photos: North Carolina Transportation Museum

Did You Know...

The first railway in North America was the Baltimore and Ohio Railroad, which began operating in 1828 with horse-drawn cars. In 1830 after a successful run with the "Tom Thumb" locomotive, the railroad switched to steam powered locomotives.

TWEETSIE RAILROAD
Blowing Rock, NC

Tweetsie makes a scenic three-mile loop through the mountains near Blowing Rock, not far from the original end-of-the-line station in Boone. Tweetsie also operates a complete train repair shop, rebuilding and restoring locomotives for other theme parks and for museums.

Meticulously maintained and now listed in the National Register of Historic Places, Tweetsie continues to delight rail fans, children, and tourists who visit the beautiful Blue Ridge Mountains of North Carolina.

The name "Tweetsie" was given to the railroad by local folks who became accustomed to the shrill "tweet, tweet" train whistles that echoed through the hills. The name stuck, and the train has been known as Tweetsie ever since.

Tweetsie's history dates back to 1866, when the Tennessee legislature granted the East Tennessee & Western North Carolina Railroad company permission for the construction of a railroad. At the outset, the ET&WNC line, which mountain humorists dubbed the "Eat Taters & Wear No Clothes" Railroad, was to operate from Johnson City, Tennessee to the iron mines just over the state line at Cranberry, North Carolina.

The narrow gauge railroad began operations in 1881 after fifty miles of track were laid through the rugged Blue Ridge chain of the Appalachian Mountains that divide the two southern states. Later, additional tracks were laid to Boone, North Carolina. In 1916 rail service was extended to that mountain community. The new line added passenger service to the formerly isolated area, and brought lumber out of the mountains.

In the summer of 1957, Tweetsie Railroad, North Carolina's first theme park, made her first run at her new location just a couple of miles away from the old railroad station in Boone. People came from all over the South to welcome her famous whistle back to the mountains.

SCHEDULES and FARES
Tweetsie Railroad is open from May through October. There are also

special-event trains. Please call or check Web site for current schedules and fares.

EQUIPMENT:
No. 12, 4-6-0 Baldwin coal steam, 1917
No. 190 2-8-2 Baldwin coal steam, 1943

CONTACT
Tweetsie Railroad
300 Tweetsie Railroad Lane
Blowing Rock, NC 28605
828-264-9061
800-526-5740
www.tweetsie.com

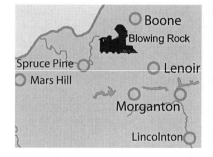

Photos: Tweetsie Railroad

Did You Know...

U.S. freight railroads are the world's busiest, moving more freight than any other country. U.S. railroads move more than four times as much frieght as do all of Western Europe's freight railroads combined.

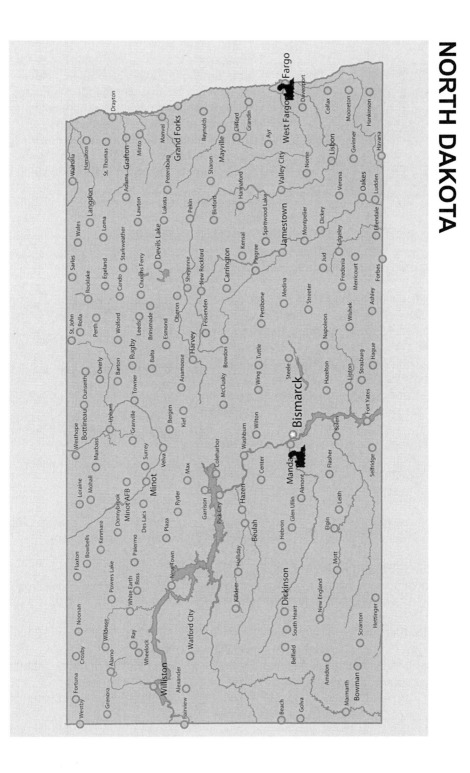

NORTH DAKOTA

BONANZAVILLE USA
West Fargo, ND

Bonanzaville USA is named after the Bonanza Farms that dotted this region in the late 19th Century as a result of Northern Pacific Railroad's efforts to develop large-scale, showcase farms of 1,000 acres or more. The farms were meant to advertise the economic potential of the land on either side of the railroad's route, in particular the land along the Minnesota, Dakota Territory border known as the Red River Valley.

Today, Bonanzaville USA recreates the magnificent history of this area's past using more than 400,000 documented artifacts indigenous to the upper Midwest showcased in 40 buildings spread over 15 acres.

You won't want to miss the Embden Depot and Train Shed. This 1900 Northern Pacific building houses an 1883 NP locomotive and caboose, a Russell snow plow and a 1930, 80-passenger coach. The water tower and railroad water column in front of the building were used by steam locomotives in downtown Fargo as well as by the Northern States Power Company.

Another building in the village is the Kathryn Depot. Here, the Spud Valley Model Railroad Club operates a model railroad covering the length of the building with a number of trains traveling throughout the hills and village of this miniature landscape.

Don't miss the opportunity to see a variety of other buildings (many moved intact from surrounding areas) that showcase the history of this important era!

SCHEDULES and FARES
The museum and village are May through October. Please call or check website for current schedules and fares.

EQUIPMENT
There are over 400,000 artifacts in the Cass County Historical Society's collection at Bonanzaville. Many of them are on display in the main museum and throughout the village.

CONTACT
Bonanzaville, USA
1351 Main Avenue West
West Fargo, ND 58078
701-282-2822
info@bonanzaville.com
www.bonanzaville.com

Photos: Bonanzaville USA

Did You Know...

According to the Association of American Railroaders, 70% of all automobiles produced in the U.S., 30% of the nation's grain harvest, and 65% of the nation's coal are moved by train. Another way to look at it is U.S. railroads carry enough cars to account for 7 out of 10 sold every year, enough wheat to make 315 loaves of bread for every American, and enough coal to supply electricity to every home in America.

NORTH DAKOTA STATE RAILROAD MUSEUM
Mandan, ND

Located on five acres in northwest Mandan, the North Dakota State Railroad Museum is filled with artifacts both large and small. Visitors can explore rolling stock and the collection of railroad timetables from railroads across the country. The museum also features a collection of photographs taken by Ron V. Nixon, a longtime Northern Pacific dispatcher.

It all began in 1974 within the Morton County Historical Society. During 1986 the Railroad Museum Historical Society was established from the original committee.

In 1985, Kenneth and Darlene Porsborg of Mandan, North Dakota, donated four acres of land for a museum, and Burlington Northern, Inc., donated the yard office. With assistance from the Morton County Historical Society, the yard office was moved to its current site. The North Dakota State Legislature in 1989 designated the museum in Mandan as the North Dakota State Railroad Museum.

SCHEDULES and FARES
The museum is open daily from Memorial Day through Labor Day. Admission to the museum is free. Please call or check website for current schedules and fares.

EQUIPMENT
The museum features a variety of cabooses, flatcars, boxcars, semaphores, and speeder shacks.

CONTACT
North Dakota State Railroad Museum
3102 37th Street NW
Mandan, ND 58554-7001
701-663-9322
www.geocities.com/ndsrm

Photos: North Dakota State Railroad Museum

OHIO

Sylvania
Conneaut
Ashtabula
Painesville
Carson
Euclid
Jefferson
Toledo
Cleveland
Kirtland
Cleveland Heights
Bryan
Waterville
Sandusky
Lorain
Independence
Defiance
Bowling Green
Elyria
Peninsula
Warren
Paulding
Norwalk
Medina
Youngstown
Struthers
Fostoria
Willard
Orrville
Akron
Findlay
Salem
Van Wert
Ashland
Canton
Lima
Mansfield
Kenton
Sugarcreek
St. Marys
Marion
Millersburg
Dover
Steubenville
Bellefontaine
Mount Vernon
Sidney
Delaware
Coshocton
Piqua
Worthington
Westerville
St. Clairsville
Troy
Upper Arlington
Hebron
Moundsville
Vandalia
Springfield
Columbus
Dayton
Grove City
Zanesville
Kettering
Lancaster
Oxford
Franklin
East Logan
Marietta
Hamilton
Wilmington
Glouster
Forest Park
Circleville
Nelsonville
Reading
Chillicothe
Athens
Cincinnati
Hillsboro
Jackson
Pomeroy
Portsmouth
New Boston
Ironton

AC & J SCENIC LINE RAILWAY
Jefferson, OH

Riders enjoy a one hour, 12-mile round trip through scenic back farm country and woods of northeastern Ohio. Enjoy travel as it once was: restful and unhurried. Many areas of the line haven't barely changed since service began in 1872. You will ride on vintage coaches that date back to the mid-1920s and first generation diesels locomotives from of the late 1940s and early 1950s.

Since August of 1872, the former New York Central route was known as the "High Grade" running to Pittsburgh and Oil City, PA in competition with the Pennsylvania Railroad. Trains from Cleveland and Buffalo used the route daily in the heyday of rail travel. Early in the 20th century, train service continued even after a merger into the New York Central System. By the 1950's, traffic had begun to decline and service was reduced to a flag stop in 1956. All service ceased through Jefferson during July of 1957. Passenger service continued using nearby Dorset and their parallel freight line.

Gradually over the years sections of the original "High Grade" were removed. The last section was removed in between Dorset to Andover, in 1988, leaving the Jefferson branch as the only remaining track in existence of the "High Grade." In 1984, Conrail abandoned the line, and it became the Ashtabula, Carson, and Jefferson Railroad. The AC & J still offers freight service and a tourist passenger line.

SCHEDULES and FARES
AC&J Scenic Line Railway runs regular excursions from mid-June through late October on Saturdays and Sundays. Regular adult fares are under $10 but may vary for special trips. Please call or check website for current schedules and fares.

EQUIPMENT
1948 Alco S2 switch engine
1950 Alco S2 switch engine
1925 Stillman heavyweight passenger coach
1926 Long Island commuter cars (2)
1950 baggage cars (2)
1956 Nickel Plate caboose

CONTACT
AC & J Scenic Line Railway
122 East Walnut Street
Jefferson, OH 44047-0517
440-576-6346
440-576-8848 (fax)
info@acjrscenic.net
www.acjrscenic.net

Photos: AC & J Scenic Line Railway

CUYAHOGA VALLEY SCENIC RAILROAD
Peninsula, OH

Today, Cuyahoga Valley Scenic Railroad operates on 26 miles of track running from independence, which is located 15 miles south of downtown Cleveland, to downtown Akron. The line runs through the heart of Cuyahoga Valley National Park, which encompasses 33,000 acres of land that is part of our National Park system. From river flood plain and steep-cut valley walls to ancient stands of evergreen, you'll journey through a world of historic sites and timeless natural processes.

Take a seat in our vintage, climate-controlled coaches, which originally saw service on the Seaboard and Santa Fe Railroads, and watch it all reveal itself: meadowlands, pines, marsh, river, ravine and wood, not to mention beaver, fox, deer, and owl. Amble through small towns. See a working 19th-century farm and a canal museum.

For thousands of years Indians used the Cuyahoga River and Valley in northern Ohio as a north-south transportation corridor. Later, the Ohio and Erie Canal provided the early settlers a slow but easy way to move bulk goods and people.

In 1880, the first steam engine chugged its way down the new Valley Railway. It was primarily built to transport coal from south of Canton to Cleveland's growing industries.

Today, the historic rails are owned by the National Park Service as part of its goal to preserve the significant cultural resources in the Cuyahoga Valley. The organization operates the excursion train through the Cuyahoga Valley National Park in cooperation with the National Park Service.

SCHEDULES AND FARES
The Cuyahoga Valley Scenic Railroad operates from mid-June through December. Adult fares range from $15-$26. Please call or check website for current schedules and fares.

EQUIPMENT
Locomotives:
No. 14 (EX. CN No. 6777) FPA-4 freight/passenger A Unit
No. 15 (EX. CN No. 6771) FPA-4 freight/passenger A Unit
B&O No. 800 (EX. CN No. 6780) FPA-4 freight/passenger
No. 6767 (CN No. 6767) FPA-4 freight/passenger A Unit
No. 365 (EX. Atlantic Coastline No. 127) C420, 1965

CONTACT
Cuyahoga Valley Scenic Railroad
1664 Main Street
Peninsula, OH 44264
800-468-4070
330-657-2642
330-657-2080 (fax)
marketing@cvsr.com
www.cvsr.com

Photos: Tom Jones, Cuyahoga Valley Scenic Railroad, and Larry Blanchard

HOCKING VALLEY SCENIC RAILWAY
Nelsonville, OH

Climb aboard the Hocking Valley Scenic Railway for a leisurely trip on an old-time passenger train through the beautiful hills of southeastern Ohio. Whether it's the blooming dogwoods of spring, summertime greenery, spectacular fall foliage, or a special winter ride with Santa Claus, you'll certainly have a train excursion to remember.

The route between Nelsonville and Logan was once a part of the original Hocking Valley Railway's Athens Branch. The railway offers diesel-powered rides through the hillside aboard vintage equipment. The coaches were built in 1927 for commuter service around Chicago, and the primary diesel locomotive used was built in 1952. You can choose either a 14-mile or a 22-mile excursion with a stop at an historic 1840s village. It is a living museum sure to fascinate your entire family.

SCHEDULES and FARES

The Hocking Valley Scenic Railway operates on weekends from Memorial Day through the first weekend in November. Special-events trains are also scheduled throughout the year, including a Santa Train in December. Group rates and special charters are available. Please call or check website for current schedules and fares. This railroad has a mobile wheelchair lift.

EQUIPMENT

No. 5833, GP-7, built in 1952
No. 4005, RS4TC, built for the US Army in 1954
No. 7315, 45-tonner built for the US Army between 1948 and 1949
No. 701, GP-10, built in 1957

CONTACT

Hocking Valley Scenic Railway
33 Canal Street
Nelsonville, OH 45764
800-967-7834
www.hvsry.org.

Photos: Hocking Valley Scenic Railway

LEBANON MASON MONROE RAILROAD
Lebanon, OH

Experience a nostalgic train ride along the Lebanon Mason Monroe (LM&M) Railroad through Warren County in Southwestern, Ohio. Walk through the train to the open-air gondola and listen to the informative conductors describe railroad history and operation, as well as a brief locomotive tour. Passengers will enjoy an authentic, historic train with fun excursions like tea party trains, mystery trains, Thomas the Tank Engine, Pumpkin Patch Express, and special Christmas and Easter trains.

SCHEDULES and FARES
Trains operate every weekend from Easter through Christmas. Weekday trips are available for schools and group tours from April through October. Tickets are available on-line and by fax. Please call or visit website for current schedules and fares.

EQUIPMENT
CNRY No. 55, GP7 locomotive
CNRY Nos. 101-104, Pullman coaches, built in 1930
CNRY No. 100, freight gondola, built in 1934

CONTACT
Lebanon Mason Monroe Railroad
127 South Mechanic Street
Lebanon, OH 45036
513-933-8022
www.lebanonrr.com

Photo: Lebanon Mason Monroe Railroad

MAD RIVER AND NKP RAILROAD MUSEUM
Bellevue, OH

The Mad River and NKP Railroad Museum houses numerous historical displays and rolling stock in its museum and on the surrounding grounds. Visit the private collection of Ted and Sarah Church, housed in three former Troop Sleepers, where you will find cases displaying various torches, buttons, badges, locks, silverware, linens and china used by the troops during WWII. The museum also has many other artifacts such as uniforms, timetables, lanterns, china, and much, much more. Take a self-guided tour through the museum and grounds, visit our gift shop, or bring large groups for a picnic and entertaining day here at the depot.

SCHEDULES AND FARES
Open daily Memorial Day through Labor Day, and through October on the weekends. Admission ranges from $4-7.

EQUIPMENT
Various rolling stock including cabooses, passenger and freight cars, engines, and much more.

CONTACT
Mad River and NKP Railroad Museum
253 Southwest St, Bellevue, OH 44811
419.483.2222
www.madrivermuseum.org
madriver@oneebellevue.com

NORTHWEST OHIO RAILROAD PRESERVATION, INC.
Findlay, OH

Northwest Ohio Railroad Preservation, Inc., is a 501(c)(3) nonprofit corporation established for the preservation, promotion, and education of railroad history in Northwest Ohio.

Visitors will experience the thrill of a coal-burning steam train ride on its nearly half mile of 15 inch gauge track. The museum's Engine 901 and passenger coaches were originally built and operated at the Israelite House of David amusement park in Benton Harbor, Michigan.

On site is a quarter-scale water tower, designed and built by volunteers. The museum's front room is used for purchaseing of train tickets and as a gift shop. In the model train room, there is a large, detailed HO model train layout.

SCHEDULES AND FARES
The museum is open from late March through December. It offers various events throughtout its season, including a Halloween train, a North Pole Express train, and a train show. Please call or check website for current schedules and fares.

EQUIPMENT
Engine 901, 1950s
Wooden boxcar from the late 1800s
1940s Plymouth switcher.
B&O caboose C2157

CONTACT
Northwest Ohio Railroad Preservation, Inc.
11600 County Road 99
Findlay, OH 45840
419-423-2995
NWORRP@bright.net
http://nworrp.org

Photos: Northwest Ohio Preservation. Inc

ORRVILLE RAILROAD HERITAGE SOCIETY
Orrville, OH

The Orrville Railroad Heritage Committee was formed in 1978 to save the town's railroad station, located at the junction of two former Pennsylvania Railroad lines. The route from Pittsburgh to Chicago via Crestline, Ohio, and Fort Wayne, Indiana, is still used by Conrail. The other line is the Orrville secondary, part of a former PRR route from Cleveland to Columbus, Ohio. This portion is still used by Conrail to serve local industries.

The society also owns the interlocking tower that controlled the junction, an ex-PRR caboose, several heritage passenger cars, and an F&ABB diesel locomotive. The society operates main line passenger excursion trains several times a year on the Wheeling & Lake Erie Railway, the Ohio Central Railroad System, and other railroads, with Amtrak specials. Steam locomotives power the excursions whenever possible.

SCHEDULES and FARES
There is no admission charge to the depot. Fares vary according to excursion. Please call or check website for current schedules and fares.

EQUIPMENT
The society's rolling stock includes an ex-PRR caboose, several heritage passenger cars, and an F&ABB diesel locomotive.

CONTACT
Orville Railroad Heritage Society
145 Depot Street
Orrville, OH 44667
330-683-2426
Questions@Orrvillerailroad.com
www.orrvillerailroad.com

Photos: Orville Railroad Heritage Committee

OKLAHOMA

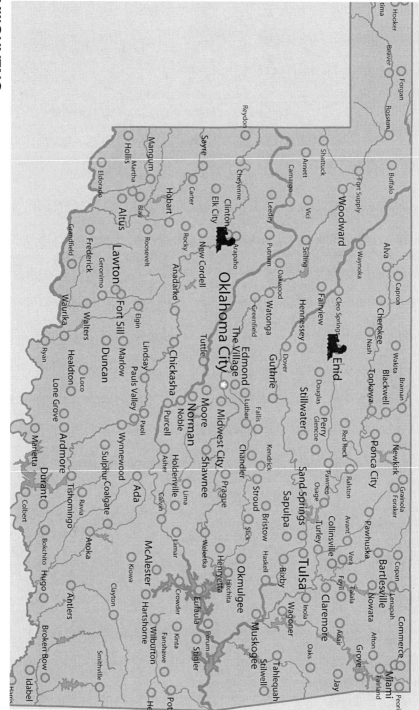

FARMRAIL SYSTEM, INC.
Clinton, OK

Farmrail System, Inc., is "Western Oklahoma's Regional Railroad." It is an employee-owned holding company managing nearly 200 miles of line. For these employees, it's a matter of earning respect for the railroad and its history.

Farmrail turns back the clock so that guests can relive "the way it was" nearly 100 years ago when the railroads came to western Oklahoma. Beautifully appointed passenger coaches re-create the experience of riding the train, but in modern-day air-conditioned comfort. Farmrail offers Quartz Mountain Flyer passenger excursions which are two-hour narrated trips with a stop in Lone Wolf.

SCHEDULES AND FARES
The Quartz Mountain Flyer leaves Quartz Mountain on select Saturdays from April through December. Adult fares are generally under $20. Please call or check website for current schedules and fares.

EQUIPMENT
2 GP-10 locomotives
1950s-era passenger coaches
A kid's car

CONTACT
Farmrail Corporation
1601 West Gary Boulevard
Clinton, OK 73601
580-323-1234
580-323-4568 (fax)
www.farmrail.com

Photos: Farmrail System Inc.

RAILROAD MUSEUM OF OKLAHOMA
Enid, OK

Housed in a former Santa Fe freight house, the Railroad Museum of Oklahoma has one of the largest collections of railroad material in the United States. Volunteers began renovating the complex in the late 1980s and say that the process is ongoing. The museum is located across the street and to the west of the Old Santa Fe Depot. Volunteers are working on oral-history presentations of how they brought the museum and railroading back to life.

The Railroad Museum of Oklahoma is one of the few railroad museums in the nation to conduct all-caboose excursions over the rails. Held twice each year, these memorable trips take riders between Enid and Drummond in September (10 miles each way) and between Enid and Okeene on a day trip as part of the annual Okeene Rattlesnake Hunt in May (35 miles each way). The train is usually made up of eight or more cabooses representing railroads that served or  continue to serve Enid, bracketed by two diesel engines from the Farmrail Railroad.

SCHEDULES and FARES
The museum is open year-round. A donation of $2 per person is suggested. Please call or check website for current schedules and fares.

EQUIPMENT
No. 1519, 1925 Frisco Baldwin 4-8-2
1965 GE 50-ton class BB switcher, operational
6 renovated cabooses from railroads that served Enid
1928 automobile boxcar
1937 three-domed riveted tank car
1930 boxcar
1920 gondola with arch-bar tracks
Amtrak lounge car

CONTACT
Railroad Museum of Oklahoma
702 N. Washington
Enid, OK 73701
580-233-3051
information@railroadmuseumofoklahoma.org
www.railroadmuseumofoklahoma.org

Photos: Railroad Museum of Oklahoma

Did You Know...

The First Trancontinental Railroad in the United States was built across North America in the 1860s, linking the railway network of the Eastern United States with California on the Pacific Coast.

OREGON

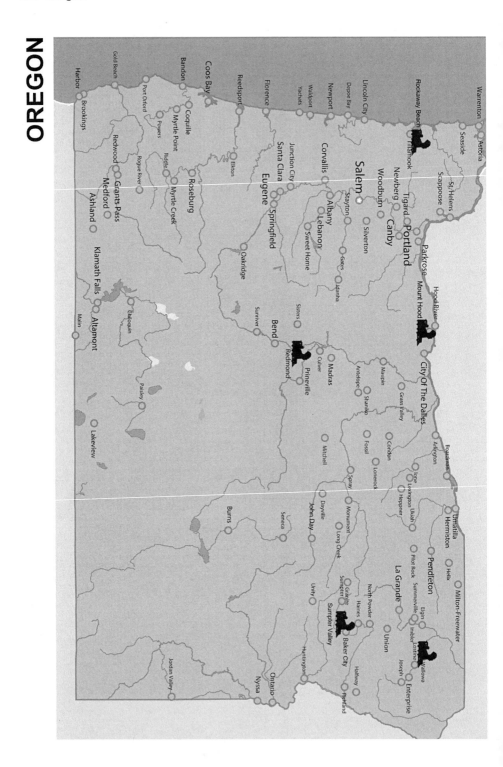

CROOKED RIVER DINNER TRAIN
Redmond, OR

The Crooked River Railroad is an 1800s western theme dinner train, featuring characters from the Wild West. On your three hour journey back in time, look for deer, cattle, and cowboys as you ride through Central Oregon's beautiful Crooked River Valley, with jagged rimrock, lush fields, and 19 miles of high desert terrain.

The staff will entertain you the moment you step aboard the western dinner train and will take you back 100 years, when trains were robbed and murder was common. All murders take place before you depart and it is up to you and your fellow passengers to solve the crime while enjoying the action, suspense, and humor.

The railway also offers Sunday Brunch and Supper trains through the Crooked River Valley. But again, don't be surprised if Jesse James and the gang interrupt things when you least expect it.

SCHEDULES and FARES
The Crooked River Dinner Train runs on Saturdays year-round, and on Fridays from June through September. Sunday Brunches and Suppers run on select dates. Adult fares, depending on your excursion, are generally under $80. Please call or check website for current schedules and fares.

CONTACT
The Crooked River Dinner Train
P.O. Box 387
Redmond, OR 97756
541-548-8630
www.crookedriverrailroad.com

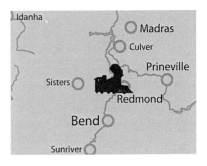

Photos: Crooked River Dinner Train

EAGLE CAP EXCURSION TRAIN
Wallowa, OR

The Eagle Cap is Oregon's newest excursion train. Your journey will take you through rugged canyons, alongside rivers, and across the Wallowa Valley. Your backdrop is the Blue and Wallowa Mountains. The train operates on a 63-mile-long railroad that links the communities of Elgin, Wallowa, Enterprise, and Joseph in Northeast Oregon.

The track, historically known as the Joseph Branch, is owned by the governments of Wallowa and Union Counties and operated by the Wallowa Union Railroad Authority, which also operates rail freight service on the track. The Eagle Cap Train excursions are run by a volunteer organization called the Friends of the Joseph Branch, using the professional train crew of the Wallowa Union Railroad.

SCHEDULES and FARES
There are at least seven excursion options varying in cost from $45 to $80 for adults and $25 to $55 for youth tickets. Travel times range from 2 to 6 hours. Please call or check website for current schedules and fares.

EQUIPMENT
2 EMD-GP-7
WURR baggage generator car
Pullman standard coaches

CONTACT
Eagle Cap Excursion Train
209 E First Street
Wallowa, OR
541-886-3200
www.eaglecaptrain.com

Photos: Bill Peek, David Yerges, and Eagle Cap Excursion Train

MOUNT HOOD RAILROAD
Mount Hood, OR

Every year, thousands of visitors enjoy this leisurely tour as part of the Mount Hood Loop, adding visits to Multnomah Falls, Bonneville Dam, and Timberline Lodge for a complete Oregon experience. The railroad offers day and evening 4-hour round-trip tours and special events throughout the season.

All trains depart from the historic depot in the town of Hood River, 60 miles east of Portland. After departing the depot, trains travel along the Hood River to a rare rail switchback, and up to the forests, meadows, and orchards of the upper valley. Mount Hood and Mount Adams supply dramatic backdrops as the track winds through the countryside.

The fun begins when you step aboard this historic train. Passengers are seated in 1910-1950-era enclosed coaches, Double Decker train car, and Upper Dome with a skylight view. Our open-air car offers an observation deck as well as seating. The trip is narrated through the valley, covering the area's history and key sights along the way. Passengers may disembark during the one-hour layover in Parkdale. Bring along a picnic, sample the local cafes, browse the gift shop, visit the Hutson Museum, or just relax and take in stunning views of Mount Hood. Lunches are available onboard the train.

Every season presents the Hood River Valley in its unique splendor. In the springtime, thousands of acres of fruit blossoms bathe the valley in soft colors, while summer brings a lushness to the foliage and blush to the ripening fruit. Autumn signals the bustle of harvest time and sets the orchards and mountains ablaze in fiery golds, oranges, and reds. Finally, winter softly blankets the sleeping landscape in white. Come join us on a scenic journey through the beautiful Northwest.

The Dinner Train: This 1940s-era train captures the nostalgia of classic American passenger train service. Meticulously restored dining cars provide a relaxing atmosphere as you enjoy delicious four-course meals prepared on board and served by friendly and attentive wait staff. If you like, we'll bring you a bottle of fine Northwest wine, chosen by our executive chef to complement your meal.

Stroll to the lounge car or just sit back and enjoy the intimate surroundings at your windowed booth. Whether you've chosen the Dinner or Brunch Train, you will find the cuisine and the service to be first class. Their "Club Car" has live bands, DJ and alternative entertainment which is also available for charters and personal events.

SCHEDULES and FARES
The Mount Hood Railroad operates from late March through December. Adult fares generally range from $27 to $82, depending on your excursion. Please call or check website for current schedules and fares.

EQUIPMENT
No. 88, GP9, EMD, 1959
No. 89, GP9, EMD, 1958
No. 1040 caboose, 1952
No. SLRG 513 Dome 1954
No. RCPX 509 Dome 1954
No. SLRG 2923 Parlor 1955
No. SLRG 2920 Coach 1955
No. SLRG 2948 Coach 1955
No. SLRG 2974 Coach 1955
No. SLRG 2968 Club Car 1955
No. RSO1 Lounge
No. RS02 dining car, 1947
No. RS03 kitchen car, 1948
No. RS04 dining car, 194

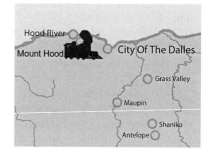

CONTACT
Mount Hood Railroad
110 Railroad Avenue
Hood River, OR 97031
800-872-4661
www.mthoodrr.com/

Photos: Mount Hood Railroad

OREGON COAST SCENIC RAILROAD
Rockaway Beach, OR

The Oregon Coast Scenic Railroad offers visitors a chance to step back in time by riding the rail behind a 1910 Heisler steam locomotive. You will be lulled into the peaceful views along Tillamook Bay and beyond to the Pacific Ocean.

Coast excursions from Garibaldi to Rockaway Beach are an hour and a half round trip, including a layover in the town opposite from where you board. You have time to explore the town, play on the beach, get an ice cream cone, or shop in the variety of boutiques.

Port of Tillamook Bay is comprised of 1600 acres of land zoned for industrial use. The facility is built around the former Tillamook U.S. Naval Station, home to one of the blimp squadrons that patrolled the Pacific coast during World War II.

The 95 miles of railroad were put in place to serve the coastal towns of Garibaldi, Rockaway Beach and Wheeler.

SCHEDULES and FARES
The Oregon Coast Scenic Railroad operates on weekends from Memorial Day to Labor Day. There are Friday excursions in July and August. Adult fares are generally under $15. There are also opportunities for Cab rides. Because of its popularity reservations are highly recommended. Please call or check website for current schedules and fares.

EQUIPMENT
Curtiss Lumber Co. No. 2
Polson Logging Co. No. 3
Stimson Mill Co. No .23
Buffelen Lumber & Mfg Co. No. 5
E.C. Schevlin Timber Co. No. 3
Deep River Logging Co. No. 7 (Skookum)
Passenger car No. 0100
Passenger car No. 0200
Caboose No. 24508

CONTACT
Oregon Coast Scenic Railroad
Hwy. 101
Rockaway Beach, OR
503-842-7972
info@ocsr.net
www.ocsr.net

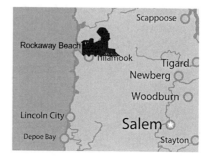

Photos: Oregon Coast Scenic Railroad

SUMPTER VALLEY RAILWAY
Sumpter Valley, Oregon

Nearly all of today's excursion and museum railroads operate on abandoned right-of-way. But the Sumpter Valley Railway is unique in that the current railroad has built the railroad itself. The roadbed and track are mostly on original Sumpter Valley Railway right-of-way, but the original track was scrapped in 1947, and most of the original roadbed eroded away. With an all-volunteer work force, the Railway has rebuilt over seven miles of track and continues to expand.

Today your trip on the Sumpter Valley Railway takes you over five miles of track to the historic gold town of Sumpter, passing through beautiful countryside to relive the glorious days of steam travel.

SCHEDULES and FARES
The Sumpter Valley Railway operates on weekends and holidays from Memorial Day through September. Trains depart from both the McEwen Station and the Sumpter Station. You may purchase either a one-way ticket or a round-trip ticket. Fares are generally under $15. Please call or check website for current schedules and fares.

EQUIPMENT
The railroad has an extensive collection of narrow gauge and standard gauge rolling stock including:
2 1920 Alco Mikado steam locomotives
1915 Heisler steam locomotive
No. 20 Union Pacific first-class coach
Wood drop-bottom gondolas
Sumpter Valley Railway caboose No. 5

CONTACT
Sumpter Valley Railroad
P.O. Box 389
Baker City, OR 97814
541-894-2268
866-894-2268
www.svry.com

Photos: Sumpter Valley Railway and Gary Collins

Did You Know...

The first flight of the Wright Flyer was 120 feet. That is 12 feet less than the length of the Union Pacific "Big Boy." Built in 1941, it is 132 feet, 9 3/4 inches long.

PENNSYLVANIA

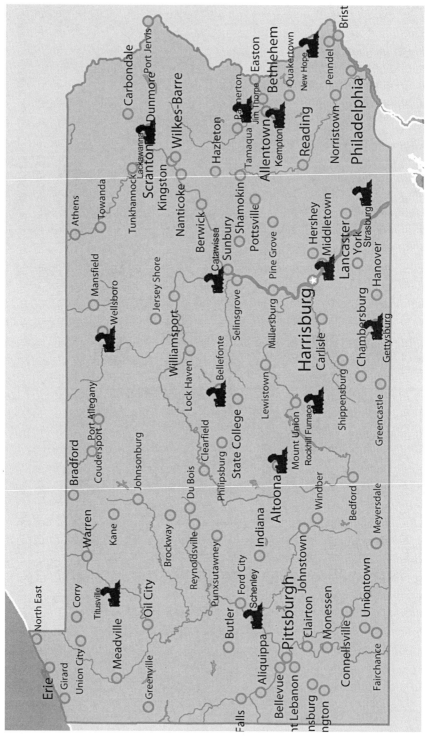

CATAWISSA RAILROAD
Catawissa, PA

About 100 miles northwest of Philadelphia, the Catawissa Branch of the Reading Railroad Lines offers Caboose Lodging--a must experience for train buffs of all ages. Ring the old steam locomotive's bell and explore the 14 cabooses and the other equipment on display.

The Caboose Lodging is unlike a hotel stay. The railroad maintained as much authenticity as possible. The very large His & Hers private bathrooms are next to the cabooses; you'll get your own keys to them. The three newer cabooses have bathrooms in them. The Catawissa Railroad is located in a park, with lots of shade trees.

SCHEDULES and FARES
Caboose Lodging is available from April to November. Reservations are required for lodging.

EQUIPMENT
12 Cabooses for rent:
13 Cabooses on display

CONTACT
Catawissa Railroad
111 Main Street
Catawissa, PA 17820
570-356-2345
www.caboosenut.com
Photos: Catawissa Railroad

Did You Know...

The Transcontinental Railroad was considered the greatest American technological feat of the 19th century.

EAST BROAD TOP RAILROAD
Rockhill Furnace, PA

The East Broad Top Railroad (EBT) operates steam-powered trains on a refurbished five-mile-long segment of its original main line. Using its historic locomotives and passenger cars, EBT trains carry passengers from the railroad's Orbisonia Station north along scenic Aughwick Creek to a picnic area at Colgate Grove. There the train is turned on a wye track for its return trip to Rockhill Furnace.

The station is located in the town of Rockhill Furnace, but in the early 1900s it was renamed for adjoining Orbisonia to avoid misdirected express shipments caused by confusion with other stations with similar names. Another wye track around the railroad's shop complex allows the train to end its trip at the station, ready for its next trip north.

The EBT was constructed in 1873-74 to exploit semi-bituminous coal deposits on the eastern side of Broad Top Mountain in south-central Pennsylvania. To save construction costs, the railroad was built to narrow gauge: The inside edges of the rails are 3 feet apart rather than 4 feet, 8 1/2 inches (U.S. standard gauge).

At the operating headquarters of the railroad, in Rockhill Furnace, the EBT developed a complex of service and shop buildings where it maintained, repaired, and constructed its equipment. The coal transported by the EBT was in high demand, and in the early 20th century the railroad constructed a modern coal-cleaning plant at Mount Union, where the coal was cleaned in the process of being transferred to the Pennsylvania Railroad's

standard guage cars. From Mount Union, Broad Top coal could then go anywhere in the country. In 1926, its peak year, the EBT transported approximately 26 million ton-miles of coal traffic--an incredible record for a narrow gauge railroad with a main line 33 miles long.

SCHEDULES and FARES
The East Broad Top Railroad runs weekend excursions from June to October. Adult fares are generally under $15. Please call or check website for current schedules and fares.

EQUIPMENT
7 steam locomotives (No. 15 in operation)
M-1 gas electric car
Speeder cars, built between 1920 and 1950
Twin cabooses, built in 1920

CONTACT
East Broad Top Railroad
P.O. Box 158
Rockhill Furnace, PA 17249
814-447-3011
814-447-3256 (fax)
www.ebtrr.com

Photos: Lance Myers, East BroadTop RR

KISKI JUNCTION RAILROAD
Schenley, PA

The Kiski Junction Railroad "hauls freight for a living and passengers for fun." Take a 1-to 1.5-hour ride along the Kiski and Allegheny Rivers in southwestern Pennsylvania. You'll hear a brief description of local history and learn how a working railroad operates.

Enjoy views of the rivers and see remnants of bygone canals, coal mines, distilleries, and railroads.

The train departs from Schenley Station and travels to Bagdad before returning. Once back in Schenley, the train pulls out on a bridge that spans the Kiski River for a view of three railroads and two rivers. You are welcome to bring your own food because most cars have tables.

SCHEDULES and FARES
The Kiski Junction Railroad operates from the first of June through the end of October on Tuesdays, Fridays and Saturdays, at 2:00 p.m. Special events include October fall leaf rides and Halloween train rides. Reservations are required for special events. Adult

fares are generally under $10. Please call or check website for current schedules and fares.

EQUIPMENT
No. 7135, Alco S1
No. 5 KJR
No. 200 KJR transfer cabin
No. 44 KJR flatcar
No. 1154 KJR coach

CONTACT
Kiski Junction Railroad
130 Railroad Street
Schenley, PA 15682
724-295-5577
info@kiskijunction.com
www.kiskijunction.com

Photos: Kiski Junction Railroad

LEHIGH GORGE SCENIC RAILWAY
Jim Thorpe, PA

The Lehigh Gorge Scenic Railway offers a 16-mile round trip on the Jersey Central Lines. Take a ride though the former Lehigh Valley Railroad. The train follows the winding Lehigh River until reaching Old Penn Haven.

The formation of the Lehigh Valley Railroad in the 1850s brought prosperity to the area as it carried anthracite coal and other goods to market and promoted a town once known as "Mauch Chunk" as an excursion destination. In the 1870s, competition came with the arrival of the Central Railroad of New Jersey and a second main line that paralleled the LVRR through the region.

In the early 20th century, the area began to experience a decline. Coal had lost its industrial importance, and the results were felt in Mauch Chunk. The decline of railroading across the country came next, causing further economic hardship in Mauch Chunk.

The widow of Olympic athlete Jim Thorpe offered her husband's name in exchange for a memorial in 1954. That gesture provided a solution to the area's woes. The citizens voted and gave their town a new name: Jim Thorpe. Today, a 20-ton monument marks his burial place on the east side of Jim Thorpe, the town. Many of the old homes and buildings are now on the National Historic Register. The recently renovated former Central Railroad of New Jersey Station is the focal point of tourism in the town today.

SCHEDULES and FARES
Lehigh Gorge Scenic Railway operates from late May through mid-December on Saturdays and Sundays. Adult fares are generally under $15. Please call or check website for current schedules and fares.

EQUIPMENT
Lehigh Gorge Scenic Railway trains are old style passenger coaches from the 1920s.

CONTACT
Lehigh Gorge Scenic Railway
P.O. Box 91
Jim Thorpe, PA 18229
570-325-8485
www.lgsry.com

Photos: Lehigh Gorge Scenic Railway

MIDDLETOWN & HUMMELSTOWN RAILROAD
Middletown, PA

Ride the train that is sure to "engineer special memories," the Middletown and Hummelstown Railroad, located just outside Hershey and Harrisburg, Pennsylvania. You may board at either the 1891 freight station in Middletown or at the Indian Echo Caverns Platform. You'll ride on 1920s vintage coaches, formerly owned by the Delaware, Lackawanna & Western Railroad.

Your 11-mile excursion follows the towpath of the historic Union Canal and along the peaceful Swatara Creek. Your narrator will relate the history of the canal, completed in 1827, and point out the location of Canal Lock No. 33; a century-old limekiln; and Horse Thief Cave. Don't miss the chance to take breathtaking pictures when you cross the 35-foot-high bridge over Swatara Creek.

SCHEDULES and FARES
Regular scheduled trains begin on Father's Day weekend through Labor Day weekend. Please call or check website for current schedules and fares.

EQUIPMENT
1941 and 1955 General Electric diesel locomotives
No. 91, former Canadian National steam locomotive, 2-6-0
1903 trolley freight car built in Middletown
Circa 1800s wooden boxcar with link and pin couplers
Trolley snow sweeper
1930s and 1940s streetcars
1906 convertible trolley, formerly used in Brooklyn, N.Y.

CONTACT
Middletown & Hummelstown Railroad
136 Brown Street
Middletown, PA 17057
717-944-4435
www.mhrailroad.com

Photos: Middletown & Hummelstown Railroad

NEW HOPE & IVYLAND RAILROAD
New Hope, PA

The New Hope and Ivyland Railroad takes you along the same route featured in the 1914 movie series *Perils of Pauline*. While onboard, you will learn that this railroad has had a few perils of its own since it started in 1962.

In its early days, the railroad offered steam passenger service, but within five years extravagant spending and heavy debt sent the company into insolvency. It had to sell off real estate, went bankrupt, and operated with only volunteer help until the Bucks County Industrial Development Corporation bought it in 1974.

Now visitors are treated to a re-creation of the Golden era of railroading through the beautiful hills and valleys of historic Bucks County, Pennsylvania. The ride is 9 miles long and lasts about 45 minutes.

SCHEDULES AND FARES
New Hope & Ivyland Railroad operates year-round. Fares vary according to excursion. Please call or check website for current schedules and fares.

EQUIPMENT
4 steam locomotives
2 diesel locomotives
10 freight cars
11 coaches
1 caboose

CONTACT
New Hope & Ivyland Railroad
32 West Bridge Street
New Hope, PA 18938
215-862-2332
215-862-2150 (fax)
info@newhoperailroad.com
www.newhoperailroad.com

OIL CREEK & TITUSVILLE RAILROAD
Titusville, PA

The Oil Creek & Titusville Railroad gives you the chance to take a 27-mile, 2.5-hour ride through "The Valley That Changed the World," thanks to the discovery of oil here. It also offers a unique evening's lodging in the adjoining Caboose Motel.

You board at the first of four stations, the Perry Street Station, and travel to the Drake Well Station in historic Drake Well Park, where additional passengers are boarded. The park includes an operating replica of Colonel Edwin L. Drake's first successful oil well. On the way to the next stop, Petroleum Centre Station, the train follows Oil Creek and passes the sites of 15 former boom towns and 60 early refineries. At the last stop, Rynd Farm Station, Oil City is just down the road. Rynd Farm is the place where Jonathan Watson became the world's first oil millionaire. You can visit the house where "Coal Oil Johnny," a famous wastrel of the oil country, grew up just below the station.

Throughout your ride, you're provided a taped commentary on the valley's history. Volunteer tour guides add their own unique interpretations. Feel free to visit the open car, on the north end of the train, or the last working railway post office, where you can mail souvenir postcards to friends and buy snacks and sandwiches. You can get off the train at Petroleum Centre and take advantage of picnic grounds, bike trails, historic sites and other recreational opportunities before boarding for the return trip to the Perry Street Station.

SCHEDULES and FARES
Trains operate on weekends from June through October, with selected weekdays added in July, August, and October. Special events include murder mystery dinner trains, Speeder Day, and holiday trains. Please call or check website for current schedules and fares.

EQUIPMENT
No. 66, the only operating railway post office in the U.S. , built in 1927
No. 75, Alco S-2 switch engine (regular use)
No. 85, Alco S-2 switch engine (standby use)
7 passenger cars Nos. 59-65, built in 1930 by Pullman Standard and named and numbered for significant people and years in the region's history
No. 827, open car, originally an express refrigerator car built in 1940

CONTACT
Oil Creek & Titusville Railroad
409 South Perry Street,
Titusville, PA
814-676-1733
ocandt@usachoice.net
www.octrr.org

Photos: Oil Creek & Titusville Railroad

RAILROAD MUSEUM OF PENNSYLVANIA
Strasburg, PA

The Railroad Museum of Pennsylvania allows visitors to explore more than 100 pieces of rolling stock, including steam, electric, and diesel-electric locomotives; passenger and freight cars; and railroad-related art and artifacts. The museum's original exhibit hall resembles an early train shed circa 1860. In 1995, in celebration of the Pennsylvania Railroad's 150th anniversary, a new addition was opened that is modeled after a glass-roofed train shed of the early 20th century.

The museum's core collection, which has been greatly expanded over the years, is an assortment of vintage locomotives and rolling stock that the Pennsylvania Railroad assembled for the 1939-40 New York World's Fairs.

SCHEDULES and FARES
The museum is open seven days a week. It is closed on Mondays from November through March except President's Day. Admission is generally under $10. Please call or check website for current schedules and fares.

EQUIPMENT
The extensive listing of rolling stock is available at the museum's website.

CONTACT
Railroad Museum of Pennsylvania
Route 741
Strasburg, PA
717-687-8628
info@rrmuseumpa.org
www.rrmuseumpa.org

Photos: Railroad Museum of Pennsylvania

RAILROADERS MEMORIAL MUSEUM
Altoona, PA

For more than a century, Altoona was one of the most important rail facilities in the United States. The city was home to the Pennsylvania Railroad's repair and maintenance shops, its locomotive construction facility, and its test department. Altoona's location at the foot of the Allegheny and its proximity to the Horseshoe Curve route over the mountains made the city a key location in the Pennsylvania Railroad's operations. By 1945 the railroad's facilities at Altoona had become the world's largest rail shop complex.

Today, you can see--through exhibits and train rides--the work involved in building such an empire. Your admission also allows you to see the Horseshoe Curve Historical National Landmark in the Allegheny Mountains, where you can marvel at one of the world's engineering feats. Experience the challenge that the Pennsylvania Railroad workers overcame in completing rail tracks through this rough terrain.

SCHEDULES and FARES
The Railroaders Memorial Museum is open from April through October. Adult admission is generally under $10. Please call or check website for current schedules and fares.

EQUIPMENT
No. 1361, one of 111 K-4 passenger locomotives built in Altoona in 1918 (one of two still in existence and the only one operating)
No. 2826, Vulcan Iron Works saddle tank locomotive
No. 6712, Baldwin Locomotive Works diesel-electric VO-660
The "Loretto," private car of Charles Schwab

CONTACT
Railroaders Memorial Museum
1300 Ninth Avenue
Altoona, PA 16602
814-946-0834
888-425-8666
admin@railroadcity.com
www.railroadcity.com

Photos: Railroaders Memorial Museum

Did You Know...

Most people think of railways as being a relatively new invention. But they started over 500 years ago, when very early versions of the railway were built in European mines.

STEAMTOWN NATIONAL HISTORIC SITE
Scranton, PA

Steamtown National Historic Site preserves an era that slipped from consciousness virtually unnoticed. Today, you can relive the age of steam railroading as these fire-breathing monsters lumber back to life. The cinders, grease, oil, steam, and people of steam railroading have returned.

In the earlier part of the 20th century, Northeastern Pennsylvania sparked rapid growth in the rail industry that ultimately extended across the United States. The Lackawanna Iron & Coal Company (LI&C) in Scranton was one of the first producers of the iron T-rail in the United States. Without the iron T-rail, the country's railway system could not have existed; and the LI&C, in turn, could not have shipped its product in the amounts needed.

The museum complex includes a Visitor Center, History Museum, Theater, Technology Museum and Roundhouse. You can also enjoy a Ranger led tour or shop in the museum store.

SCHEDULES and FARES
The Steamtown National Historic Site is open seven days a week,year-round, with the exception of Thanksgiving, Christmas Day, and New Year's Day. The Park entrance fee, which includes admission to the Railroad Yard, Theater, History Museum, Roundhouse, and Technology Museum, is $6 for ages 17 and older. Children 16 and under must be accompanied by a parent or guardian.

Excursion fares are not included in the park entrance fee and vary by excursion. Please call or check website for current schedules and fares.

EQUIPMENT
Steamtown has an extensive collection of equipment including:
28 passenger cars
11 freight cars
25 locomotives
11 maintenance of way

CONTACT
Steamtown National Historic Site
150 South Washington Avenue
Scranton, PA 18503
570-340-5200
570-340-5235 (fax)
www.nps.gov/stea

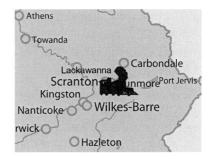

Photos: NPS and

STRASBURG RAIL ROAD
Strasburg, PA

The golden age of steam railroading and the rich cultural heritage of the Lancaster Amish come together at the historic Strasburg Rail Road. Founded in 1832, this is America's oldest short-line railroad and a designated Lancaster County Heritage Site.

Board one of our beautifully restored wooden coaches, pulled by a huge, coal-burning steam locomotive, and relive the wonder and magic of days gone by as you enjoy the spectacular beauty of the Amish farmland. The Strasburg Rail Road is a hands-on experience of men and machinery. It's no amusement park re-creation of our past. The station, buildings, and trains are the real thing.

Choose from five unique riding options. Surround yourself in Victorian splendor and indulge yourself with a selection of elegant confections and beverages aboard the first class parlor car Marian. Get cozy in our deluxe Henry K. Long lounge car, featuring solid cherry interior and authentic stained-glass accents. Make a reservation for lunch or dinner in the Lee E. Brenner dining car, the oldest wooden dining car still in operation. Tour the scenic surroundings with a wide-open view of the countryside and neighboring Amish farms aboard the open-air car. Even the standard coaches are beautifully restored in authentic Victorian style. For a glimpse of how railroad presidents and other dignitaries traveled, you can book a summer excursion aboard the President's Car, circa 1913. Enjoy wine, hors d'oeuvres, dessert, coffee, and tea as the train travels the tracks.

On the 45-minute narrated round trip, you'll learn the story of the Strasburg Rail Road, pass right through farms of our Amish neighbors, and even have a chance to get off the train and enjoy your own picnic lunch in Groff's Grove. After your ride, take a ride aboard a miniature steam locomotive or test your own power on a vintage pump car. Explore the Railroad Museum of Pennsylvania, just across the road, featuring a world-class collection of more than 100 historic locomotives and railcars. Visit our gift shops and discover an impressive selection of railroad memorabilia, children's toys, and distinctive merchandise for every rail fan. Visit the restaurant, pick up a boxed lunch for the grove, or make a reservation to eat a light lunch or a full dinner aboard the train's dining car.

SCHEDULES and FARES
The Strasburg Rail Road operates from mid-February through the end of December and fares vary. Its website includes listings for special tours and excursions. Please call or check website for current schedule and fares.

EQUIPMENT
The Strasburg rolling stock includes Engines 31, 89, 475, and 90, which pull the vintage trains.

CONTACT
Strasburg Rail Road
Route 741 East
Strasburg, PA 17579
717-687-7522
717-687-8421 (Dining Car Reservations)
717-687-6193 (Group Information)
www.strasburgrailroad.com

Photos: Strasburg Rail Road

THE ROCKHILL TROLLEY MUSEUM
Rockhill Furnace, PA

The Rockhill Trolley Museum is Pennsylvania's first operating trolley museum. Its demonstration electric railway offers visitors a three-mile round trip which is representative of a rural Pennsylvania trolley line. The trolleys meet the narrow gauge steam trains of the EBT. The scenic ride rambles through the countryside and along the Black Log Creek, encountering a number of historic sites (iron furnace, logging railway, iron mine, and the remains of a quarry trestle), and ends in Black Narrows.

In October of 1960, an old trolley from Johnstown, Pennsylvania, was selected for preservation and was moved to the East Broad Top Railroad at Rockhill Furnace, Pennsylvania. During the next two years, car 311 was restored and overhead wire was installed over a short portion of standard gauge track. Operation began in the fall of 1962. From these meager beginnings, the Rockhill Trolley Museum has continued to grow.

All the people who work at the museum are volunteers. All share an affection for trolleys and a desire to see them preserved. Members come from all walks of life. They staff the museum store and also work on tracks; restore, maintain and opreate cars; and perform administrative duties.

SCHEDULES and FARES
The museum is open to the public on weekends and holidays from Memorial Day weekend through October. Please call or check website for current schedules and fares.

EQUIPMENT
Over 30 trolleys, from around the world
Additional pieces of equipment

CONTACT
Rockhill Trolley Museum
P.O. Box 203
Rockhill Furnace, PA 17249
814-447-9576 (weekends)
610-965-9028 (weekdays)
www.rockhilltrolley.org

Photos: Rockhill Trolley Museum

TIOGA CENTRAL RAILROAD
Wellsboro, PA

The excursion and dinner trains of the Tioga Central Railroad are reminiscent of passenger travel as it existed in America fifty to sixty years ago. This experience is provided in a scenic setting of exceptional beauty by a carrier with twenty-four years of experience and outstanding records in safety and reliability.

At a comfortable twenty miles per hour, trains skirt two large wetland areas rich in wildlife, pass through beautiful fields and forests, follow sparkling streams, and traverse a 2-mile shoreline of the beautiful Hammond Lake.

Tioga Central's excursion trains provide fun for the whole family. Youngsters enjoy the sights from the open observation car and have fun visiting the club car and gift shop. Seniors recall train rides taken in years past, and forgotten family memories return. Friendly volunteer crew members, who thoroughly enjoy what they do, are always ready to contribute to passenger enjoyment.

You will board at Wellsboro Junction, three miles north of Wellsboro, Pennsylvania, on Route 287. Wellsboro itself is worth a trip from almost anywhere, with its quaint gaslights, tree-lined streets, friendly people, gracious homes, and Main Street shopping.

On the dinner train excursion, your meal is prepared in the classic manner, right on the train and under the supervision of an executive chef. You are seated at a table for four. The dinner trains depart Wellsboro Junction at 5:30 p.m. on Saturday evenings only, and the ride is a 42-mile, 2.5-hour round trip to the New York State border at Lawrenceville.

Power for the trains is provided by first-generation Alco diesel-electric locomotives: an S-2, an RS-1, and an RS-3u. Tioga Central takes particular pride in maintaining these authentic early diesels.

SCHEDULES and FARES
The Tioga Central Railroad operates from Memorial Day weekend through October. The dinner train is in operation from early June through the end of October. Excursion fares vary. Please call or check website for current schedules and fares.

EQUIPMENT
Locomotives:
TIOC 14, Alco S-2, Schenectady 1947
TIOC 62, Alco RS-1, Schenectady 1950
TIOC 506, Alco RS-3, Schenectady 1952
Passenger Cars:
TIOC 300, open-sided observation car Ives Run
TIOC 365, 64-seat dining car Norris Brook
TIOC 370, 48-seat diner/kitchen Crooked Creek
TIOC 410, Head-end power car
TIOC 500, club car Canyon Club,
NYC 2930, deluxe coach

CONTACT
Tioga Central Railroad
P.O. Box 269
Wellsboro, PA 16901
570-724-0990
info@tiogacentralcom
www.tiogacentral.com

Photos: Tioga Central Railroad

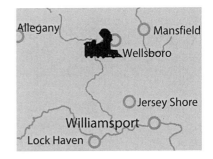

WANAMAKER, KEMPTON & SOUTHERN RAILROAD
Kempton, PA

The Wanamaker, Kempton & Southern Railroad is located in scenic Berks County. Most people call it the "Hawk Mountain Line" because of its proximity to the famous bird sanctuary. On this excursion you may catch a glimpse of one or more of the 20,000 hawks, eagles, and falcons that migrate through the area each fall.

The WK&S has been open since 1963 thanks to hardworking volunteers. As of 2006 they were continuing to build track in and around our storage shed. They are making improvements to the shed as well. Visitors may also see them working on a wooden-sided caboose or a passenger car. The WK&S has two steam locomotives (tank engines) and three diesel locomotives pulling the trains. When they are used, you can expect your 6 mile trip to last around 40 minutes.

SCHEDULES and FARES
WK&S train rides are offered on weekends from May through October, with special events throughout the year, including a Santa Special weekend in December. You can rent a caboose for a birthday party, private charters can be arranged at any time, and educational school trips are available in May. Fares are generally under $10. Please call or check website for current schedules and fares.

EQUIPMENT
5 locomotives
6 coaches
5 freight cars
3 cabooses
Note: Not all of WK&S rolling stock is on the active roster.

CONTACT
WK&S, Inc.
42 Community Center Drive
Kempton, PA 19529-0024
610-756-6469
info@kemptontrain.com
www.kemptontrain.com

Photos: Wanamaker, Kempton & Southern Railroad

Did You Know...

The average 150-car freight train traveling at 59 km/h needs about 960 meters to stop. At 100 km/h, the same freight train needs about 2,500 meters to stop.

RHODE ISLAND

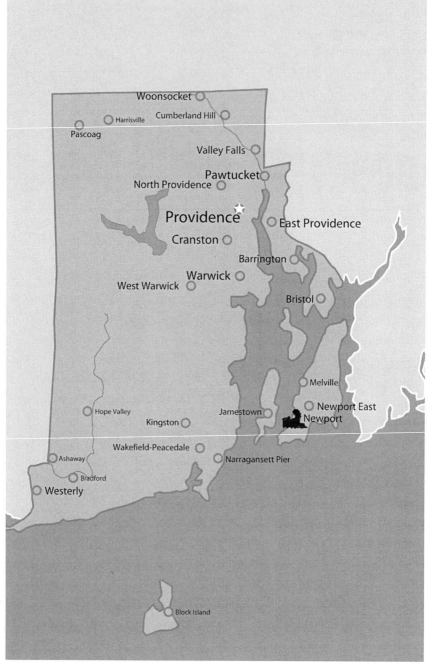

NEWPORT DINNER TRAIN
Newport, RI

In years gone by, dining aboard a luxury railcar was a statement of elegance and privilege. The Newport Dinner Train allows travelers of today to relive those times. Meticulously restored vintage railcars quietly reflect the nostalgia and aura of the "Golden Age of Railroading." Each car seats 72 guests and is lavishly appointed with plush velvet draperies, parlor carpeting, and incandescent lighting. The Cabaret Dining Pullman Car seats 48 guests. All seats are window seats from which to view the magnificent sunset on Narragansett Bay.

The sentimental journey begins as your coach pulls away from the historic depot in downtown Newport. Travel takes you through tunnels of lush greenery that open up to the breathtaking image of the super aircraft carriers Forrestal and Saratoga, which are proudly docked at the Newport Naval Base in Middletown. The bay beckons with its beautiful view of sailing vessels. After dinner, cocktails are offered to complement your dessert and your unique dining adventure. The 22-mile trip lasts 2.5-hours.

SCHEDULES and FARES
The Newport Dinner Train operates from May through December. Lunch trains are offered on Thursdays and Saturdays from May through September. Fares normally range from $30 to $70. Reservations are required. Please call or check website for current schedules and fares.

CONTACT
Newport Dinner Train
19 America's Cup Avenue
Newport, RI 02840
800-398-7427
401-841-8700
info@newportdinnertrain.com
www.newportdinnertrain.com

Photos: Newport Dinner Train

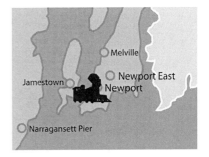

SOUTH CAROLINA

SOUTH CAROLINA RAILROAD MUSEUM
Winnsboro, SC

Do you want to take your children or grandchildren for a ride on a real passenger train? Visit a red caboose, an authentic dining car and a Pullman? Then spend the day at the South Carolina Railroad Museum.

Your train ride is a 10-mile round trip to Rion over a portion of the former Rockton & Rion Railway. The route was built in the late 1800s as a quarry line to haul world-famous Winnsboro blue granite from the quarry to the Southern Railway at Rockton.

The South Carolina Railroad Museum, Inc., was established in 1973 by a group of dedicated railroad enthusiasts from the Columbia and Charleston, South Carolina, areas. In 1983, the museum received by way of donation the former Rockton and Rion Railway located in Fairfield County, South Carolina, from Martin Marietta Aggregates. The museum named the line the Rockton, Rion, and Western Railroad (RR & W).

Plans call for the construction of a locomotive shop and an equipment-maintenance area as well as display tracks. Ultimately the museum plans to have educational train excursions over the entire 11.5-mile route, exhibitions of freight and passenger train operations, and a library of railroad-related publications.

SCHEDULES and FARES
The museum and the train are open on the first and third Saturday of the month from June through October and on special-events days. Adult fares are generally under $15. Please call or check website for current schedules and fares.

EQUIPMENT
No. 44, steam locomotive once belonging to the Hampton & Branchville Railroad
Nos. 2015 and 2028, SW-8s, built in 1950
Nos. 2049 and 2076, RS4TC1As, built in 1954, rebuilt in 1995
No. 33, GE 44-ton, former PRR, built in 1946
No. 76 Porter 50-ton U.S. Navy, built in 1951

CONTACT
South Carolina Railroad Museum
110 Industrial Boulevard
Winnsboro, SC 29180
803-635-4242
803-635-9893 (recorder information)
info@scrm.org
www.scrm.org

Photos: South Carolina Railroad Museum

Did You Know...

An eight car passenger train traveling at 100 km/h requires about 1,070 meters to stop. When traveling at 130 km/h, a stopping distance of about 1,825 meters is required.

SOUTH DAKOTA

Camp Crook

Buffalo

Belle Fourche
Spearfish
Deadwood
Lead
Sturgis
Newell

Hill City
Keystone
Keystone
Hermosa
Custer
Fairburn
Pringle
Hot Springs
Edgemont
Oelrichs
Ardmore
Pine Ridge
Batesland
Martin

Rapid City
Box Elder
Wall
Wasta

Bison

Isabel

Timber Lake

Faith
Dupree
Eagle Butte

Philip
Cottonwood
Interior
Belvidere
Midland
White River

Draper
Murdo
Presho
Reliance
Oacoma

Winner
Colome
Burke
Carter
Mission
St. Francis

Chamberlain
Kimball

McIntosh
McLaughlin

Mobridge
Akaska
Gettysburg
Lebanon
Seneca
Orient
Faulkton

Hoven
Bowdle
Roscoe
Loyalton

Mound City
Herreid
Eureka
Selby
Wetonka
Ipswich

Long Lake
Frederick
Westport
Claremont
Veblen

Aberdeen
Sisseton
Pierpont
Grenville
Peever

Blunt
Highmore
Harrold
Wessington
St. Lawrence

Fort Pierre
Pierre

Agar
Onida

Northville
Mellette
Redfield
Ashton
Warner
Tulare
Rockham

Webster
Marvin
Florence
South Shore
Turton
Clark
Hazel
Goodwin
Brandt
White

Watertown
Bancroft
De Smet
Arlington
Carthage

Platte
Corsica
Armour
Dimock
Stickney
Alexandria
Salem

Woonsocket
Wolsey
Cavour
Alpena
Huron
Doland

Tripp
Olivet
Tyndall
Freeman
Dolton
Humboldt
Tea

Mitchell
Madison
Brookings
Flandreau
Nunda
Trent
Dell Rapids

Lake Andes
Bonesteel
Ravinia

Yankton
Vermillion
Sioux City

Sioux Falls
Canton
Irene

Jennings

BLACK HILLS CENTRAL RAILROAD
Hill City, SD

The Black Hills Central Railroad operates the 1180 train and has significant history in the development of the American Frontier specifically in the Black Hills of South Dakota. The isolated line that the Black Hills Central Railroad operates today is the only remnant left of the 106.4 mile High Line from Edgemont to Deadwood. This High Line serviced the mines, lumber industry and hauled passengers from its construction in 1890 to 1983.

The equipment yard in Hill City and the track to Keystone are well preserved and carefully maintained. The line is surrounded by the Black Hills. The route has many vistas of Harney Peak, which is the highest point between the Alps and the Rockies, Elkhorn Mountain and Granite Cliffs where mountain goats frequent.

SCHEDULES and FARES
The trains run from May through October. Adult fares are generally under $20. Please call or check website for details and special events.

EQUIPMENT
No. 104 Baldwin 2-6-2 saddle tank, 1926
No. 7 Baldwin 2-6-2, 1919
No. 110 Baldwin 2-6-6-2
2 open-air coaches, 1880s-1910

CONTACT
Black Hills Central Railroad
P.O. Box 1880
Hill City, SD 57745
605-574-2222
605-574-4915 (fax)
office@1880train.com
www.1880train.com

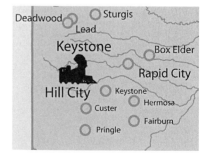

Photos: Black Hills Central Railroad

PRAIRIE VILLAGE, HERMAN & MILWAUKEE RAILROAD
Madison, SD

The Prairie Village, Herman & Milwaukee Railroad is part of the historic Prairie Village. The railroad began with the purchase of an 0-4-0T narrow gauge locomotive in 1969. The Whilimine Victoria No. 7 was built by Orenstein & Koppel in 1927 in Berlin. Folks at the village used it to give rides to schoolchildren and their chaperons.

In 1987 the present track was laid, using the original rail from the Madison, South Dakota switch yard. The first rail laid was stamped 1887. This new track renewed interest in the little train and in the possibility of laying track to include the entire village grounds. Around this time, someone donated a crane to the village. Volunteers restored it and used it to build the 2-mile track that visitors are enjoying today while touring the turn-of-the-century village.

SCHEDULES AND FARES
Prairie Village is open from May through September. Adult admission fees/fares are generally under $10. Group rates are available. Please call or visit website for details.

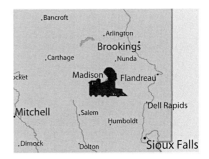

EQUIPMENT
RS4TC-1 Baldwin Whitcomb 60T No. 4002, Serial No. 61232
GE 80T 8-wheel diesel-electric, U.S. Air Force No. 1687 Locomotive
NP No. 29 Russell snowplow, 1950s wedge snowplow (on static display for touring)

CONTACT
Prairie Historical Society
P.O. Box 256
Madison, SD 57042
605-256-36441
800-693-3644
prariev@rapidnet.com
www.prairievillage.org

Photos: Prairie Village, Herman & Milwaukee Railroad

Did You Know...

When completed in 1882, the Kinzua Railroad Bridge near Mount Jewett, in Pennsylvania, was aclaimed "the highest and longest railroad viaduct in the entire world." Rising 301 feet from the valley floor at its center, with a total length of 2,100 feet.

TENNESSEE

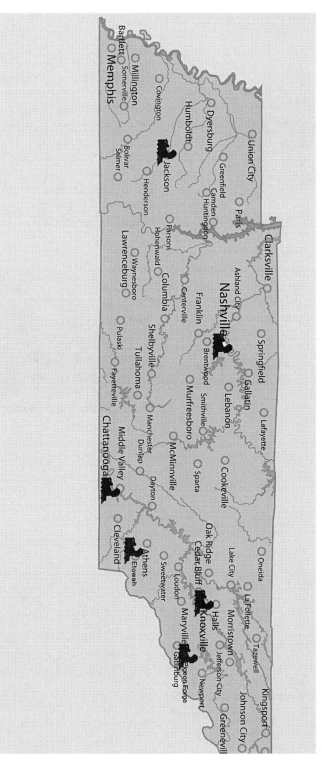

Memphis
Bartlett
Millington
Somerville
Bolivar
Selmer
Covington
Humboldt
Dyersburg
Greenfield
Union City
Jackson
Camden
Huntingdon
Paris
Henderson
Parsons
Hohenwald
Lawrenceburg
Waynesboro
Columbia
Centerville
Ashland City
Clarksville
Nashville
Franklin
Brentwood
Springfield
Gallatin
Lafayette
Pulaski
Fayetteville
Shelbyville
Tullahoma
Manchester
Murfreesboro
Smithville
Lebanon
Cookeville
Sparta
Dunlap
McMinnville
Oneida
Lake City
Chattanooga
Middle Valley
Dayton
Cleveland
Athens
Etowah
Sweetwater
Oak Ridge
Cedar Bluff
Loudon
Halls
Maryville
Knoxville
Gatlinburg
Pigeon Forge
Newport
Jefferson City
Morristown
LaFollette
Tazewell
Johnson City
Kingsport
Greeneville

CASEY JONES HOME AND RAILROAD MUSEUM
Jackson, TN

The accident made him a legend and the song made him immortal. Visit the Casey Jones Home and Railroad Museum and find out why he was a hero. Climb aboard Engine No. 382 and ring the bell just as Casey did.

At Casey Jones home, restored to look as it did at his untimely death on April 30, 1900, you can watch a video about the man and the legend. See railroad artifacts from the early days when the rails were king and the engineers were the astronauts of their day.

In 2006, the museum celebrated its Golden Anniversary, 50 years since the death of Casey Jones. If you want to know more about his life and times, this is the museum for you.

SCHEDULES and FARES
The Casey Jones Home and Railroad Museum is open daily year-round. Admission is generally under $5. Please call or check website for current schedules and fares.

EQUIPMENT
Rogers 4-6-0 locomotive
1800s M&O baggage car
IC caboose
1890s sleeper car

CONTACT
Casey Jones Home and Railroad Museum
30 Casey Jones Lane
Jackson, TN 38305
731-668-1223
800-748-9588
cjtrainstore@iwon.com
www.caseyjones.com

Photos: Casey Jones Home & Railroad Museum

DOLLYWOOD EXPRESS TRAIN
Pigeon Forge, TN

The Dollywood Express Train takes you on a 5-mile trip through the Great Smoky Mountain Foothills. The train is pulled by an authentic 110-ton coal-fired steam engine. The ride takes 20 minutes, with one departure per hour. In one day these trains burn 110 tons of coal and carry up to 550 people.

The engineer sounds the whistle and your mountain excursion is underway. It is a breathtaking journey where you'll enjoy pastoral scenery and some of the most beautiful views that nature has to offer. Close your eyes and enjoy a fascinating trip back in time when travel in and out of the mountains of Pigeon Forge relied on trains like the Dollywood Express.

Many celebrities and their families have taken a trip aboard the Dollywood Express. The train is one of Dolly Parton's favorite rides, and she can sometimes be seen riding up front with the engineer when she visits Dollywood.

SCHEDULES and FARES
This outdoor attraction is available to people in the amusement park. The fare is included in the park admission. The Dollywood Express runs from April through December.

EQUIPMENT
Dollywood's rolling stock includes Klondike Katie (1943) and Cinderella (1938). Both are authentic 2-8-2 Baldwin steam locomotives originally built for the U.S. Army.

CONTACT
Dollywood Express Train
1020 Dollywood Lane
Pigeon Forge, TN 37863-4101
865-428-9486
publicity@dollywood.com
www.dollywood.com

Photos: Dollywood Express Train

SOUTHERN APPALACHIA RAILWAY MUSEUM
Knoxville, TN

The Southern Appalachia Railway Museum (SARM) is a nonprofit organization dedicated to preserving, restoring, and operating historical railroad equipment. It is also dedicated to the preservation of the railroad history of the Southern Appalachia region.

Turn back the clock and return to the heyday of passenger railroading with the Southern Appalachia Railway Museum's Secret City scenic excursion train. The train winds along Poplar Creek and Highway 327 in the beautiful hills and valleys of East Tennessee. It travels a former Southern Railway branch line through the former Manhattan Project K-25 facility.

Each round trip is approximately 14 miles and lasts about one hour. The trains are pulled by 1950s vintage Alco diesel locomotives. Seating is in an air-conditioned coach and dining car, both restored to their 1940s glory. If you'd like, you can charter a caboose for up to 10 people or charter the entire train!

SCHEDULES and FARES
The museum is open and the train runs on selected weekends from April through December. Ticket prices are generally under $20 for adults. Special events and dinner trains are also available. Reservations are highly recommended for any excursion. Please call or check website for current schedules and fares.

EQUIPMENT
5 locomotives
7 passenger cars
7 freight cars

CONTACT
Southern Appalachia Railway Museum
P.O. Box 5870
Knoxville, TN 37928
865-241-2140
www.southernappalachia.railway.museum

TENNESSEE CENTRAL RAILWAY MUSEUM
Nashville, TN

Headquartered in the former Tennessee Central Railway's Master Mechanic's office, the Tennessee Central Railway Museum's goal is to preserve, restore, interpret, and operate historic railroad equipment for the education of the public. The building houses offices, a library, and a rapidly expanding collection of railroad material, including the largest collection of Tennessee Central Railway artifacts to be found anywhere.

One of the main attractions is a fully restored Operation Lifesaver caboose, used to promote safety at railroad highway crossings. After exploring the stationery history, climb aboard the train and watch Tennessee roll past your wide sightseeing window. The museum's streamlined coaches feature air conditioning and comfortable reclining seats. The passenger excursions are done in cooperation with the Nashville & Eastern Railroad.

SCHEDULES and FARES
The museum is open year-round on Tuesdays, Thursdays, and Saturdays. Admission is free. Train excursions run from April through December. Please call or visit website for details.

EQUIPMENT
EMD E8A TCRX 5764
EMD SW8 TC 52
Former ATSF coaches
TCRX 4711, 4717, 4719, 4733, 4739
Budd buffet-diner cars TCRX 3113 and 3119
Budd slumber coach

CONTACT
Tennessee Central Railway Museum
220 Willow Street
Nashville, TN 37210
615-244-9001
615-244-2120
hultman@nashville.com
www.tcry.org

Photos: Tennessee Central Railway Railroad

TENNESSEE VALLEY RAILROAD
Chattanooga, TN

The Tennessee Valley Railroad has three different excursions.

1) The **Missionary Ridge Local** is a 55-minute ride departing regularly from Grand Junction Station. The train takes you along an original railroadline which carried passengers into Chattanooga before the Civil War. Along the way you'll get to experience a variety of scenery and one of Tennessee's oldest railroad tunnels.

2) The **Chickamauga Turn** is a 5 hour roundtrip ride to historic Chickamauga, GA. Layover time allows passengers to stroll through the quaint one stoplight downtown area, visit the Chickamauga Depot which houses a regional history museum and large model train display. On your stroll you will probably pass the Civil War cannons that stand guard over the main intersection in town

3) The **Dixie Land Excursion** operates on select weekends, especially in the fall when the 100 mile round-trip "Autumn Leaf Special" runs from Chattanooga to Summerville, GA, and includes lunch aboard a restored 1924 dining car.

SCHEDULES and FARES

The Tennessee Valley Railway operates from March through November. Fares and departure times vary according to excursion. Please call or check website for current schedules and fares.

EQUIPMENT

Steam locomotive No. 610
Alco RSD1 or EMD GP7 diesel-electrics (operates when steam is not available)

CONTACT

Tennessee Valley Railroad
4119 Cromwell Road
Chattanooga, TN 37421
423-894-8028
423-894-8029 (fax)
info@tvrail.com
www.tvrail.com

Photos: Tennessee Valley Railroad

THE CHATTANOOGA CHOO CHOO
Chattanooga, TN

It's a train...it's a song...it's a hotel! Located at the original Terminal Station, the Chattanooga Choo Choo Holiday Inn transports its guests to the golden age of the railroad era. You can sleep aboard an authentic Victorian train car, or stroll through the formal rose gardens nestled among the sleeper cars.

Treat yourself to Dinner in the Diner, our gourmet restaurant set aboard a railcar, complete with Victorian décor, an elegant menu, and an intimate setting. You will quickly agree that "nothing could be finer."

Model railroad enthusiasts can visit the Model Railroad Museum, one of the largest HO-gauge model railroads in the world. Boasting 3,000 feet of track, 120 locomotives, 1,000 freight cars, 80 passenger cars, and numerous structure and landscape pieces, this museum is guaranteed to delight the child in all of you! Much more awaits guests at this historic 24-acre vacation complex.

SCHEDULES and FARES
Please call or check website for current schedules and fares.

CONTACT
The Chattanooga Choo Choo
1400 Market Street
Chattanooga, TN 37402
423-266-5000
frontdesk@Choochoo.com
www.choochoo.com

Photos: The Chattanooga Choo Choo

THREE RIVERS RAMBLER
Knoxville, TN

Climb aboard the Three Rivers Rambler for an excursion filled with stories of historical interest and unrivaled scenery. Your 11-mile, 1 1/3-hour trip takes you over the Knoxville & Holston River Railroad.

You leave from the Volunteer Landing on the Knoxville Riverfront and travel parallel to the river through farmland, local industries, historic landmarks, and active businesses.

At the head of the Tennessee River, where the Holston and French Broad Rivers meet to form the Tennessee, the train crosses the Holston River on the famous Three Rivers Trestle. At the Ashbury Quarry outside Marbledale, the train makes a brief stop while the locomotive is switched from one end of the train to the other for your return journey. Just after starting back, the Rambler pauses on the trestle for a breathtaking view.

SCHEDULES and FARES
The Three Rivers Rambler is open from April through August on Saturdays and Sundays. The Pumpkin Express runs on select weekends in October, and the Christmas Express runs on select weekends in December. Fares are generally under $20. Please call or check website for current schedules and fares.

EQUIPMENT
"Lindy," No. 203, Baldwin 2-8-0, built in 1925
"Resplendent," Pullman office car, built in 1925
"Trustworthy" and "Intrepid," coaches, built in 1932
"Forthright," open-air car built in 1940 (converted flatcar)
"Desire," caboose

CONTACT
Three Rivers Rambler
Volunteer Landing
Knoxville, TN 37902
865-524-9411
Info@threeriversrambler.com
www.threeriversrambler.com

Did You Know...

Measured in ton-miles, freight railroads carry 42% of the nation's intercity freight.

HIWASSEE RIVER RAIL ADVENTURE
Etowah, TN

The Tennessee Valley Railroad Museum has partnered with the Tennessee Overhill Heritage Association to offer tourist rail services along the historic L & N "Old Line" from Etowah, Tennessee through the scenic Hiwassee River Gorge.

This is one of the most remote and beautiful locations in the Tennessee/Georgia/North Carolina tri-state area. The standard "Loop" trip is a 3-hour, 50-mile round trip to Farner that includes spectacular views of the Hiwassee River and traverses the famous Hiwassee Loop. Along the route, planners originally needed to gain elevation in a short distance as the tracks climbed a gentle mountain. Their solution was to form the tracks into a corkscrew spiral, making almost two complete revolutions and passing over itself on a 60-foot trestle.

In addition to the frequent rides to Farner, special "double-length" trips run beyond Farner to the joint towns of Copperhill, Tennessee and McCaysville, Georgia. The "Copperhill" trips are a 100-mile round-trip all day excursion, with a layover allowing passengers to shop or eat on their own. Don't miss an opportunity to ride an historic route with amazing scenery.

SCHEDULES and FARES
Hiwassee River Rail Adventures operate from April to November. Fares and departure times vary according to excursion. Please call or check website for current schedules and fares.

EQUIPMENT
1950s diesel locomotives and passenger cars

CONTACT
Hiwassee River Rail Adventures
4119 Cromwell Road
Chattanooga, TN 37421
423-894-8028
423-894-8029 (fax)
info@tvrail.com
www.hiwassee.tvrail.com

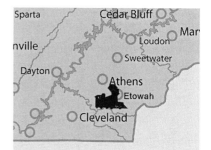

Photo: Hiwassee River Rail Adventures

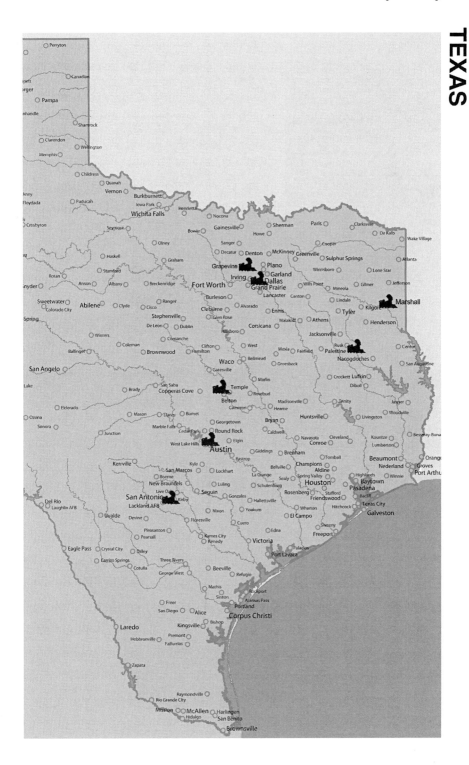

TEXAS

AUSTIN STEAM TRAIN ASSOCIATION
Austin, TX

The Austin Steam Train takes passengers over the first railroad line into Austin. The association offers passengers year-round excursion choices and two ways to travel. A coach ticket puts you into 1920s coach cars. A lounge ticket reserves a seat in a climate-controlled streamline lounge car.

The original and most popular ride, the Hill Country Flyer, is the round-trip excursion from Cedar Park to Burnett through Texas hill country. On this ride, you'll feel as though you escaped the 21st century, passing rivers and ranches along the way.

The Bertram City Flyer and the River City Flyer are other excursion options. The River City Route changed in 2006 allowing passengers to ride over the historic line of the first railroad into Austin.

SCHEDULES and FARES
The Austin Steam Train is in operation every weekend. Fares vary according to excursion choice.Please call or check website for current schedules and fares.

EQUIPMENT
Passenger Cars:
Southern Pacific 786
Alco Diesel 442
Coach Cars:
Pennsylvania Railroad P70 coach
Lounge Cars:
City of Chicago
Eagle Cliff
Santa Fe 1334
Private Charter Only:
Santa Fe caboose
Boonesborough

CONTACT
Austin Steam Train Association
P.O. Box 1632
Austin, TX 78767
512-477-8468
512-477-8633 (fax)
info@austinsteamtrain.org
www.austinsteamtrain.org

Photos: Austin Steam Train Association

GRAPEVINE VINTAGE RAILROAD
Grapevine, TX

The Grapevine Vintage Railroad rides over some 21 miles of the historic Cotton Belt Route between Grapevine and the Fort Worth Stockyards. Passengers enjoy the experience of train travel as it was in the days of the expanding West. This route was the first serious attempt to develop an extended railroad system on the North American continent. The Cotton Belt Route arrived in Grapevine in 1888. Grapevine's depot served the community until 1972, when it was officially closed by the company. Passenger service along this route was discontinued about 1930.

The second excursion choice is the Trinity River Route, which goes from the Fort Worth Stockyards to 8th Avenue. After arriving in Fort Worth from Grapevine, the locomotive pulls onto the circa 1925 turntable to head south for a 10-mile trek along the famous Chisholm Trail. The train travels across the western edge of downtown Fort Worth to the southwestern area of the city, crossing both the West and Clear Forks of the Trinity River on large trestles that

offer spectacular views of the Fort Worth skyline not seen from city streets.

SCHEDULES and FARES
Train runs from February through December generally Fridays through Sundays. Fares vary according to excursion. The range is from $10 to $20 for adults. Please call or check website for current schedules and fares.

EQUIPMENT
Coaches
1896 steam locomotive ("Puffy")
1953 GP-7 diesel locomotive
1920s and 1930s Victorian style coaches

CONTACT
Grapevine Vintage Railroad
709 South Main Street
Grapevine, TX 76051
817-410-3123
twayne@ci.grapevine.tx.us
www.tarantulatrain.com

Photos: Grapevine Vintage Railroad

Did You Know...

The Union Pacific Railroad headquartered in Omaha, Nebraska, is the largest railroad network in the United States.

MUSEUM OF THE AMERICAN RAILROAD
(Formerly the Age of Steam Railroad Museum)
Dallas, TX

The Age of Steam Railroad Museum is now the Museum of the American Railroad. It is still located in Fair Park in Dallas and has one of the oldest and most comprehensive heavyweight passenger car collections in the United States.

The collection includes lounge cars, Pullman sleeping cars, and a dining car. Over 30 pieces of historic railroad equipment-- including steam, diesel and electric locomotives; cabooses; historic structures; and artifacts-- make this one of the finest railroad museums in the United States. Be sure to see the restored MKT dining car and "Glengyle," the oldest all-steel, all-room Pullman.

The museum notes that the name change coincides with an ambitious strategic plan to expand the museum's collection of railroad history and technology. Programs will emphasize the American Railroad as an institution and its effect on our lives past, present and future.

SCHEDULES and FARES
The museum is open year-round from Wednesdays through Sundays. During the State Fair of Texas, it is open daily. Admission is generally under $10. Special events include a murder mystery dinner aboard a diner, Family Fun Day, Railroadiana Auction, State Fair picnic, and more. Please call or check website for current schedules and fares.

EQUIPMENT
No. 4018, "Big Boy," Union Pacific
No. 6913, "Centennial," Union Pacific
No. 4501 Frisco
Pullman sleeping cars
Santa Fe M.160 and FP-45

CONTACT
Museum of the American Railroad
1105 Washington Street, Fair Park
Dallas, TX 75315
214-428-0101
214-426-1937 (fax)
info@dallasrailwaymuseum.com
www.dallasrailwaymuseum.com

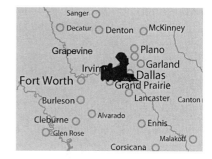

Photos: Museum of the American Railroad

RAILROAD AND HERITAGE MUSEUM
Temple, TX

The Railroad and Heritage Museum of Texas is housed in the 1910 Gulf, Colorado & Santa Fe depot in downtown Temple. The museum features early Santa Fe station equipment and furniture, including a working telegraph for train orders. You can also see everything from a rail handcar to lanterns to blacksmithing tools to period clothing. Photographs of railroad depots, rolling stock, rail lines, and local sites and people from the 1880s are included.

The Springer Collection has thousands of railroad timetables, passes and books from railroad lines in the United States, Canada, Mexico, and a few other countries. The Temple Santa Fe Engineer Records is a large collection of thousands of GCSF & ATSF engineer completion reports and linen tracings of work accomplished between 1908 and 1980 for the Southern Division of the railway. The Pounds Collection is a complete set of Santa Fe timetables from ATSF and all the subsidiary railroads purchased by the Santa Fe.The Dienst Collection is a history of Temple and central Texas collected by Dr.

Alexander Dienst from the 19th and early 20th centuries.

SCHEDULES and FARES
The Railroad and Heritage Museum is open year-round on Tuesdays through Saturdays. Adult admission is generally under $5. Please call or check website for current schedules and fares.

EQUIPMENT
Locomotives:
No. 3423 Santa Fe Baldwin steam locomotive, built in 1921
No. 2301 Santa Fe Alco diesel locomotive, built in 1937. Believed to be the oldest surviving Santa Fe diesel locomotive
Cabooses:
No. 1556 Santa Fe, dated 1927
MKT 140, Missouri Pacific
Pullman sleeper-1913 "Clover Glade"
SLSF WWII Pullman troop sleeper
Missouri Pacific boxcar
Three depots built between 1907 and 1912

CONTACT
Railroad and Heritage Museum
315 W. Avenue B
Temple, TX 76501
254-298-5172
254-298-5171
www.rrhm.org

Photos: Railroad and Heritage Museum

Did You Know...

The average 150-car freight train traveling at 59 km/h needs about 960 meters to stop. At 100 km/h, the same freight train needs about 2,500 meters to stop.

TEXAS & PACIFIC RAILWAY MUSEUM
Marshall, TX

On November 13, 1999, the restored Texas & Pacific Depot in Marshall was dedicated and opened to the public as the T&P Railroad Museum and Amtrak Station. The station is a stark change from the vandalized eyesore that was there for nearly 25 years.

The T&P Depot now combines historical preservation with modern function. The museum is on the second floor. The depot in was built in 1912 as a passenger station and to house the general administrative offices of the railroad's eastern region. It was the focal point of a once vast 66-acre shop complex, totaling 57 structures including a roundhouse, car shops, water tower, and a warehouse. The Marshall shops were built on land belonging to the city of Marshall, but provided to the T&P railroad for free use, as long as the depot remained an active station. Of the Marshall shop buildings, the 7,500 square-foot, three story depot is now the only survivor.

SCHEDULES and FARES
The Texas & Pacific Depot is open Wednesdays through Sundays. Admission to the museum is generally under $5. Please call or check website for current schedules and fares.

EQUIPMENT
No. 25687 UP caboose

CONTACT
Texas & Pacific Railway Museum
800 N. Washington Street
Marshall, TX 75670
903-938-9495
www.marshalldepot.org

TEXAS STATE RAILROAD
Rusk and Palestine, TX

The Texas State Railroad, Est. 1881, is the "Official Railroad of Texas" and is truly a "Texas Treasure!" The Texas State Railroad is operated by American Heritage Railways, owners of the Durango and Silverton Narrow Gauge Railroad in Durango, CO and the Great Smoky Mountains Railroad in Bryson City, NC. This historic train travels through the scenic piney woods and hardwood creek bottoms of East Texas. The Texas State Railroad offers both steam and diesel train excursions reminiscent of days gone by. Passengers may board excursion trains at either the Rusk or Palestine depots where southern hospitality is the norm. These depots were built with an eye for detail and the elegance of Victorian charm. Both Depots have beautiful parks, picnic areas, a concession, and a gift shop. The Rusk Depot offers visitors a beautiful 15-acre fishing lake and a full-service campground facility to enhance a four-season vacation experience.

FARES AND SCHEDULES
The Texas State Railroad offers train excursions year-round with special events and dinner trains throughout the year. Special Events include: The Polar Express™ Train Ride, The Lone Ranger® Train Ride, The Little Engine

That Could™ Rail Tour, Peanuts™ - The Valentine Express, Peanuts™ - The Easter Beagle Express, Peanuts™ - The Great Pumpkin Patch Express, and Day Out With Thomas™. Ticket prices start at $19 for Children and $36.50 for Adults. Upgrades available. Enjoy Cab Rides and Caboose Charters. Group Discounts available. Check online for schedule and information or call the reservation office.

EQUIPMENT
Five Steam Locomotives
Engine 201, a 4-6-0 built in 1901 by A. L. Cooke
Engine 300, a 2-8-0 built in 1917 by Baldwin

Engine 400, a 2-8-2 built in 1917 by Baldwin – Under Restoration
Engine 500, a 4-6-2 built in 1911 by Baldwin – Under Restoration
Engine 610, a 2-10-4 built in 1927 by Lima – Static Display
Three Diesel Engines built between 1944 & 1953

CONTACT
Texas State Railroad
PO Box 166
Rusk, TX 75785
888-987-2461
903-683-2561
info@TexasStateRR.com
www.TexasStateRR.com

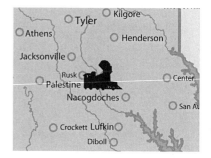

Photos: Texas State Railroad

TEXAS TRANSPORTATION MUSEUM
San Antonio, TX

Volunteers opened the Texas Transportation Museum in 1964. Today, volunteers still maintain the museum, with the Longhorn & Western Railroad as its centerpiece. The museum is housed in an antique depot, formerly located in Converse, Texas, which was built in 1913. It contains two steam engines, two diesels, a passenger car, a business car, and a variety of other rolling stock, including cabooses and motor cars.

When you visit the museum, your train will be pulled for one-third mile behind a Baldwin Rs4 switcher with an MP bay-window caboose. The museum's goal is to collect, preserve, and display transportation equipment and related items. Artifacts date back to the late 1800s when the first steam train arrived. There are also several model-train layouts and road vehicles on site.

SCHEDULES and FARES
The Texas Transportation Museum is open Thursdays through Sundays. The trains run Saturdays and Sundays. The museum is closed on select national holidays. Please call or check website for current schedules and fares.

EQUIPMENT
No. 6, 1910 Baldwin "Consolidation," class 2-8-0 locomotive
No. 1, 1925 Baldwin yard switcher 0-4-0 locomotive
44-ton, WWII-era diesel-electric engine
1954 Baldwin diesel-electric engine
No. 404, Santa Fe business car
Pullman McKeever sleeper car
Variety of other rail cars and cabooses

CONTACT
Texas Transportation Museum
11731 Wetmore Road
San Antonio, TX 78247
210-490-3554
www.txtransportationmuseum.org

Photos: Texas Transportation Museum

Did You Know..

The more than 600 freight railroads operating today in Canada, Mexico, and the United States are vital to North America's economic health.

UTAH

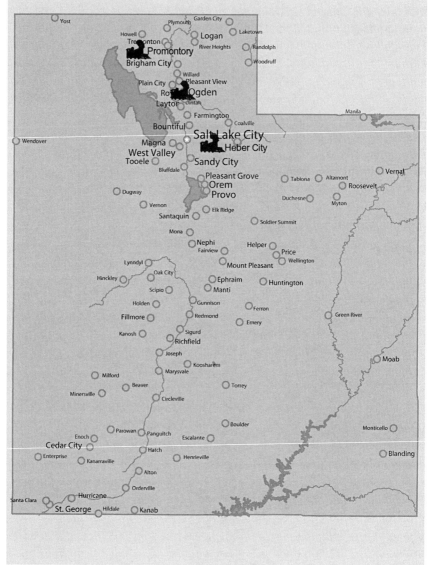

Yost
Plymouth
Garden City
Laketown
Howell
Logan
Trementon
Promontory
River Heights
Randolph
Brigham City
Woodruff
Willard
Plain City
Pleasant View
Roy
Ogden
Layton
Uintah
Manila
Farmington
Coalville
Bountiful
Wendover
Salt Lake City
Magna
Heber City
West Valley
Tooele
Sandy City
Bluffdale
Pleasant Grove
Vernal
Tabiona
Altamont
Dugway
Orem
Roosevelt
Provo
Duchesne
Vernon
Myton
Elk Ridge
Santaquin
Soldier Summit
Mona
Nephi
Helper
Fairview
Price
Lynndyl
Wellington
Mount Pleasant
Hinckley
Oak City
Ephraim
Huntington
Scipio
Manti
Holden
Gunnison
Ferron
Fillmore
Redmond
Green River
Emery
Kanosh
Sigurd
Richfield
Joseph
Moab
Koosharem
Milford
Marysvale
Beaver
Torrey
Minersville
Circleville
Boulder
Monticello
Parowan
Panguitch
Enoch
Escalante
Cedar City
Hatch
Enterprise
Henrieville
Blanding
Kanarraville
Alton
Orderville
Santa Clara
Hurricane
St. George
Hildale
Kanab

GOLDEN SPIKE NATIONAL HISTORIC SITE
Promontory, UT

The Golden Spike National Historic Site commemorates the construction and completion of the first transcontinental railroad. Situated on a broad, wind-swept basin separating the Promontory Mountains from the North Promontory Range, Golden Spike NHS preserves and interprets an historic event unequaled in American history and a landscape relatively unchanged by the passage of time.

There are daily programs offered by Rangers on the historical significance of the site and the driving of the last spike of the world's first transcontinental railroad on May 10, 1869. Just beyond the Visitor Center is the Last Spike Site, where the Union Pacific and Central Pacific rails were joined. Almost two miles of track lay on the original roadbed, and here the working replicas of the Jupiter and No. 119 locomotives make steam demonstration runs daily from May through September.

Also at the historic Last Spike Site, visitors are invited to step back in time to join Leland Stanford, Dr. Thomas Durant, General Grenville Dodge, and others for special living-history re-creations of the original Golden Spike ceremony. A favorite event among many visitors to Golden Spike, these reenactments take place on Saturdays and holidays from mid-May through Labor Day.

SCHEDULES and FARES
Entrance fees are based on vehicles (commercial and noncommercial). Please call or check website for current schedules and fares.

EQUIPMENT
Jupiter and No.119 locomotives

CONTACT
Golden Spike National Historic Site
P.O. Box 897
Brigham City, UT 84302
435-471-2209
www.nps.gov/gosp/home.html

Photos: Golden Spike National Historical Site

HEBER VALLEY RAILROAD
Heber City, UT

Featured On:
GREAT SCENIC RAILWAY JOURNEYS

At the Heber Valley Railroad's depot, the track seems to stretch out across the valley for as far as you can see. It actually only goes 16 miles. But many say it's the most scenic 16 miles in all of Utah.

Today the Heber Valley Railroad operates two steam engines year-round, offering a variety of exciting excursions for young and old alike. During the winter, passengers can enjoy the beauty of the snow-covered fields, a frozen lake, and a breathtaking glacier-carved canyon. Steam billows up in the frosty, air creating a beautiful sight for all to enjoy.

In summer, train enthusiasts can look forward to daily train schedules. On Friday and Saturday evenings, guests can enjoy either a Murder Mystery or the Sunset Special Barbecue train. A variety of seasonal events are planned, such as the Haunted Canyon Halloween train and the popular North Pole Christmas train which re-creates Chris Van Allsburg's award-winning children's story "The Polar Express."

Back in 1899 the track ran all the way into Provo, Utah, and the line belonged to the Denver & Rio Grand

Western Railroad. It was primarily a freight-hauling line and had the distinction of carrying more livestock out of the Heber Valley in the 30s and 40s than anywhere in the nation.

The railroad fell on hard times but gained worldwide notoriety as a result of its participation in the 2002 Winter Olympic Games. For the first time in Olympic history, three steam locomotives, two from the Heber Valley Railroad and one on loan from the Nevada Northern Railway, carried the Olympic flame some 4.5 miles.

SCHEDULES and FARES

The Heber Valley Railroad operates year-round. Schedules and fares vary according to the excursion. Please call or check website for current schedules and fares.

EQUIPMENT

Nos. 618 and 75 2-8-0 Baldwin steam, 1907
No. 1813 MRS-1 EMD
No. 1218 Davenport 44-ton
Nos. 270 and 250 Lackawanna coaches
No. 248 Clinchfield
Nos. 365, 366, 501, and 504 open-air cars
No. 700 UP caboose
Nos. 7508 and 7510 DRGW coaches

CONTACT

Heber Valley Railroad
450 South 600 West
Heber City, UT 84032
435-654-5601
801-581-9980
www.hebervalleyrr.org

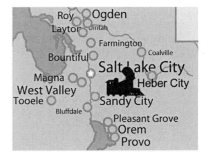

Photos: Heber Valley Railroad

OGDEN UNION STATION
Ogden, UT

The Ogden Union Station was a hub for transcontinental rail travel for 50 years. Today it serves as a monument to the railroad of old. Museums, an art gallery and even a satellite police station are housed in the depot now. The Utah State Legislature and the Ogden City Council provided funds to renovate the station for public use.

Ogden's first depot was built in 1869 out of lumber by the Union Pacific Railroad Company. The old wooden depot was replaced by a brick Victorian one in 1889. Public transport between downtown and the station was by mule-drawn trolley.

A fire that started on the second floor destroyed the station in 1923. Some effort was made to restore the burned-out building, but ultimately it was demolished and a completely new station was built. The current building was completed in 1924. During the height of World War II, Union Station saw thousands of servicemen pass through.

SCHEDULES and FARES
The museum is open year-round, Monday through Saturday. Adult admission is generally around $5. Please call or check website for current schedules and fares.

EQUIPMENT
No. 833, Union Pacific 4-8-4
X-26 turbine

CONTACT
Ogden Union Station
2501 Wall Avenue
Ogden, Utah 84401
www.theunionstation.org

Photos: Ogden Union Station

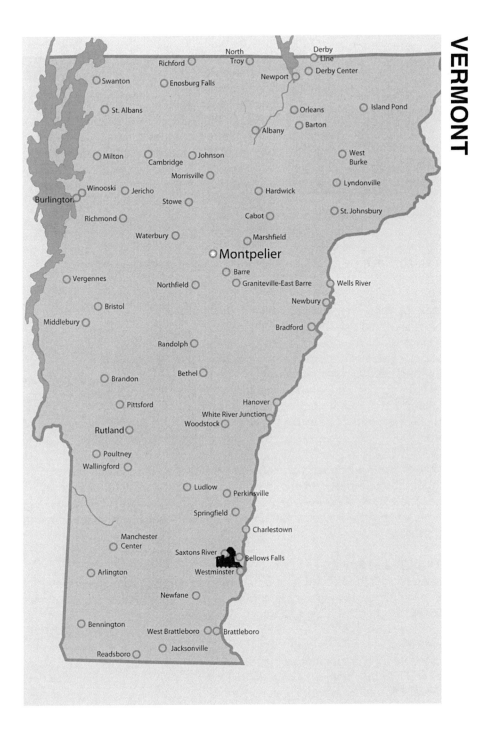

GREEN MOUNTAIN RAILROAD
Bellows Falls, VT

Climb aboard the Green Mountain Flyer for a trip from Bellows Falls to Chester. Your journey begins at the Bellows Falls Union Station, built in the 1850s and today featuring a waiting room and ticket office restored to look as they did in the 1940s. Your trip will take you through the scenic southern Vermont countryside in restored coaches pulled by a vintage diesel locomotive. You'll travel along the Connecticut and Williams Rivers, with spectacular views of Brockway Mills Gorge and two historic covered bridges. During your stop at the Chester Depot, you'll have time to explore the 1852 train station and the restored 1941 bay-window caboose on display in the depot's parking lot.

The Vermont Valley Flyer leaves Manchester Depot and travels along the Battenkill River to North Bennington. You ride in gleaming vintage stainless-steel passenger coaches built in the 1930s through 1950s. All coaches are enclosed, air conditioned, and run rain or shine. Manchester offers many specialty shops and an old-fashioned diner within walking distance.

The White River Flyer departs from Union Depot in White River Junction, offering four round-trip excursions to Norwich and the Montshire Museum of Science. The excursion will travel along the majestic Connecticut River with a panoramic view of the White Mountain foothills and a causeway that serves as a wildlife sanctuary.

SCHEDULES and FARES
The Green Mountain Railroad is open Tuesday to Sunday from late June through mid-October. Fares vary according to excursion. Please call or check website for current schedules and fares.

EQUIPMENT
Green Mountain Flyer locomotive
Champlain Flyer locomotive
White River Flyer locomotive
Restored passenger cars and coaches

CONTACT
Green Mountain Railroad
54 Depot Street
Bellows Falls, VT 05101
800-707-3530
802-463-3069
railtour@vermontrailway.com
www.rails-vt.com

Photos: Green Mountain Railroad

Did You Know...

The Canadian National Railway is the largest railway in Canada, in terms of both revenue and the physical size of its rail network, and is currently Canada's only transcontinental railway company, spanning Canada from the Atlantic to the Pacific coast.

VIRGINIA

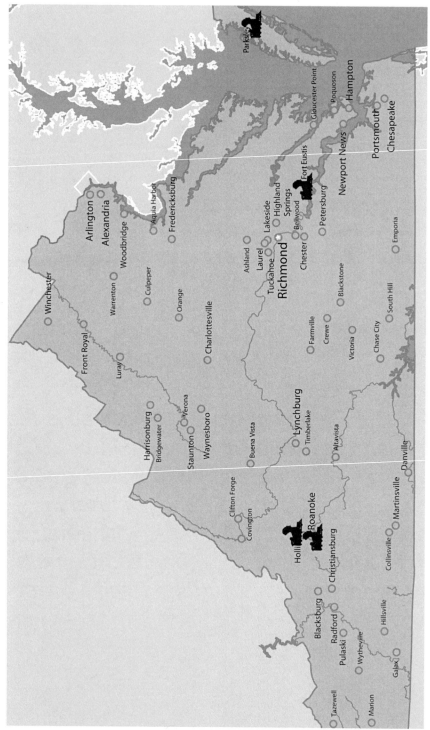

Parksley

Gloucester Point
Poquoson
Hampton

Newport News
Portsmouth
Chesapeake

Fort Eustis
Petersburg

Arlington
Alexandria

Woodbridge

Aquia Harbot

Fredericksburg

Highland
Springs
Lakeside
Bellwood
Chester

Emporia

Winchester

Warrenton

Culpeper

Orange

Ashland
Laurel
Tuckahoe
Richmond

Blackstone

Front Royal

Charlottesville

Luray

Farmville
Crewe
Victoria
Chase City
South Hill

Harrisonburg
Bridgewater
Verona
Staunton
Waynesboro

Buena Vista

Lynchburg
Timberlake

Altavista

Clifton Forge

Covington

Danville

Holli
Roanoke
Christiansburg

Collinsville
Martinsville

Blacksburg
Radford
Pulaski
Wytheville

Hillsville

Tazewell

Galax

Marion

EASTERN SHORE RAILWAY MUSEUM
Parksley, VA

The Eastern Shore Railway Museum features a 1906 New York, Philadelphia and Norfolk (later Pennsylvania) Railroad passenger station, an 1890s maintenance-of-way tool shed full of tools and other railway artifacts, a turn-of-the-century crossing guard shanty, and railcars lined up on the museum's sidings.

It was founded in 1988 and is located in the center of Parksley's business district. Parksley was founded in 1886 as the Philadelphia and Norfolk Railroad was built and passed through the middle of the Delmarva Peninsula. People rode the train to Cape Charles and then took a passenger ferry to Norfolk. Freight cars were also loaded from the rails to the barges and automobiles came soon thereafter, keeping the railroad very busy. Passenger service did stop at the Parksley Depot but is alive again thanks to a downtown revitalization project.

SCHEDULES and FARES
The Eastern Shore Railway Museum is open daily year-round except on Wednesdays (November through March), Thanksgiving Day, Christmas Day, and New Year's Day. Admission is under $5 for adults. Please call or check website for current schedules and fares.

EQUIPMENT
RF&P post office car, 1920s
No. 473 NKP caboose, 1962
No. 2783 Wabash caboose, 1949
No. 8011 Seaboard Airline diner car
RF&P Fairfax River, 1950
Pullman Diplomat parlor/observation car, 1927

CONTACT
Eastern Shore Railway Museum
P.O. Box 135
Parksley, VA 23421
757-665-RAIL
www.chincoteaguechamber.com/i-rail.htm

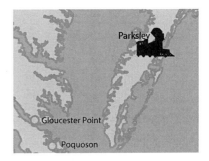

Photos: Eastern Shore Railway Museum

O. WINSTON LINK MUSEUM
Roanoke, VA

One of only two museums in the United States dedicated to a single photographer, the O. Winston Link Museum is housed in the former Norfolk and Western passenger station and is located in the heart of the railroad district of Roanoke, between the Hotel Roanoke, Norfolk Southern shops, and Virginia Museum of Transportation. The Link Museum celebrates the life and work of O. Winston Link, a Brooklyn native and self-taught photographer, whose most historically notable work documented the end of the steam locomotive era running on the Norfolk and Western Railway.

The Link Museum's self-guided tour is rich with insight and nostalgia from the days when Norfolk and Western was running steam through Roanoke and so many other small towns surrounding it. One and a half to two hours are suggested to examine the photographs, see the film (30 min) about the life of O. Winston Link, and experience Linkπs audio recordings and other exhibits relating to the railroad and photography. The Link Museum

also boasts a plentiful Museum Store, filled with unique railroad and regional merchandise, including apparel, books, DVDs, prints, posters, and children's items.

SCHEDULES AND FARES:
The O. Winston Link Museum is open daily except on Thanksgiving Day, Christmas Day, New Year's Day, and Easter. Admission to the museum is $5 for adults, $4 for seniors, and free for children under 3. The museum offers a joint admission with the Virginia Museum of Transportation that is $12 for adults, $10 seniors, and $8 for children 12 and under.

COLLECTION:
The O. Winston Link Museum permanent collection features more than 300 black and white images of the end of the steam locomotive era on the Norfolk and Western Railway taken between 1955 and 1960 by O. Winston Link. The

collection also includes Link's audio recordings, interactive lighting exhibits, Link's original darkroom equipment, a recreation of an old general store (with actual artifacts from Link's photographs), Link's cameras, and a 30 minute documentary film on the life and work of O. Winston Link.

CONTACT:
O. Winston Link Museum
101 Shenandoah Ave NE
Roanoke, VA 24016
540-982-5465
Www.linkmuseum.org

US ARMY TRANSPORTATION MUSEUM
Fort Eustis, VA

The rail collection at the US Army Transportation Museum represents the Army's role in train operations and maintenance from World War II to the mid-1970s. Pieces of equipment are moved around periodically to exercise them and are also removed for painting. As a result, individual cars are sometimes absent. The first use of the rail was during the Civil War in 1863, for transporting troops and supplies. During World Wars I and II, the Army teamed up with commercial railroads to move troops and supplies both at home and in Europe. Railway training was moved to Fort Eustis, in 1951, when a newly formed Transportation Corps rail-training moved from Wyoming, Louisiana, and Mississippi to Fort Eustis.

The 774th Transportation Group (Railway) provided training at Fort Eustis and included two battalions: the 714th Railway Operating Battalion and the 763rd Railway Shop Battalion. The 714th was the last active Army rail battalion, being absent only during its Korean service. During cutbacks after the Vietnam War, all active Army rail battalions were inactivated, and today they are only in the Reserves.

SCHEDULES and FARES
The museum is open year-round except on Mondays and federal holidays. Admission is free. Please call or check website for current schedules and fares.

US ARMY TRANSPORTATION MUSEUM
Fort Eustis, VA

EQUIPMENT
Steam locomotive 2-8-0 No. 607 & Tender, 1945
Steam locomotive 0-6-0 No.V-1923
Ambulance ward car No. 89568
Railway crane, locomotive, steam, wrecking
Railway flatcar, 50-Ton
Railway flatcar, 40-Ton
Railway snowplow-spreader-ditcher car
Railway tank car, petroleum
Railway caboose

CONTACT
US Army Transportation Museum
300 Washington Boulevard, Besson Hall
Fort Eustis, VA 23604-5260
757-878-1115
757-878-5656 (fax)
bowerba@eustis.army.mil
www.eustis.army.mil/

Photos: US Army Transportation Museum

VIRGINIA MUSEUM OF TRANSPORTATION, INC.
Roanoke, VA

The Virginia Museum of Transportation features diesel, steam, and electric locomotives, railcars, trolleys, carriages, automobiles, trucks, aviation, and rockets. Permanent exhibits include a pictorial history of the Norfolk & Western Railroad; African American heritage on the Norfolk & Western Railroad; and the Claytor Brothers, Virginians who were instrumental in building America's railroad. There is also an O-gauge train layout, four tiers of tracks, and trains with viewing levels for all sizes.

The museum's Resource Library & Archives houses a

wonderful collection of items related to the history and development of transportation in Virginia and throughout the world. It includes former Norfolk & Western Railway President Frederick J. Kimball's personal copy of the 1890 N&W annual report, two 1850s editions of *Railroad Journal* magazine, early survey reports, early Virginia railroad annual reports, and a wealth of statistical information relating to the transportation of goods and people. The Library & Archives also has an outstanding collection of Norfolk & Western blueprints and a number of N&W company photographs.

SCHEDULES and FARES
The Virginia Museum of Transportation is open seven days a week year-round. Adult admission is under $10. Please call or check website for current schedules and fares.

EQUIPMENT
No. 611, N&W class J locomotive
No. 1470, DC Transit Company PCC streetcar, built in 1945
No. 763, Nickel Plate Road class-S-2 locomotive
No. 1135, N&W Alco C-630 diesel locomotive
No. 6, N&W class-G-1 locomotive
No. 4919, Panama Canal Electric towing locomotive
No. 4, Virginian class SA locomotive

CONTACT
Virginia Museum of Transportation, Inc.
303 Norfolk Avenue SW
Roanoke, VA 24016
540-342-5670
570-342-6898
info@vmt.org
www.vmt.org

Photos: Virginia Museum of Transportation

WASHINGTON

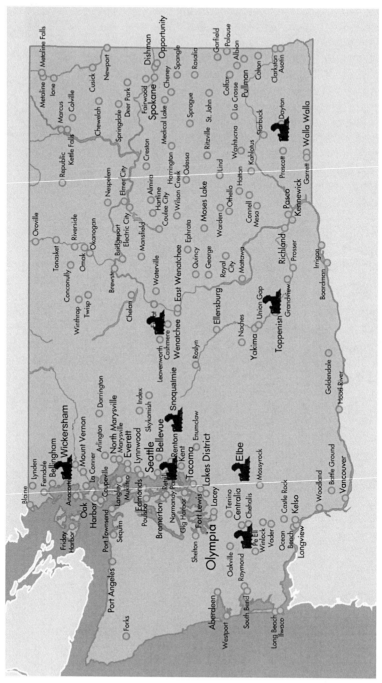

Metaline Falls
Metaline
Ione
Metaline
Marcus
Newport
Cusick
Colville
Chewelah
Dishman
Opportunity
Kettle Falls
Spangle
Springdale
Deer Park
Fairwood
Garfield
Palouse
Republic
Cheney
Rosalia
Albion
Spokane
Medical Lake
Colfax
La Crosse
Colton
Creston
Sprague
Pullman
Clarkston
Kettle Falls
Almira
Harrington
St. John
Asotin
Oroville
Nespelem
Elmer City
Hartline
Coulee City
Odessa
Ritzville
Starbuck
Dayton
Tonasket
Riverside
Wilson Creek
Lind
Washtucna
Walla Walla
Conconully
Omak
Brewster
Mansfield
Moses Lake
Hatton
Garrett
Winthrop
Okanogan
Electric City
Almira
Warden
Connell
Kahlotus
Prescott
Twisp
Bridgeport
Ephrata
Othello
Mesa
Pasco
Chelan
Waterville
Quincy
Royal
City
Kennewick
East Wenatchee
George
Mattawa
Richland
Prosser
Irrigon
Wenatchee
Ellensburg
Grandview
Boardman
Leavenworth
Cashmere
Roslyn
Yakima
Union Gap
Snoqualmie
Naches
Toppenish
Darrington
Index
Skykomish
Wickersham
Arlington
North Marysville
Bellingham
Mount Vernon
Marysville
Bellevue
Enumclaw
Lynden
La Conner
Everett
Renton
Elbe
Ferndale
Oak
Harbor
Lynnwood
Seattle
Kent
Mossyrock
Goldendale
Anacortes
Coupeville
Edmonds
Tacoma
Blaine
Langley
Mukilteo
Bremerton
Lakes District
Hood River
Friday
Harbor
Port Townsend
Poulsbo
Normandy Park
Gig Harbor
Lacey
Sequim
Renton
Fort Lewis
Tenino
Port Angeles
Shelton
Olympia
Centralia
Castle Rock
Chehalis
Woodland
Oakville
Pe Ell
Winlock
Battle Ground
Forks
Raymond
Vader
Vancouver
Ocean
Beach
Kelso
Aberdeen
Castle Rock
Longview
Westport
South Bend
Long Beach
Ilwaco

CHEHALIS-CENTRALIA RAILROAD AND MUSEUM
Chehalis, WA

The Chelhalis-Centralia Railroad Association was formed in 1986 by a group of local citizens whose goal was to restore a 1916 logging locomotive that had been placed in a Chehalis park 30 years earlier. By the summer of 1989, scheduled operations had begun.

The railroad is presently one of only a few steam-powered standard gauge tourist railroads in Washington. The trains operate over a nine-mile section of track that extends southwest of Chehalis. This historic rail line was previously operated by the Milwaukee Road, and later the Chehalis Western Railroad. A ride on the Chehalis-Centralia Railroad is a pleasant, scenic, and relaxing journey back in time. We invite you to ride with us and enjoy the sights and sounds of steam railroading as it used to be. You have options ranging from short excursions to dinner trains.

SCHEDULES and FARES

The Chehalis-Centralia Railroad Association operates trains from Memorial Day weekend through mid-October. There are also numerous special event trains in the off season. Fares vary according to excursion. Please call or check website for current schedules and fares.

EQUIPMENT
No. 15, 2-8-2 Mikado, Baldwin
No. 602, ex-Union Pacific coach
No. 601, ex-Union Pacific coach-diner
No. 801, open car

CONTACT
Chehalis-Centralia Railroad Association
1945 S. Market Boulevard
Chehalis, WA 98523
360-748-9593
info@SteamTrainRide.com
www.steamtrainride.com

Photos: Chehalis Centralia Railroad Association, Dave LaClair

CHELAN COUNTY HISTORICAL SOCIETY/
CASHMERE MUSEUM AND PIONEER VILLAGE
Cashmere, WA

In 1955 Willis Carey had a dream and he had cancer, and it was going to be a race to see which won. During his lifetime he amassed a personal collection of Native American artifacts, historic relics, antiques and curios that was famous throughout Central Washington. As his cancer progressed he lamented to friends there was no place to house his treasures after his death. The word spread among the local businessmen and the Chamber of Commerce, led by John McDonald, began exploring the possibilities of building a local public museum for the Carey artifacts. On a late summer day the committee visited the terminally ill Willis Carey at his home to acquaint him with the proposal. McDonald later reported that "tears of joy streamed down Carey's face" when he realized his collection might be preserved for the people of Cashmere. He immediately called for paper and pen and on the spot signed over his entire treasure. He died the next day. On August 31st, 1955, Cashmere mourned the death of Willis Carey, and his passing set into motion a project that would ultimately involve an estimated 600 citizen volunteers, and nearly four years of community action to create an institution we now recognize as the Cashmere Museum.

John McDonald, Eric Braun, Cecil Hawker and Robert Murray, along with Robert Eddy set about inventorying and cataloging the collection. By late 1955, The City of Cashmere had acquired Smith Grove, a four-acre parcel of land next to the Wenatchee River. By 1956, construction was started on what is now the basement of the Cashmere Museum. Monies were raised locally, much of which was by selling $2.00 membership to the Chelan County Historical Society. The work of the volunteers had begun, and they went door to door through out the county soliciting money. $20,000 got the project started by building the

basement to house the artifacts. The first cabin to be dismantled and rebuilt was in November 1957. The Assay office was in the path of the Blewett Pass Highway project. In May, 1959, Explorer Post #88, led by Dr. Ed Meyer, moved a second pioneer cabin onto the village green and the Cashmere Women's Club was busy landscaping the grounds. A Great Northern Caboose, Pullman car, Ticket office and Section House became the John McDonald Railroad. By 1959, the village had acquired several more cabins, and in the years that followed the museum and village had begun to evolve. The country store, Treadwell school-house and the Horan Cabin as well as the Miller Trading Post and Slawson Cabin arrived in 1972. The Weaver Cabin and Stoffel Waterwheel were installed in 1973. It was a spectacular sight watching the waterwheel come from Monitor by helicopter.

SCHEDULES AND FARES:
The Cashmere Museum and Pioneer Village is open from 10:00am to 4:00pm seven days a week from March through October. Special arrangements may be made to tour during the winter months when the site is closed. Please call for more information or for reservations.

CONTACT:
Chelan County Historical Society
600 Cotlets Way
Cashmere, WA 98815
509-782-3230
pioneer49@verizon.net
www.cashmeremuseum.org

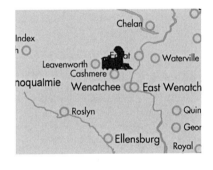

DAYTON DEPOT
Dayton, WA

The Dayton Depot is the oldest surviving train depot in the state. Originally built in 1881, it is now restored and houses a museum. Revolving exhibits are featured in the upstairs gallery. It is listed on Local State and National Registers of Historic Places.

The depot has been altered only slightly in the 120 years of its existence. It is a two-story framed structure with a cross frame gable shake roof. The second story, formerly the station master's quarters, provides access to the balcony running on three sides of the building. The wood brackets that support the balcony are a prominent feature of the structure.

A three-sided bay window on levels of the north side provides a view of the tracks to the east and west. The interior walls are the original beaded board, typical of the area. All of the rooms have high ceilings and wainscoting. The freight scale is intact and usable.

SCHEDULE AND FARES
The Dayton Depot is open year-round. Admission to the first floor is free. The fee for guided tours and gallery exhibits is under $5 for adults. Please call or check website for current schedules and fares.

EQUIPMENT
The caboose outside of the Dayton Depot is part of the Union Pacific train that serviced Dayton.

CONTACT
Dayton Depot
222 East Commercial Street
Dayton, WA 99328
509-382-2026
http://dayton.bmi.net/

Photos: Dayton Depot

LAKE WHATCOM RAILWAY
Wickersham, WA

At the Lake Whatcom Railway visitors ride steam trains that are almost 100 years old. Ride the little railroad speeder for a 1.5-hour trip along the shore of Lake Whatcom. You are also able to explore some ancient wooden freight cars from the Great Northern Railway housed on the premises.

The Lake Whatcom Railway is a dedicated living preservation of the Pacific Northwest's railway heritage. For political reasons the railway currently uses a diesel locomotive. The passenger coaches date to the early 1900s and were used for many years on the Northern Pacific passenger trains out of Seattle. Some ancient wooden freight cars from the Great Northern Railway are also on the premises.

SCHEDULES and FARES
The Lake Whatcom Railway operates from July through September, with special holiday runs. The summer trains run on Tuesdays and Saturdays. Adult fares are under $15. Please call or check website for current schedules and fares.

EQUIPMENT
Passenger coaches dated to the early 1900s

CONTACT
Lake Whatcom Railway
P.O. Box 91
Acme, WA 98220
360-595-2218
www.lakewhatcomrailway.com

Photos: Lake Whatcom Railway

MT. RAINIER SCENIC RAILROAD
Elbe, WA

The Mt. Rainier Scenic Railroad operates in Elbe, Washington, about 70 miles southeast of Seattle and 45 miles southeast of Tacoma on tracks owned by the city of Tacoma. The railroad runs a 1.5-hour excursion in the summers from Elbe to Mineral Lake, which is only 13 miles from the entrance to Mt. Rainier National Park.

On a clear day, you will experience a beautiful vista of Mount Rainier as we cross the Nisqually River Bridge. On a cloudy day, you will know the mountain is still there, as the Nisqually is fed directly from the huge Nisqually glacier, Mt. Rainier's year-round blanket of white. Also on occasion, we will see herds of majestic Roosevelt elk grazing in nearby pastures along our route.

The railroad was originally started in 1981 by the Western Forest Industries Museum, a non-profit organization dedicated to the preservation and display of working equipment used in the forest industry during the steam-logging era.

SCHEDULES AND FARES:
The Mount Rainier Scenic Railroad runs Friday through Sunday, June through October. During July and August it runs Thursday through Sunday. There are more than 20 special events during the season. Adult fare starts at $20. Please call or check website for current schedules and fares.

EQUIPMENT
Rod 2-8-2 Porter, 1924
Rod 2-8-2T Alco, 1929
Geared Climax, 1928
3-truck Climax
3-truck Pacific Coast Shay, 1929
3-truck West Coast Special Heisler, 1930
3-truck Rayonier Willamette, 1929

CONTACT:
Mt. Rainier Scenic Railroad
PO Box 250
Mineral, WA 98355
888-STEAM-11
360-492-5588
www.mrsr.com

Photos: Mt. Rainier Scenic Railroad

NORTHERN PACIFIC RAILWAY MUSEUM
Toppenish, WA

Take a 20-mile round-trip ride on the former Northern Pacific White Swan branch line in a train operated by the Northern Pacific Railway Museum. The museum is housed in the 1911 former Northern Pacific railroad depot. For 50 years the Toppenish railroad depot served as the transportation center of the community. In 1961, as other modes of transportation became more popular, rail service was discontinued. Workers boarded the depot up in 1981. Rail fans came to its rescue in the late 1980s and after many volunteer hours the museum reopened on July 4, 1992.

This same group ultimately purchased the depot and adjacent freight house from Burlington Northern Railroad. The freight house has been converted into an engine house. At the time of publication, workers were restoring a 1930s vintage freight train to display the importance of railroad transportation to early western development. Today's 20-mile excursion from Harrah to White Swan allows visitors to relive history, and maybe even get involved in the effort to preserve it.

SCHEDULES and FARES
The Northern Pacific Railway Museum is open daily from May through October. Admission to the museum is under $5. Excursion fares are generally under $15. Please call or check website for current schedules and fares.

EQUIPMENT
No.1364,1902 NP Baldwin 4-6-0
150-ton locomotive built in 1953
2 1920s P70 heavyweights
No. 588, 1947 Northern Pacific coach

CONTACT
Northern Pacific Railway Museum
10 South Asotin Avenue
Toppenish, WA 98948
509-865-1911
www.nprymuseum.org

Photos: Northern Pacific Railway Museum

NORTHWEST RAILWAY MUSEUM
Snoqualmie, WA

The Northwest Railway Museum operates the Snoqualmie Valley Railroad, an interpretive railway program. The museum was founded in 1957 as the Puget Sound Railway Historical Association. In September 1999 the name was formally changed to the Northwest Railway Museum. It is the largest and most comprehensive railway museum in Washington State.

The museum is housed in a restored 1890 Queen Anne-style Snoqualmie Depot, and you purchase your train tickets from the original ticket window. This 5-mile common-carrier railroad allows museum visitors to experience an antique railroad coach ride through the Upper Snoqualmie Valley to Snoqualmie Falls.

SCHEDULES and FARES

The museum is open seven days a week, year round. It is closed on Thanksgiving, Christmas, and New Year's Day. The train operates from April through October. Special events are scheduled throughout the operating season. There is no charge to enter the museum. You can ride the regular train for under $10. Please call or check website for current schedules and fares.

EQUIPMENT
No. 1, Weyerhaeuser Timber Company locomotive
No. 89601, Army Medical Service hospital kitchen car
No. 201, Kennecott Copper Company locomotive
No. 10, Northern Pacific Railway rotary snowplow
No. 7320, "Cecil the Diesel," United States Navy locomotive
Polson Logging 4-yard side-dump car

CONTACT
Northwest Railway Museum
38625 SE King Street
Snoqualmie, WA 98065
425-888-3030
info@trainmuseum.org
www.trainmuseum.org

Photos: Northwest Railway Museum

CHELATCHIE PRAIRIE RAILROAD
Yacolt, WA

The Chaltchie Prairie Railroad is operated by an all-volunteer association that maintians the equipment, track, and staff the trains. The railroad operates on the north end of a former Northern Pacific branch line that runs from the BSNF in Vancouver to a 6 miles north of Yacolt. During a typical run the train passes through woodlands, a 300-foot tunnel and across a trestle and bridge over the north fork of the Lewis River. Trips last about 1.5-hours, including a 20-minute stop where passengers can view the steam engine and take a short hike over a beautiful little waterfall.

SCHEDULES and FARES
All trains depart from Yacolt. Tickets may be purchased at the railroad or over the phone. Please call or check website for current schedules and fares.

EQUIPMENT
Nos. 16 and 803, Alco 2-8-2T Minaret steam engines, built in 1929
Heavyweight coaches
Wide-vision cabooses
Open-air cars

340 Washington

CONTACT
Chelatchie Prairie Railroad
P.O. Box 1271
Battle Ground, WA 98604
360-686-3559
360-750-0451 (fax)
admin@bycx.com
www.bycx.com

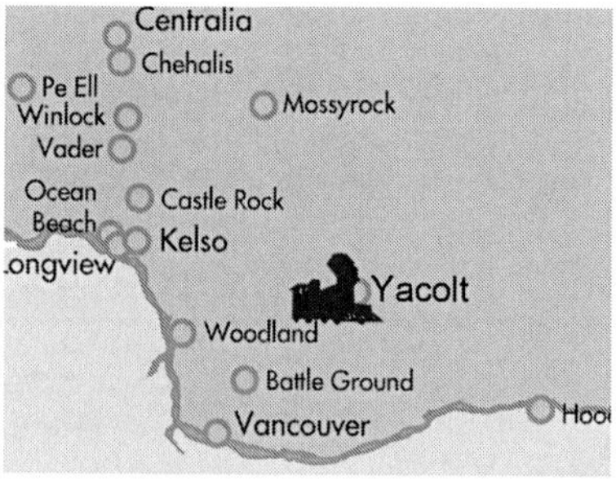

Did You Know...

There are approximately 150,000 miles of railroad track in the United States; nearly all are standard gauge.

The Alaska Railroad has a mainline over 470 miles long and is well over 500 miles, including branch lines and sidings.

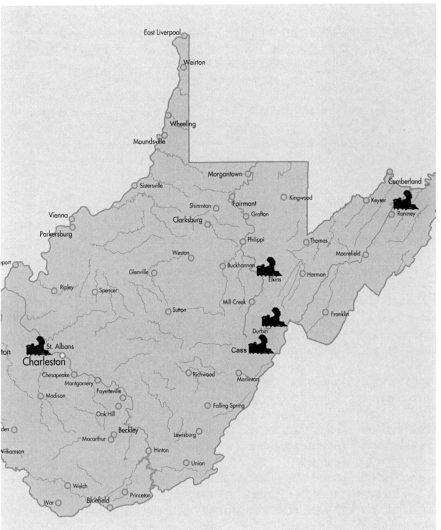

CASS SCENIC RAILROAD
Cass, WV

Nestled in the mountains of West Virginia, Cass Scenic Railroad State Park offers excursions that transport you back in time to relive an era when steam-driven locomotives were an essential part of everyday life. Trips to Cass are filled with rich histories of the past, unparalleled views of a vast wilderness area, and close-up encounters with the sights and sounds of original steam-driven locomotives.

The town of Cass remains relatively unchanged. The restored company houses now rented as vacation cottages, add to the charm and atmosphere of the town. From the company store and museum to the train depot, you'll find an abundance of things to do prior to your departure on the historic Cass Railroad.

The Cass Scenic Railroad is the same line built in 1901 to haul lumber to the mill in Cass. The locomotives are the same Shay locomotives used in Cass, and in the rainforests of British Columbia for more than a half-century. Many of the passenger cars are old logging flat-cars that have been refurbished.

The railroad offers several trips for you to choose from. The Whittaker Station trip travels four miles up the track from Cass. Visitors can rest, eat lunch, and take a tour of the authentic logging camp recreated by the volunteers of the Mountain State Railroad & Logging Historical Association. The Bald Knob trip travels 11 miles up the mountain from Cass. The Bald Knob area has a climate similar to Canada and is abundant in plants typical to the Canadian wilderness. At an elevation of 4,842 feet, it is the third highest point in West Virginia. The overlook at Bald Knob provides panoramic views into two states.

SCHEDULES AND FARES:
Cass Scenic Railroad operates from Friday of Memorial Weekend in May through the last Sunday in October. Advance ticket purchase is strongly recommended. Please call or check website for current schedules and fares.

EQUIPMENT
Invented to do the impossible, the Shay logging locomotive was designed to

climb the steepest grades, swing around hairpin curves and negotiate frail temporary tracks. In addition, they had to haul incredibly heavy loads, from woods to mill. Power was all-important.

No. 2 Shay, 1928
No. 4 Shay, 1922
No. 5 Shay, 1905
No. 6 Shay, 1945
No. 7 Shay, 1920
No. 9 Climax, 1919
No. 6 Heisler, 1929
No. 11 Feather River Shay, 1923

CONTACT:
Cass Scenic Railroad State Park
Physical location:
Rt. 66, 252 Main Street, Cass WV
Mailing address:
PO Box 130, Green Bank WV 24944
Cass, WV 24927
800-CALL WVA
304-456-4300
304-456-4641 (fax)
cassrailroadsp@wv.gov
www.cassrailroad.com

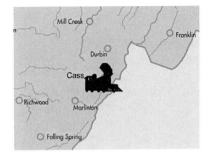

Photos: Cass Scenic Railroad

DURBIN & GREENBRIER VALLEY RAILROAD
Durbin, West Virginia

Durbin & Greenbrier Valley Railroad offers a 102-mile round trip on the Tygert Flyer that takes you along two rivers, underneath Cheat Mountain, and through a long "S" curve tunnel. There is also the Cheat Mountain Salamander railbus ride, an 80-mile trip across the top of the Cheat Mountain range. Both of these trains converge from opposite directions for a stop at "High Falls of the Cheat River".

Our flagship train, the Durbin Rocket, is now powered by a 1910 Climax steam locomotive for the 10.5 mile round trip into the heart of the Greenbrier River wilderness. The Durbin & Greenbrier Valley Railroad, Inc. was formed in 1996 in an attempt to save the abandoned 15 mile rail line between Durbin and Cass, WV.

SCHEDULES and FARES
The Durbin & Greenbrier Valley Railroad operates from May through October. Fares and schedules depend on excursion choice. Please call or check website for current schedules and fares.

EQUIPMENT
Locomotives:
No. 1, Little Leroi, a 1936
No. 3,1910 55-ton Climax Manufacturing Company steam
No. M-3, circa 2000, Edwards Railway Motor Car Co
No. 41, 1959 Alco
No. 67, 1952, EMD
No. 82, 1948, EMD
No. 303, 1950, Alco
Passenger Cars:
Pullman coaches- Nos. 512, 537, 1827, 1801, and 1802
Open observation car No. 202
Cabooses Nos. 4 and 5, ex-B&ORR, No. 1800, ex-WM Rwy

CONTACT
Durbin & Greenbrier Valley Railroad, Inc.
PO Box 44
Durbin, WV 26264
304-456-4935
877-MTN-RAIL
877-686-7245
www.mountainrail.com

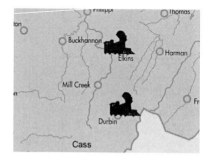

Photos: Durbin & Greenbrier Valley Railroad

NEW RIVER TRAIN
Huntington, WV

The New River Train excursion through the New River Gorge in southern West Virginia promise to be an unforgettable trip. As one of the newest national parklands, the "Grand Canyon of the East" along the New River is usually aglow in fall colors in mid-to-late October. It is during this peak autumn foliage time that the trains traverse the former Chesapeake & Ohio mainline from Huntington, WV to Hinton, WV and back, allowing for a front-row seat to some of the most spectacular scenery in the country.

Landmarks and scenic locations on the route include downtown Charleston and the State Capitol building, WVU Tech in Montgomery, Kanawha Falls, Hawks Nest Dam and Bridge, the famous New River Gorge Bridge at Fayetteville, Grandview, Stretcher Neck Tunnel, Sandstone Falls, and numerous historical artifacts and towns from the New River's rich coal mining era. The New River Train is operated by the Collis P. Huntington Railroad Historical Society in conjunction with Amtrak and CSX.

SCHEDULES and FARES
The New River Train only operates four days in October. Please call or check website for current schedules and fares.

EQUIPMENT
6108 Seaboard Diner, Budd of Philadelphia in 1948.
NYC-38 full length lounge car
Braddock Inn A Lounge/Parlor Car

CONTACT
New River Train
1323 8th Avenue
Huntington, WV 25701
304-453-1641
newrivertrain@aol.com
www.newrivertrain.com

Photos: New River Train

POTOMAC EAGLE SCENIC RAILROAD
Romney, WV

As it glides along the banks of the South Branch of the Potomac River, the Potomac Eagle provides passengers with a leisurely view of the magnificent West Virginia wilderness. The on-board narrator points out the historic eighteenth century farmsteads and battle sites that line the river, as well as the wildlife that inhabits the region.

The 3-hour excursion also includes traveling through The Trough, a 7-mile gorge inaccessible to all except the train and canoeists. In addition to enjoying the tranquil beauty of the Trough, passengers can also experience the thrill of seeing the American bald eagle in its natural habitat. Attracted by its clear water, abundant fish, and remote location, bald eagles have made the Trough a permanent nesting area. Eagles are sighted on over 90% of trips.

The Potomac Eagle offers both coach and first class service. Coach passengers ride in open-window cars and may purchase sandwiches, snacks, and drinks in the concession car. They may also bring their own picnic baskets on-board. First class passengers ride in our air-conditioned club cars and are served a full meal during the trip. In addition to the 3-hour ride, the Potomac Eagle also operates several all-day excursions and special evening trains.

The Potomac Eagle is located on Route 28 about 1.5 miles north of Romney, West Virginia. Driving times are about 1 hour from Winchester, VA and 45 minutes from Cumberland, MD.

SCHEDULES and FARES
The Potomac Scenic Railroad operates from May through October. Adult fares range from $30 to $100. Please call or check website for current schedules and fares.

EQUIPMENT
Open-window coaches and table cars
Open gondola
Air-conditioned, first class club cars
Diesel locomotives

CONTACT
The Potomac Eagle Train Station
Route 28 North
Romney, WV 26757
304-822-7464 (train days)
304-424-0736 (reservation line)
304-485-5901 (fax)
http://www.potomaceagle.info

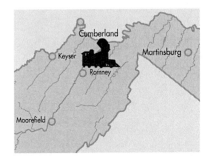

Photos: Potomac Eagle Scenic Railroad

Did You Know...

The Mount Hood Railroad operates on a line with one of the last five remaining railroad switchbacks in use in the United States.

WISCONSIN

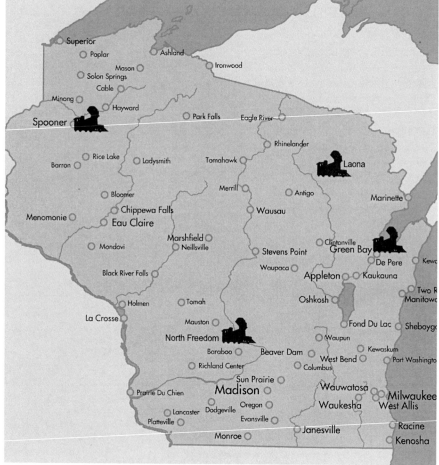

Superior
Poplar   Ashland
Mason ○   Ironwood
○ Solon Springs
Cable ○
Minong ○
○ Hayward
Spooner

Park Falls   Eagle River ○

Rhinelander ○

○ Rice Lake   ○ Ladysmith   Tomahawk ○
Barron ○   Laona

○ Bloomer   Merrill ○   ○ Antigo
Chippewa Falls   Marinette ○
Menomonie ○   Eau Claire   ○ Wausau

Marshfield ○   ○ Clintonville
○ Mondovi   ○ Neillsville   ○ Stevens Point   Green Bay
                                    Waupaca ○   ○ De Pere   Kewc
Black River Falls ○   Appleton ○ ○ Kaukauna

                                                                Two R
○ Holmen   ○ Tomah   Oshkosh ○   Manitowc
La Crosse ○
            Mauston ○   ○ Fond Du Lac ○ Sheboyg
North Freedom   ○ Waupun
        Baraboo ○   Beaver Dam ○   Kewaskum ○
        Richland Center ○   West Bend ○   ○ Port Washingto
                                ○ Columbus
                Sun Prairie ○
○ Prairie Du Chien   Madison ○   Wauwatosa ○
                    Oregon ○   Waukesha   Milwaukee
        ○ Lancaster Dodgeville ○   West Allis
Platteville ○   Evansville ○
                                Janesville ○   Racine
        Monroe ○   Kenosha

CAMP FIVE MUSEUM
Laona, WI

Every summer, visitors to Camp Five reconnect with Northern Wisconsin's fascinating history by traveling to the original logging site on the "Lumberjack Special" train. The train is pulled by a 1916 Vulcan-built steam locomotive.

Your trip begins at a Nineteenth Century Soo Line depot. The depot was moved to Laona from its original location in Dunbar, Wisconsin. Passengers on the Lumberjack Special enjoy the wonderful Northwoods, streams and numerous natural wildflower areas. Upon arrival, visitors are delighted to find Camp Five nestled in a natural setting surrounded by hundreds of acres of farmland and forest.

Numerous attractions and activities await the disembarking passengers, including a working blacksmith shop, displays of logging antiquities (which features an extensive display of logging currency), early transportation memorabilia, a harness shop, a walk through a lush forest and a tour aboard a guided surrey.

In 1914, the Connor Lumber & Land Company created a farm in Laona to raise cattle, produce and draft horses for area lumber camps. Today, all of these lumber company farm buildings still stand as part of the Camp Five Museum complex. It is a unique site in Wisconsin and has been added to the National Registry of Historic Places by the United States Department of the Interior.

SCHEDULES and FARES
The Summer Season at Camp Five Museum is from late June through late August on Mondays to Saturdays. The fall season extends to October but is limited. The Lumberjack Special runs 4 excursions a day either from Camp Five to Laona and back or vice versa. Visitors should give themselves two hours to explore and ride the train. Please call or check website for current schedules and fares.

EQUIPMENT
4-spot "Lumberjack Special,"1916 locomotive
The "Rat River",1912
The "Otter Creek", 1911, rebuilt in 1941
Two 18 passenger cabooses, 1965 and 1966, Duluth, Mesabi, and Iron Range railroad
Soo Line's Caboose No.147.

350 Wisconsin

CONTACT
Camp Five Museum Foundation
5480 Connor Farm Road
Laona, WI 54541
715-674-3414
mverich@camp5museum.org
www.camp5museum.org

Photos: Camp Five Museum

MID-CONTINENT RAILWAY HISTORICAL SOCIETY
North Freedom, WI

The Mid-Continent Railway Historical Society, also known as Mid-Continent Railway Museum, is an outdoor, living museum and operating railroad. Workers have recreated the small town/short line way of life during the "Golden Age of Railroading," spanning the years 1880-1916. The museum has been in operation since 1963.

Founded in 1959 as the Railway Historical Society of Milwaukee, its sole purpose has been to perpetuate the heritage of steam railroads through the operation and display of authentic railroad equipment. The first attempt to fulfill this mission took place at Hillsboro, Wisconsin, in 1962. But the rules of the rail line owner required the fledgling group to pull its coaches with gas power and leave the steamers for display only.

In 1963 the society purchased 4.2 miles of track from the Chicago & Northwestern Railroad and moved its

operations to North Freedom, Wisconsin. That year society members offered steam train rides under their new name, the Mid-Continent Railway Historical Society, Inc.

Today visitors can take a memorable, seven-mile, 50-minute round-trip ride on a former branch line of the Chicago & Northwestern Railway through the scenic Baraboo Hills. Passengers ride in restored steel coaches built in 1915. An authentically-attired conductor will call "all aboard!" before the train leaves from an historic wooden depot built in 1894. At the end of the line, passengers may detrain to get a look inside the cab of the locomotive from a viewing platform.

SCHEDULES and FARES
The Mid-Continent Railway is open from May through October. Fares vary according to the excursion. Please call or check website for current schedules and fares.

EQUIPMENT
14 steam locomotives
6 diesel/other locomotives
23 wooden passenger trains
15 steel passenger trains
24 wooden freight cars
8 steel freight cars
21 cabooses

CONTACT
Mid-Continent Railway Historical Society
E8948 Diamond Hill Road
North Freedom, WI 53951
608-522-4261
inquiries@midcontinent.org
www.midcontinent.org

Photos: Mid Continent Railway Historical Society

NATIONAL RAILROAD MUSEUM
Green Bay, WI

The National Railroad Museum allows you to sit in the cab of the Union Pacific Big Boy, the world's largest steam locomotive, or view General Eisenhower's World War II command train and the sleek 1955 General Motors Aerotrain.

Even though it's 50 years old, the General Motors (GM) Aerotrain still wows rail enthusiasts. The builder's model is an original piece from the mid-1950s used to showcase GM's design for the futuristic Aerotrain. The model, like the prototype, has one locomotive and 10 passenger coaches. GM designed the train using existing technologies from its various divisions. The concept was to create a rail vehicle that would be economical to build and maintain as well as offer aesthetic appeal to the traveling public.

This museum is one of the America's oldest and largest dedicated to the history of railroading. From exhibits to rolling stock to a ride in vintage equipment, there is something for every railroad enthusiast! There is also a model railroad layout, a theater presentation and an 85-foot observation tower for you to explore.

SCHEDULES and FARES
The museum is open year-round on Mondays through Sundays. It is closed on New Year's Day, Easter, Thanksgiving, Christmas Eve and Christmas Day. The train ride is only available from May through September. Several special events are scheduled throughout the year, including Rocky Mountain Rail Adventure, Terror on the Fox, Great Pumpkin Train, Civil War Reenactment, Festival of Trees, Santa Train and more. Please call or check website for current schedules and fares.

EQUIPMENT
No. 4017, Union Pacific Big Boy
No. 4890, Pennsylvania GG-1
General Motors Aerotrain - locomotive and two passenger cars
General Eisenhower's World War II command train

CONTACT
National Railroad Museum
2285 South Broadway
Green Bay, WI 54304-4832
920-437-7623
staff@nationalrrmuseum.org
www.nationalrrmuseum.org

Photos: National Railroad Museum

WISCONSIN GREAT NORTHERN RAILWAY
Spooner, WI

The Wisconsin Great Northern Railroad is an historic excursion and dinner train operating on 20 miles of former Chicago & Northwestern Railroad track between the northern Wisconsin towns of Spooner and Springbrook along the Namekagon River. This family-oriented attraction combines vintage railroad equipment with exciting special events to entertain and educate rail fans of all ages.

The railroad, that operates today, was founded on April 1, 1997. Today, the railroad operates locomotives from the 1940's and a fleet of mahogany interior passenger cars built between 1910 and 1930. The cars have been tastefully rebuilt to give passengers the flavor of rail travel from this time period.

The railroad was first laid through the wilderness that became Spooner in 1879, and for the next century Spooner was an important division point. At one time nearly 75% of the residents worked for the railroad and 22 passenger trains stopped here each day. The History of the Line is the story of the railroad that lived, died, and was reborn here in Spooner.

SCHEDULES and FARES
Trains operate from May through October and many special events are scheduled throughout the operating season. Dinner trains include a family pizza train, hobo trains, Empire Builder's Lunch and Dinner with the Outlaws. Other trains include Family Picnic Trains, Spooner Rodeo Train Robberies, Railroad

SCHEDULES and FARES cont.

Heritage Days, Majestic Fall Colors and the Great Pumpkin Train. Please call or check website for current schedules and fares.

EQUIPMENT

Locomotives:

Nos. 400 and 423, 1949 EMD F-7A, No. 423

No. 862, 1940 EMC SW1

No. 26, "East Lexington," passenger car, built by Pullman in 1925

No. 28, "Arrowhead," built as an 80-seat coach in 1912 by American Car and Foundry Company

No. 32, D&NM "Apostle Isle," built by Pullman in 1918

No. 34, WGN "Presque Isle," built in 1918 by Pullman

No. 112, "Namekagon Club," built as a mail and express car in 1912

CONTACT

Wisconsin Great Northern Railroad
426 North Front Street
Spooner, WI 54801
715-635-3200
office@spoonertrainride.com
www.spoonertrainride.com

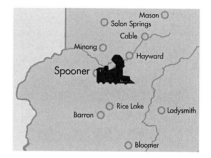

Photos: Wisconsin Great Northern Railroad

Did You Know...

The Baltimore & Ohio Railroad is one of the oldest railroads in the US, and includes the oldest operational bridge in the world.

WYOMING

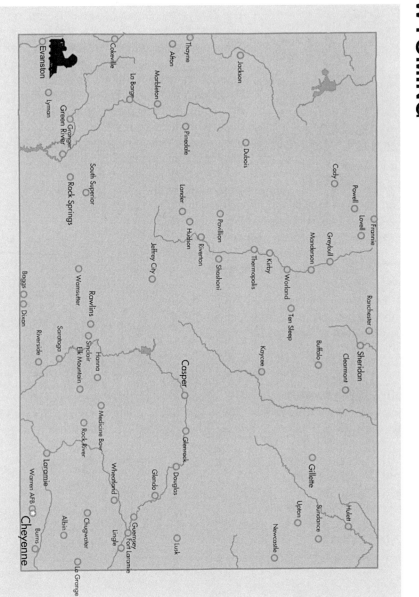

CHEYENNE DEPOT MUSEUM
Cheyenne, WY

The Cheyenne Depot Museum is housed in the last grandiose Union Pacific Depot that was constructed in the 19th century. The Cheyenne Union Pacific Depot was recognized in March 2006 as a National Historic Landmark. It was designed by noted American architect Henry Van Brunt. The depot is significant not only for its architect, but because it was an important link in the transcontinental railroad.

The Cheyenne Depot Museum strives to exhibit the great link between Cheyenne and the American railroad. The town of Cheyenne was established when the Union Pacific chose to go through the Rockies by way of Wyoming. The original settlers of Cheyenne were there because of the railroad. The museum displays this great rail history through historic photographs and exhibits. The depot is a display of America's rail history and the way the railroad connected the East and the West to form the America of today.

SCHEDULES and FARES
The Cheyenne Depot Museum is open seven days a week, year round. Hours of operation vary. Please call or check website for current schedules and fares.

CONTACT
Cheyenne Depot Museum
121 West 15th Street
Cheyenne, WY 82001
307-632-3905
307-632-0614 (fax)
www.cheyennedepotmuseum.org

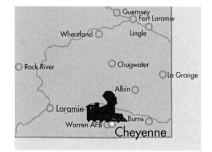

Photos: Cheyenne Depot Museum

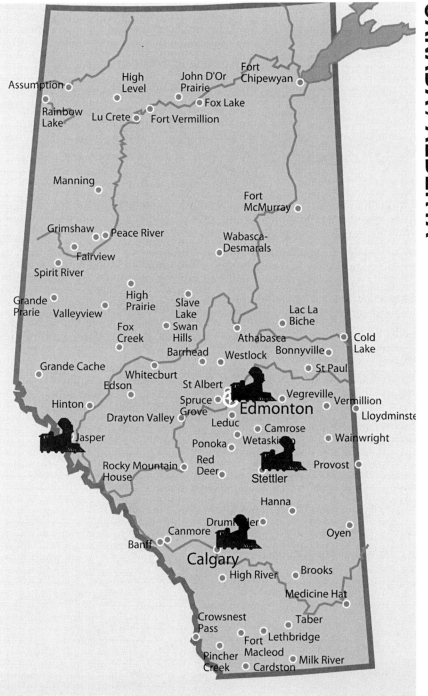

Assumption

High
Level

John D'Or
Prairie

Fort
Chipewyan

Fox Lake

Rainbow
Lake

Lu Crete

Fort Vermillion

Manning

Fort
McMurray

Grimshaw

Peace River

Wabasca-
Desmarals

Fairview

Spirit River

Grande
Prarie

Valleyview

High
Prairie

Slave
Lake

Lac La
Biche

Fox
Creek

Swan
Hills

Athabasca

Bonnyville

Cold
Lake

Grande Cache

Barrhead

Westlock

St Paul

Whitecburt

Edson

St Albert

Vegreville

Vermillion

Hinton

Spruce
Grove

Edmonton

Lloydminste

Drayton Valley

Leduc

Jasper

Camrose

Ponoka

Wetaski

Wainwright

Rocky Mountain
House

Red
Deer

Provost

Stettler

Hanna

Drum   ler

Canmore

Oyen

Banff

Calgary

High River

Brooks

Medicine Hat

Crowsnest
Pass

Taber

Fort
Pincher   Macleod
Creek

Lethbridge

Cardston

Milk River

ALBERTA PRAIRIE RAILWAY
Stettler, AB

Alberta Prairie offers one day adventures on board a real steam or diesel powered train. The train leaves Stettler, Alberta, and returns 5-6 hours later. All excursions include a full-course buffet meal, on board entertainment and maybe even a train robbery. During your journey you will travel through the rolling hills and trees of Alberta's parkland.

During both legs of each excursion, professional performers entertain passengers in their seats. For those passengers who want to feel the gentle Alberta air, you can spend time in the open-air coach. Others prefer to be entertained while enjoying a 'cool one' in the Lone Star Saloon. Snack foods and refreshments are available and the train is fully licensed.

SCHEDULES and FARES
The Alberta Prairie Railway is open April through October. Adult fares range from $60 to $140 U.S. Special events and "Fine Dining" trains are also available. Please call or check website for current schedules and fares.

EQUIPMENT
Locomotives:
1920 Baldwin No. 41 steam 2-8-0
1958 General Motors No.1259 Diesel SW-1200 RS
1944 Montreal Locomotive No.6060 steam Mountain Class 4-8-2

CONTACT
Alberta Prairie Railway Excursions
P.O. Box 1600
Stettler, AB
T0C 2L0
403-742-2811
info@absteamtrain.com
www.absteamtrain.com

Photos: Alberta Prairie Railway

FORT EDMONTON PARK
(Edmonton Radial Railway Society)
Edmonton, AB

One of Edmonton's premier attractions, Fort Edmonton Park brings to life four distinct time periods during the country's development from a fur trade post to a booming metropolitan centre after the First World War. The park features more than 75 structures, many of which are the originals. Costumed interpreters operate the site.

Free steam engine train and streetcar rides are available but you can also hitch a ride on a wagon, stagecoach, or pony and buggy. The streetcar rides are operated by the Edmonton Radial Railway Society. The Society, through volunteer efforts, preserves and interprets the history of streetcars in the area.

SCHEDULES and FARES
Schedules and fares vary according to excursion. Please call or check website for current schedules and fares.

EQUIPMENT
1919 Baldwin
No.107 2-6-2
Oakdale & Gulf Railway (restored to 1905 appearance)

CONTACT
Fort Edmonton Park
PO Box 2359
Edmonton, AB
T5J 2R7
780-496-8787
780-496-8797(fax)
attractions@edmonton.ca
www.gov.edmonton.ab.ca/fort

Photos: Fort Edmonton Park

HERITAGE PARK HISTORICAL VILLAGE
Calgary, AB

Travel back in time and discover the treasures of Western Canada's past at Heritage Park. All the sights and sounds of pre-1914 life are recreated at Canada's largest living historical village.

Heritage Park features over 66 acres of parkland, over 150 historical exhibits, thousands of artifacts, and lively interpretive activities. Stroll down relaxing Main Street 1910 and let the aroma of freshly baked bread draw you into the Alberta Bakery. Ride the rails behind a real thundering steam locomotive. Framed by the majestic Rockies, you'll pass through billowing trees and near blue water for breathtaking views and a true western experience. You can also board the S.S. Moyie for a steamwheeler cruise on the Glenmore Reservoir and enjoy the thrills of the antique midway.

SCHEDULES and FARES
Heritage Park is open late May through Labor Day. Adult day passes are generally under $15 U.S. Please call or check website for current schedules and fares.

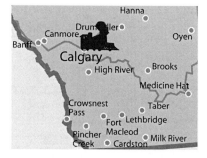

EQUIPMENT
Locomotives
1909 port steam 0-4-0T (2)
1902 No. 3 Vul Steam 0-4-0T
1905 No. 4 CP CPR steam 0-6-0
1942 No. 2023 USA ALCO steam 0-6-0
1944 No. 2024 Lima steam 0-6-0
1949 No. 5931 CPR MLW steam 2-10-4
1944 No. 7019 CPR 1 MLW S2 1000

CONTACT
Heritage Park Historical Village
1900 Heritage Dr. S.W.
Calgary, Alberta
T2V 2X3
403-268-8500
403-268-8501 (fax)
sales@heritagepark.ab.ca
www.heritagepark.ca

Photos: Heritage Park Historical Village

ROYAL CANADIAN PACIFIC
Calgary, AB

The signature Royal Canadian Pacific journey is the Golden/Crowsnest Excursion. This is a 6-day, 5-night, 650 mile loop starting from Calgary, Alberta. The train travels through Banff National Park in the Canadian Rockies, through the Columbia River Valley and back to Calgary via the Crowsnest Pass and Lethbridge.

The Royal Canadian Pacific route follows the historic CPR line that was completed in 1885 to form Canada's first transcontinental railway. Construction of the CPR through the rugged Canadian West was considered one of the greatest engineering feats of that period.

Today, guests enjoy world-class catering on board the train. Meals are served in elegant dining cars with white glove service. Special dietary needs can be accommodated.

SCHEDULES and FARES
Excursions range from $3,750 to $7,000 based on the trip and occupancy. Please call or check website for current schedules and fares.

EQUIPMENT
1953 Locomotive No.1400 General Motors CPR diesel
Observation day car: "Mount Stephen" w. dining capacity 12 persons
4 business cars
Sleeping car: "NR Crump"

CONTACT
Royal Canadian Pacific
133 9th Avenue SW
Calgary, AB T2P 2M3
877-665-3044 (North America)
403-508-1400 (direct)
403-508-1409 (fax)
info@royalcanadianpacific.com
www.cprtours.com

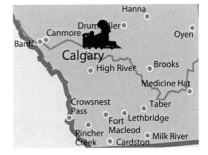

Photos: Royal Canadian Pacific

VIA RAIL CANADA/THE SKEENA
Jasper, AB

VIA Rail Canada operates Canada's national passenger rail service with up to 492 trains weekly on 12,500 kilometres of track, connecting over 450 Canadian communities. With approximately 3,000 employees, VIA carries more than 4 million passengers a year. Of all the runs, one of the most popular is the Skeena.

VIA Rail's Skeena takes you on a 2-day, 725 miles trip between Jasper National Park, in the heart of the Canadian Rockies, and Prince Rupert on the Pacific coast, with an overnight stop in Prince George. There are no on-board sleeping accommodations, but passengers can book their own accommodations in Prince George. The Skeena offers travelers the chance to experience the region's scenery and Native culture.

You have your choice of travel classes Comfort class (economy) is available year round and lets you discover the region at the best possible price. Totem class is available only in peak season (from mid-May to late September) and includes meals and exclusive access to Park car and its panoramic dome. Totem Deluxe class, is also available only in the peak season includes meals and, as an exclusive benefit, a seat throughout the journey in the new Panorama car, which is fully-glass enclosed.

VIA Rail Canada offers train trips in these other regions as well: The Rockies and Pacific region, the Prairies and northern Manitoba, Ontario, Quebec, and the Atlantic region.

SCHEDULES and FARES
Schedules and fares depend on the route chosen. Please call or check website for current schedules and fares.

EQUIPMENT
Park car - Stainless steel lounge dome observation car.
Panorama car - Fully-glass enclosed car
Comfort car - Stainless steel coach car

CONTACT
The Skeena
607 Connaught Dr
Jasper, AB
T0E 1E0
888-VIA-Rail
888-842-7245
800-268-9503 (TTY)
www.viarail.ca

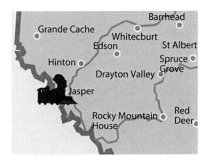

Photos:Via Rail Canada - The Skeena

Did You Know...

Guatemala has 200 miles of operating 914 mm narrow gauge railroads between Guatemala City and Puerto Barrios, managed by US based Railroad Development Corporation.

CANADA / BRITISH COLUMBIA

Dease Lake

Fort Nelson

Stewart

Fort St John
Hudson's Hope
Dawson Creek
New Hazelton   Chetwynd
Mackenzie
Terrace   Smithers
upert   Tumbler Ridge
timat   Houston
Burns Lake   Fort St James
Fraser Lake
Vanderhoof
Prince George

McBride
Quesne
Wells
Bella Coola   Valumount

Williams Lake

100 Mile House

lardy
t Alice   Ashcroft   Revelstoke   Golder
Port McNeill   Lillooet
Campbell River   Kanoloops   Salmon Arm   Invermere
Courtenay   Powell   Whistler   Merritt   Vernon   Nakusp
River
Port Alberni   Squamish   Kelowna   rd
Tofino   Vancouver   Summerland   Nelson   Steele
Ucluelet   Hope   Penticton   Cranbrook
Parksville   Abbotsford   Castlegar
Nanaimo   Osoyoos   Trail   Creston
Ladysmith   Sicney
Duncan   Saanich
Victoria

ALBERNI PACIFIC RAILWAY
Port Alberni, BC

The Alberni Pacific Railway is the rail operating part of the Western Vancouver Island Industrial Heritage Society located in Port Alberni on Canada's beautiful Vancouver Island.

Your train leaves from a restored 1912 CPR Station in downtown Port Alberni to the McLean Mill National Historic Site about 6 miles away. This scenic trip winds through the city and then out into the surrounding forest on its way to the restored and operating steam sawmill and lumber camp. The McLean Mill has sawmill demonstrations, guided theatrical tours, stage shows, food and a gift shop.

The Society has been active in restoring both railway rolling stock and other industrial artifacts such as logging trucks, lumber carriers, graders and numerous small pieces of equipment. It is made up of a group of volunteers that registered as a society in 1983. The Society operated the railway along the industrial waterfront in Port Alberni until 2000. The McLean Mill run began in 2001.

SCHEDULES and FARES
The Alberni Pacific Railway runs from mid-June through Labour Day. All fares include Mill admission. Adult fares are generally under $25. Reservations are not required but are recommended for groups of 15 or more. Please call or check website for current schedules and fares.

EQUIPMENT
1929 Baldwin 2-8-2T logging locomotive
42-ton Shay locomotive No.2
x-CPR--Alco RS3 No.8427
GE 44 ton No.11
Five rebuilt CN cabooses for passenger cars
1928 Westminster Ironworks "Buda" gas switcher
1924 Plymouth switcher No.107

CONTACT
Alberni Pacific Railway
Site 125, C14
Port Alberni, BC
V9Y 7L5
250-723-1376
250-723-5910 (fax)
email@alberniheritage.com
www.alberniheritage.com

Photos: Alberni Pacific Railway

BRITISH COLUMBIA FOREST DISCOVERY CENTRE
Duncan, BC

One hour north of Victoria, just north of Duncan, the BC Forest Discovery Centre makes a great day-trip. The 40-hectare (100-acre) site includes a recreational railway, indoor and outdoor exhibits as well as forest and nature trails.

The early 1900's steam train and gasoline electric locomotive provide visitors with an unforgettable experience on a 2.2 kilometer figure-eight loop of narrow gauge track while offering an introduction and overview of the site. Whistle stops throughout the scenic grounds let you explore on foot and still ride the train back to the entrance at Alderlea Station. Ride through the Douglas Fir forest, pass by the train sheds and sawmill, cross the timber trestle over Somenos Lake, and watch as engines take on water from an 1880s-style water tower.

SCHEDULES and FARES
The British Columbia Forest Discovery Centre is open from mid-April through October. Train rides are no longer included with admission to the Centre. Unlimited train rides are available. Please call or check website for current schedules and fares.

EQUIPMENT
Bloedel Stewart & Welch No. 1, Old One-Spot 42 ton standard Class "B"
Hillcrest Lumber Company No. 1 28 ton Class "B" 2-truck locomotive
Shawnigan Lake Lumber Company No. 2 23-25 ton Class "B" Climax locomotive
Mayo Lumber Company No. 3 50 ton standard Class "B" Hillcrest Lumber
Company No. 9 45 ton standard Class "B" Climax locomotive
Locomotive No. 25 3 foot narrow gauge 0-4-0 saddle tank engine
Locomotive No. 24 3 foot narrow gauge 0-4-0 saddle tank
No. 27 Speeder 2-truck 3 foot narrow gauge eight wheel speeder
White Pass No. 1 3 foot narrow gauge diesel electric
Plymouth No. 26 11 ton 3 foot narrow gauge locomotive
Sandy No. 23 Plymouth 3 foot narrow gauge Plymouth locomotive
Witcome No. 9 Standard 110 ton diesel electric locomotive

CONTACT
BC Forest Discovery Centre
2892 Drinkwater Road
Duncan, BC,
V9L 6C2
250-715-1113
250-715-1170 (fax)
bcfm@islandnet.com
www.bcforestmuseum.com

Photos: British Columbia Forest Discovery Centre

CANADA MUSEUM OF RAIL TRAVEL
Cranbrook, BC

The Canada Museum of Rail Travel in Cranbrook, British Columbia houses a very specialized railway heritage collection. It is the result of one person with a vision and enough dedication to inspire the people around him. Garry Anderson wrote a thesis while at the University of British Columbia involving Cranbrook's downtown "cityscape" potential. This potential included heritage landmark features for preservation. Although the project is now a wrold class historic railway, it was originally going to involve only a car or two that would be just enough to give the town an added reminder of its railway heritage.

Today, Cranbrook boasts perhaps the only yard left on the Canadian Pacific Railway (CPR) system with its original octagonal wooden water tower, plus operating turntable, roundhouse, and a two-story wooden station from the turn of the century (albeit modernized). Although the modern part of this story began in the 1970's, the railway in Cranbrook began in 1898 because of the arrival of the Canadian Pacific Railway. Visitors to the museum get to revisit the past and see how it has impacted the present.

SCHEDULES AND FARES
The Canadian Museum of Rail Travel is open year round. Please call or check website for current schedules and fares.

EQUIPMENT
Trans Canada Limited, 1929
Soo-Spokane Train Deluxe, 1907
"CP" Strathcona, 1927
Redvers, 1928

CONTACT
Canada Museum of Rail Travel
57 Van Horne Street S.
Cranbrook, BC
V1C 1Y7
250-489-3918
mail@trainsdeluxe.com
www.trainsdeluxe.com

Photos: Canada Museum of Rail Travel

FORT STEELE RAILWAY
Steele, BC

Visitors to Fort Steele Heritage Town board the steam train and are transported back in time to an era when huge man-made machines made every person a triumphant master of nature. The roar and rush of escaping steam, the clatter of the rails and the winsome call of the whistle will take you to places you will remember forever. The 2 km steam train ride takes you to a scenic viewpoint overlooking Fort Steele and the Kootenay River. Passengers board the train at the Fort Steele Steam Railway Station.

Over the next several years Fort Steele Heritage Town intends to expend time and energy bringing the railway operation to focus on the glory days of East Kootenay railway logging in the 1920s. This exhibit will continue to grow in excitement, interest and interpretive possibilities.

SCHEDULES and FARES
The park is open year-round as weather permits. The trains run from July through September. Please call or check website for current schedules and fares.

CONTACT
Fort Steele Heritage Town
9851 Highway 93/95
Fort Steele, BC
V0B 1N0
250-417-6000
250-489-2624 (fax)
info@fortsteele.bc.ca
www.fortsteele.ca

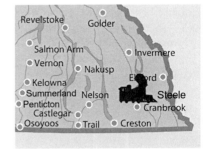

Photos: Phalley

KETTLE VALLEY STEAM RAILWAY SOCIETY
Summerland, BC

The Kettle Valley Steam Railway offers a 90 minute journey through the scenic beauty of Summerland in the heart of British Columbia's fruit and wine region – the Okanagan Valley. One of B.C.'s few operational steam railways, it takes passengers along the only preserved section of the historic Kettle Valley Railway line constructed between 1910 and 1915. The KVSR 's locomotive #3716 was built in 1912. Not only does she have 100 years under her cow catcher – she is the only Canadian Pacific Railway 2-8-0 consolidation N2b steam locomotive still working today. The #3716, also named the "Spirit of Summerland", pulls two vintage passenger coaches and three open air cars. Friendly, informative guides bring the history of the railway alive as the train steams along hillsides overlooking picturesque orchards and vineyards and onto the Trout Creek Bridge which is 238 feet above the canyon floor. It is the highest steel girder bridge built on the original KVR line.

The Kettle Valley Steam Railway is operated by the Kettle Valley Railway Society, a non-profit, charitable organization that welcomes memberships in order to continue the preservation and operation of this important historic site.

SCHEDULES and FARES
The Kettle Valley Steam Railway operates from May through October (limited schedule). There are a variety of special events including the Great Train Robbery & BBQ on specified dates during the season. Please call or check website for current schedule and fares

EQUIPMENT
1912 N2b Consolidation No. 3716 Montreal Locomotive Works, Quebec, Canada 2-8-0
1956 Alco Diesel - #803-S6, 6 cylinder 251B Prime Mover- 900 HP
1966 Alco Diesel - #804- T6DL 400 MODEL 251B Prime Mover -1000 HP

CONTACT
Kettle Valley Steam Railway
180404 Bathville Road, Summerland BC, V0H
1Z0
Phone 250-494-8422 /
Toll free in North America 877-494-8424
kvr@telus.net www.kettlevalleyrail.org
Photos: Doug Campbellinformation@ketteval-
leyrail.org
www.kettlevalleyrail.org

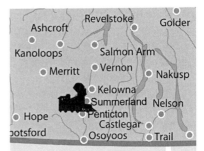

Photos: Kettle Valley Steam Railway

WEST COAST RAILWAY HERITAGE PARK
Vancouver, BC

The origin of the West Coast Railway
Association (WCRA) can be traced back to
1958 when the steam engine was in its last
days. As history was passing before their
eyes, the pioneers of the Association began
meeting on a regular basis and started
acquiring a collection of rail cars and artifacts.
Over the years the Association has grown and
evolved but its purpose remains the same: to
collect, preserve and restore railway cars and
artifacts and operate a licensed railway. Both of these goals are accomplished at
the West Coast Railway Heritage Park and with West Coast Rail Tours.

The West Coast Railway Heritage Park is the largest in Western Canada and a
major attraction with excellent tourist and rail-fan facilities. It is situated in an

area of outstanding natural beauty about one
hour north of Vancouver by car. The extensive
tour program attracts passengers who enjoy
the romance and prestige of train travel
throughout British Columbia. The tours are a
must for railway enthusiasts, photography
buffs, geography devotees, and those who just
want to explore more of British Columbia. The
choices for excursions are extensive and can
suit any pocketbook.

SCHEDULES and FARES
There are various tours scheduled from late April through October from departure locations in the Vancouver area. Please call or check website for current schedules and fares.

EQUIPMENT
13 locomotives
16 passenger cars
15 freight cars

CONTACT
West Coast Railway Association
Box 2790 Stn Terminal
Vancouver, BC
V6B 3X2
604-898-9336 (Heritage Park)
604-524-1011 (In Vancouver)
www.wcra.org

Photos: West Coast Railway Heritage Park

Did You Know...

A heritage railway, preserved railway, or tourist railroad is a term used for a railway that is run as a tourist attraction, usually by volunteers, and seeks to recreate railway scenes of the past.

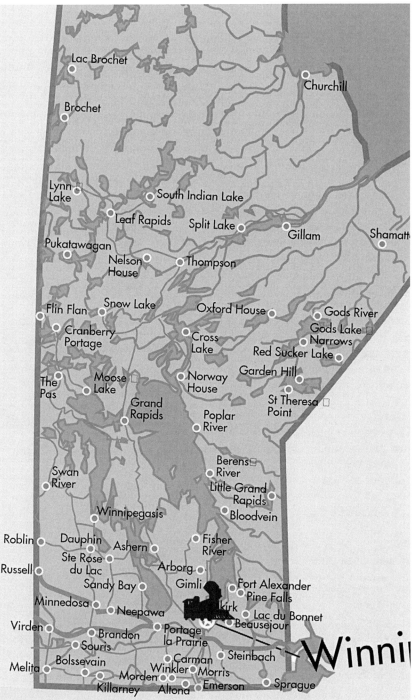

Lac Brochet

Churchill

Brochet

Lynn Lake

South Indian Lake

Leaf Rapids

Split Lake

Gillam

Shamatt

Pukatawagan

Nelson House

Thompson

Flin Flan

Snow Lake

Oxford House

Gods River

Cranberry Portage

Cross Lake

Gods Lake Narrows

Red Sucker Lake

The Pas

Moose Lake

Norway House

Garden Hill

St Theresa Point

Grand Rapids

Poplar River

Swan River

Berens River

Little Grand Rapids

Winnipegasis

Bloodvein

Roblin

Dauphin

Ashern

Fisher River

Russell

Ste Rose du Lac

Arborg

Sandy Bay

Gimli

Fort Alexander
Pine Falls

Minnedosa

Neepawa

kirk

Lac du Bonnet

Virden

Portage la Prairie

Beausejour

Brandon

Souris

Melita

Bolssevain

Carman

Steinbach

Winkler

Morris

Morden

Killarney

Altona

Emerson

Sprague

Winni

PRAIRIE DOG CENTRAL RAILWAY
Winnipeg, MB

A visit to Prairie Dog Central Railway means a trip aboard a vintage train. It gives visitors an idea of how early settlers got around. As they travel in the comfort of a fully restored, historic wooden coach, built between 1901 and 1913. History surrounds them, as they imagine former dignitaries, farmers and prime ministers, who once traveled this same route.

The Prairie Dog Central is pulled by either of two vintage locomotives, an 1882 steam engine or a 1952 vintage diesel, depending upon availability. Both locomotives played an important role in shaping Canadian heritage in the transportation industry. Other than by horse and wagon, the railway was once the only way to cross this vast land. Expect to spend two and a half hours touring the countryside.

SCHEDULES and FARES
The Prairie Dog Central Railway is open mid May to late September. Adult fares are generally under $20. There are numerous excursions, including dinner trains available. Please call or check website for current schedules and fares.

EQUIPMENT
Ex-CN Bunkcar No. 68593, built in 1911 by
   Canadian Car & Foundry Co. for the Grant Trunk Railway as No. 19552,
   Converted to Foreman's Car in 1941
Ex-CN hopper car used for coal storage
Ex-CN Boxcar No. 70733, built in 1905 for the Central Vermont by Western Steel Car & Foundry Co

CONTACT
The Vintage Locomotive Society INC.
P.O. Box 33021 RPO Polo Park
Winnipeg MB R3G 3N4
204-832-5259
866-751-2348
204-255-6641 (fax)
info@pdcrailway.com
www.vintagelocomotivesociety.mb.ca/index.html

Photos: c. 2005-2007 The Vintage Locomotive Society, Inc.

WINNIPEG RAILWAY MUSEUM
Winnipeg, MB

The Winnipeg Railway Museum houses vintage locomotives and other artifacts from the Prairie region. One of the highlights of the museum is the Countess of Dufferin. This locomotive, built in 1872, was first owned by Northern Pacific and used to build a portion of the Canadian Pacific Railway. Other highlights include a CNR caboose and a snow plow unit.

The museum also has an exhibit on the history of the Hudson Bay Railway which includes photographs, maps, and memorabilia.

The Winnipeg Railway Museum is operated by the Midwestern Rail Association, an organization committed to preserving the history and legacy of the railroads of the Prairie region.

SCHEDULES and FARES
The Winnipeg Railway Museum is open year-round on Saturdays and Sundays. From June through September, it is also open on Fridays. Admission for adults is generally under $5. Please call or check website for current schedules and fares.

EQUIPMENT
1958 CN GMD1 No.1900 diesel locomotive
1922 Mack rail bus - donated by Winnipeg Hydro, 1993
1946 Packard track inspection car - once operated by the Greater Winnipeg Water District Railway and the CPR
1921 CN 7188 combine car (colonist's car) - donated by CN Rail in 1975
1972 CN 79553 steel caboose - donated by CN Rail in 1993
1941 Chevrolet fire truck - donated by CN Rail
Whiting Class 5-TN track mobile - donated by Manitoba Hydro in 976
1922 CP Wood Express Refrigerator Car 5641
1926 CP Wood Express Refrigerator Car 5664
Pre-1930 CNR Wood Baggage Car 77573 - donated by CN Rail in July, 1975
1929 CNR WOOD single sheathed boxcar 74703 - donated by CN Rail in July, 1975
1911 CN 51031 Jordan Spreader - donated by CN Rail

CONTACT
Winnipeg Railway Museum
123 Main Street
Winnipeg, MB
R3C 1A3
204-942-4632
www.wpgrailwaymuseum.com/

Photos: Winnipeg Railway Museum

Did You Know...

The Middleton Steam Railway, located in England, is the world's oldest working railway. It was founded in 1758 and is now a heritage railway run by enthusiasts. The railway now operates passenger services on weekends and on public holidays over a 1 mile track.

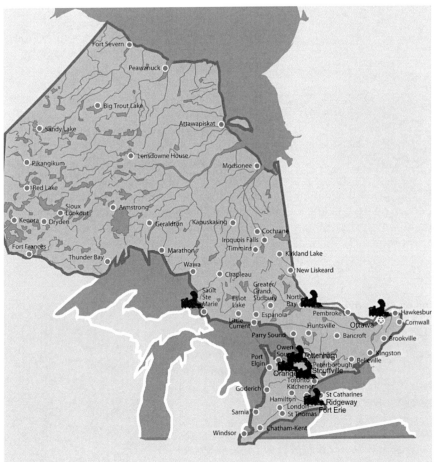

Fort Severn

Peawanuck

Big Trout Lake

Attawapiskat

sandy Lake

Lansdowne House

Moosonee

Pikangikum

Red Lake

Sioux
Lookout

Armstrong

Kenora Dryden

Geraldton Kapuskasing

Cochrane

Fort Frances

Iroquois Falls
Timmins

Thunder Bay

Marathon

Kirkland Lake

Wawa

New Liskeard

Chapleau

Greater/
Grand
Sudbury

Sault
Ste
Marie

Elliot
Lake

North
Bay

Espanola

Pembroke

Hawkesbur

Little
Current

Huntsville

Ottawa

Cornwall

Parry Sound

Bancroft

Brookville

Owen
Sound

Tottenham

Kingston

Port
Elgin

Peterborough
Stouffville

Belleville

Orange

Toronto
Kitchener

Goderich

Hamilton

St Catharines
Ridgeway
Fort Erie

Sarnia

London
St Thomas

Windsor

Chatham-Kent

ALGOMA CENTRAL RAILWAY / AGAWA CANYON TOUR TRAINS
Sault Ste. Marie, ON

The Agawa Canyon Tour Train operates daily, June to mid-October. Most visitors come to see the fall colors from mid-September through mid-October. During the Agawa Canyon tour you will relax in comfortable picture window coaches and enjoy breakfast and lunch in full service dining cars.

This 114-mile narrated journey just might take your breath away as you travel over towering trestles, alongside pristine northern lakes and rivers, and through granite rock formations. The area is known as the mixed forests of the Canadian Shield, a land made famous by Canada's most notable landscape artists - the Group of Seven. There is a two-hour stop in Agawa Canyon Park, where you can enjoy scenic hikes, cascading waterfalls or a quiet picnic lunch beside the Agawa River.

The Railway also offers a variety of other wilderness-by-rail adventures, from the one-day winter "Snow Train" tour to a "Tour of the Line" on its regular passenger train to Hearst, Ontario. You can also journey to remote wilderness fishing lodges, spend the night in a "Camp Car", or even take a "Tracks to Trails" snowmobile adventure.

The Algoma Central Railway was originally established in 1899 by American industrialist Francis H. Clergue. He wanted to open up the hinterland and transport the vast resources of timber and minerals to fuel his budding industries in Sault Ste. Marie. Though raw materials and freight are still the backbone of the Railway, it has become known worldwide for the Agawa Canyon train tours.

SCHEDULES and FARES
The Algoma Central Railway operates from June to mid-October. Schedules and fares vary according to excursion. Please call or check website for current schedules and fares.

EQUIPMENT
Locomotive CN Rail
GP 40's and SD 75's
28 refurbished coaches and 2 diners. The majority of which were built for C.N.R.
by Can Car in Montreal between 1952 and 1954
Private Car Agawa built by Barney & Smith in Dayton, Ohio, in 1913

CONTACT
Algoma Central Railway/Passenger Sales
129 Bay Street
Sault Ste. Marie, ON
P6A 6Y2
705-946-7300
800-242-9287
705-541-2989 (fax)
www.agawacanyontourtrain.com

Photos: Algoma Central Railway Agawa Canyon Tour Trains

Did You Know...

*The North American Railway
Foundation was formed to explore,
nurture and support railway safety,
efficiency and technology and to
educate and preserve the history of
railroads in the United States
and Canada.*

CANADA SCIENCE AND TECHNOLOGY MUSEUM
Ottawa, ON

This museum is the largest of its kind in Canada and features exhibits about all types of transportation - including rail. Visitors will learn about Canada's rail history as well as its present day operations.

Visitors to the museum get a hands-on look at artifact-rich exhibits featuring marine and land transportation, astronomy, communications, space, domestic technology, and computer technology. The museum's exhibits show how science and technology have changed Canada and influenced its people.

SCHEDULES and FARES
The Canada Science and Technology Museum is open daily from early May through Labor Day, then on Tuesday through Sunday from Labor Day to April. It is closed on Christmas Day. Admission to the museum includes a free train ride in July and August. Admission is generally under $10. Please call or check website for current schedule and fares.

EQUIPMENT
1923 Shay steam locomotive
No. 6510 passenger locomotive
Nos. 2560, 4001, 4284, 2542, 5320, 5542, 5304, 9552 9500, 5320, 4284, 1646, and 2542 diesel-electric Montreal locomotives

CONTACT
Canada Science and Technology Museum
P.O. Box 9724
Ottawa, ON
K1G 5A3
613-991-3044
613-991-9207 (TTY)
cts@technomuses.ca
www.sciencetech.technomuses.ca

Photos: Canada Science and Technology Museum

CREDIT VALLEY EXPLORER TOUR TRAIN
Orangeville, ON

The Credit Valley Explorer Tour Train offers a ride through Southern Ontario with highlights that include a 1,146 foot long railway trestle bridge spanning the Credit Valley and the Forks of the Credit River. This 70km adventure travels along the same route established 127 years ago.

Each season offers unique views and different tour train services through the heart of the Credit Valley. Known for its rolling hills, deep valleys, unsurpassed fall colors and for being the headwaters of four major river systems, the Hills of Headwaters region provides a spectacular backdrop for the Credit Valley Explorer's journey.

Passengers will enjoy the Credit Valley Explorer's first-class seating, large picture windows and complimentary refreshments, all in a comfortable climate-controlled environment. Tours include interpretive commentary and a souvenir mile-by-mile printed tour guide.

SCHEDULES and FARES
The Credit Valley Explorer Tour Train operates year-round. Fares and departure times vary by excursion. Please call or check website for details.

EQUIPMENT
GP9 locomotives

CONTACT
Credit Valley Explorer Tour Train
P.O. Box 351
Orangeville, ON
L9W 2Z7
888-346-0046
www.creditvalleyexplorer.com

Photos: Credit Valley Exploer Tour Train

FORT ERIE RAILROAD MUSEUM
Ridgeway, ON

At the Fort Erie Railroad Museum visitors can climb into the cab and sit where engineers once commanded the mighty locomotive. The caboose is also open for visitors to stroll through and marvel at the rough comforts of this compact "mobile home". The Canadian National Railway Ridgeway Station, c.1910, and the 1873 B-1 Grand Trunk Railway Station feature railroading exhibits, a reference library and a gift shop. Visitors will also see a "fireless" steam engine, telegraphic equipment, and other artifacts representing Fort Erie's railroad history.

The Niagara Region has enough in natural beauty and attractions to keep travelers entertained for weeks! From Niagara Falls and the beautiful sand beaches of Lake Erie to the Welland Canal, wine regions and the Shaw festival, there is truly something for the whole family.

SCHEDULES and FARES
The Fort Erie Railroad Museum is open daily June through August. The museum is closed September to May. Adult entrance fees are generally under $5.

EQUIPMENT
(On Display)
Locomotive CN No. 6218
Caboose CN No. 79138

CONTACT
Fort Erie Museum Board
400 Central Avenue,
Fort Erie, ON
L2A 6E2
905-894-5322
905-894-6851 (fax)
museum@forterie.on.ca
www.forterie.on.ca/

Photos: Fort Erie Railroad Museum

POLAR BEAR EXPRESS
North Bay, ON

The Polar Bear Express departs Cochrane for an incredible 186-mile journey to the Arctic Tidewater at Moosonee. The train travels along the "old highways" of the fur trade, the historic Abitibi and Moose rivers, while enjoying the scenery of sparsely populated forests, tranquil lakes and muskeg, or peat bog.

At Moosonee, visitors will begin to understand the realities of this frontier community by taking a freighter canoe across the Moose River to Moose Factory, founded more than 300 years ago by the Hudson's Bay Company. During your train trip, enjoy the on-board services including dinners, snacks and the entertaiment/activity car.

The Polar Bear Express is owned and operated by the Ontario Northland Transportation Commission.

SCHEDULES and FARES
The Polar Express runs everyday, except Monday, from mid June through late August. Adult fares are generally under $100. Please call or check website for current schedules and fares.

EQUIPMENT
The Polar Bear Express consists of passenger cars, a dining car, a smoking lounge, an entertainment car, and a snack car.

CONTACT
Ontario Northland
555 Oak Street East
North Bay, ON
P1B 8L3
800-268-9281 (toll free in Canada & US)
705-495-4745 (fax)
choochoo@polarbearexpress.ca
www.polarbearexpress.ca/

Photos: Polar Bear Express

SOUTH SIMCOE RAILWAY
Tottenham, ON

The South Simcoe Railway offers excursions that travel through scenic, rolling countryside through the Beeton Creek Valley, from Tottenham to Beeton, Ontario. Tottenham is located about 50 minutes north of Toronto.

Passengers travel in restored 1920's coaches over the rails of a century-old branchline that once connected Hamilton with Barrie and Collingwood. Excursion trains are pulled by one of two restored, authentic steam locomotives. Historic locomotive No.136 was built in 1883, when Sir John A. Macdonald was Prime Minister of Canada, and helped to build the transcontinental railway that joined the country together in 1885. The excursions are highlighted by the conductor's friendly, informative commentary that both adults and children will enjoy.

SCHEDULES and FARES
South Simcoe Railway operates from May through October. Adult fares are generally under $15. Please call or check website for current schedules and fares.

EQUIPMENT
No. 136 Rogers Locomotive Works 4-4-0, built in 1883
No. 1057 Canadian Locomotive Company 4-6-0, built in 1912
Vintage open window bay coaches dating to the 1920s

CONTACT
South Simcoe Railway Heritage Corp.
P.O. Box 186
Tottenham, ON
L0G 1W0
905-936-5815
info@steamtrain.com
www.steamtrain.com

Photos: South Simcoe Railway Heritage Corp.

YORK-DURHAM HERITAGE RAILWAY
Stouffville, ON

The York-Durham Heritage Railway operates a tourist train on the old railway line from Uxbridge to Stouffville. It is a 12-mile excursion that began in the 1990s. For authenticity none of the coaches are air conditioned, but all the windows open. The railway is run entirely by volunteers, very few of whom earn their living with a railway. Although the rail line dates back to the 1800s, the York-Durham Heritage Railway, as we know it, was founded in 1986. Founding members dreamed of operating a tourist train on the old railway line from Stouffville to Uxbridge and beyond. It took ten years for the York-Durham Heritage Railway to become a reality. Ten years of hard work, disappointments, dedication and persistence by the many individuals involved made this railway happen.

SCHEDULES and FARES
The York-Durham Heritage Railway schedule varies but adult fares are generally under $20. Please call or visit website for current schedules and fares.

EQUIPMENT
RS-3 No. 1310, built by Montreal Locomotive Works (MLW) in 1951
RS-3 No. 22, built by Montreal Locomotive Works (MLW) in 1955
RS-11 No. 3612, built by American Locomotive Co. (ALCO) in 1956
Coach No. 4960, built by Pullman in 1919, originally built as a Colonist sleeper
Baggage car No. 9636, built by National Steel Car in 1957
Coaches Nos. 3232 and 3209 are former CN day coaches

386 Canada/Ontario

CONTACT
York-Durham Heritage Railway
P.O. Box 462
Stouffville, ON
L4A 7Z7
905-852-3696
info@ydhr.on.ca
www.ydhr.on.ca

Photos: York-Durham Heritage Railway

Did You Know...

The Strasburg Rail Road, located near Strasburg, Pennsylvania, is a steam locomotive-powered tourist railroad in the heart of Pennsylvania dating back to 1832. In 2008, the Strasburg Rail Road celebrated 50 years as a tourist railroad.

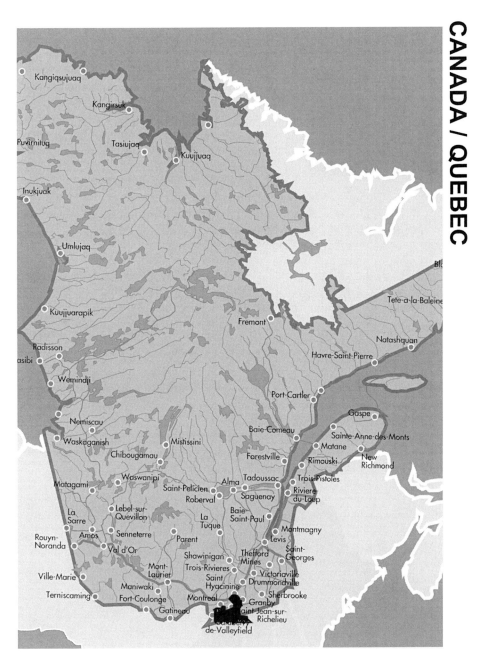

CANADIAN RAILWAY MUSEUM
St. Constants, QU

The Canadian Railway Museum has developed an interactive way for visitors to learn the history of railways in Canada. The garden train operates daily while the observation streetcar, nicknamed the Golden Chariot, runs when the weather permits. And every Sunday, a passenger train takes visitors for a short trip.

The museum, which opened in 1961, is home to the largest collection of railway equipment in Canada. In fact, the National Museums of Canada recognized it in 1978 as being the specialized museum in Canadian Railway history. The Museum is run by a dedicated group of volunteers: The Canadian Railroad Historical Association.

SCHEDULES and FARES
The Canadian Railway Museum is open from the end of June through late April. Adult entrance fees are generally under $15. Please call or check website for current schedules and fares.

EQUIPMENT
The collection includes 142 railway vehicles, some of which are unique, including the oldest surviving Canadian-built steam locomotive (CP 144), the largest steam locomotive built in Canada and the last to be built for a Canadian standard gauge railway (CP 5935).

CONTACT
Canadian Railway Museum
110 St-Pierre Street,
St. Constants, QU
J5A 1G7
450-632-2410
450-638-1563 (fax)
info@exporail.org
www.exporail.org

Photos: Canadian Railway Museum

List of Other Railway-Related Sites and Attractions

ALABAMA

Foley Railway Museum
Site Location: 125 E Laurel Ave, Foley AL 36536
Phone: 251-943-1818
Website: www.foleyrailroadmuseum.com
E-Mail: foleymuseum@gulftel.com

Fort Payne Depot Museum
Site Location: 105 Fifth St NE, Fort Payne AL 35968
Phone: 256-845-5714
Website: www.fortpaynedepotmuseum.com
E-Mail: depotmusem@bellsouth.net

Wales West Light Railway
Site Location: 13650 Smiley St, Silverhill AL 36576
Phone: 888-569-5337
Website: www.waleswest.com
E-Mail: redandkfd@hotmail.com

ALASKA

Tanana Valley Railroad
Site Location: 2300 Airport Way, Fairbanks AK 99708
Phone: 907-459-7421
Website: www.ftvrr.org
E-Mail: ftvrr.inc@gmail.com

ARIZONA

Gadsden-Pacific Division Toy Train Operating Museum
Site Location: 3975 N Miller, Tucson AZ 85754
Phone: 520-888-2222
Website: www.gpdToyTrainMuseum.com
E-Mail: lEnglish@aol.com

Goldfield Ghost Town
Site Location: 4650 N. Mammoth Mine Rd, Goldfield AZ 85219
Phone: 480-983-0333
Website: www.goldfieldghosttown.com
Karrels' Double K Ranch Bed & Breakfast
Site Location: 330 N Smokey Topaz Ln, Tucson AZ 85749
Phone: 520-749-5345
Website: www.doublekranch.com

Maricopa Live Steamers
Site Location: 22822 N 43rd Ave, Phoenix AZ 85310
Phone: 623-925-1811
Website: www.maricopalivesteamers.com

McCormick-Stillman Railroad Park
Site Location: 7301 E Indan Bend Rd, Scottsdale AZ 85250
Phone: 480-312-2312
Website: www.therailroadpark.com

Sierra Madre Express
Site Location: 4415 S Contractors Way, Tucson AZ 85726
Phone: 800-666-0346 or 520-747-0346
Website: www.sierramadreexpress.com
E-Mail: adventure@sierramadreexpress.com

Southern Arizona Transportation Museum
Site Location: 414 N Toole Ave, Tucson AZ 85701
Phone: 520-623-2223
Website: www.tucsonhistoricdepot.org
E-Mail: ContactUs@TucsonHistoricDepot.org

ARKANSAS

Frisco Depot Museum – Mammoth Spring State Park
Site Location: Highway 9 and Highway 63, Mammoth Spring AR72554
Phone: 870-625-7364
Website: www.arkansasstateparks.com/mammoth-spring
E-Mail: mammothspring@arkansas.com

CALIFORNIA

Billy Jones Wildcat Railroad
Site Location: 110 Blossom Hill Rd, Los Gatos CA 95032
Phone: 408-395-7433
Website: www.bjwrr.com
E-Mail: bjwrr1@aol.com

Cable Car Museum
1201 Mason St, San Francisco CA 94108
415.474.1887
www.cablecarmuseum.org

Calico & Odessa Railroad
Site Location: 36600 Ghost Town Rd, Yermo CA 92398
Phone: 760-254-2117
Website: www.calicotown.com

Folsom Valley Railway/Folsom City Zoo
Site Location: 121 Dunstable Way, Folsom CA 95630
Phone: 91-983-1873
Website: www.folsomvalleyrailway.com

Fort Humbolt State Park
Site Location: 3431 Fort Ave,Eureka CA 95502
Phone: 707-445-6567
Website: timberheritage.org
E-Mail: info@timberheritage.org

Knott's Berry Farm
Site Location: 8039 Beach Blvd, Buena Park CA
Phone: 714-220-5200
Website: www.knotts.com
E-Mail: info@knotts.com

Irvine Park Railroad
Site Location: 1 Irvine Park Rd, Orange CA 92862
Phone: 714-220-5200
Website: www.irvineparkrr.com

Laws Railroad Museum
Site Location: Silver Canyon Rd, Bishop CA 93515
Phone: 760-873-5950
Website: lawsmuseum.org

Lomita Railroad Museum
Site Location: 2137 W 250th St, Lomita CA 90717
Phone: 310-326-6255
Website: www.lomita-rr.org
E-Mail: f.bilyeu@lomita.com

Los Angeles Live Steamers Railroad Museum
Site Location: 5202 Zoo Dr, Los Angeles CA 90027
Phone: 323-662-8030
Website: www.lals.org

National City Depot
Site Location: 922 W. 23rd St, National City CA
      91950
Phone: 619-474-4400
Website: www.sdera.org/depot.shtml

Nevada County Narrow Gauge Railroad and
      Transportation Museum
Site Location: 5 Kidder Ct, Nevada City CA 95959
Phone: 530-470-0902
Website: www.ncngrrmuseum.org
E-Mail: contact@ncngrrmuseum.org

Orange County Model Engineers
Site Location: 2480 Placentia Ave,
      Costa Mesa CA 92628
Phone: 949-54-TRAIN
Website: www.livesteamclubs.com

Poway-Midland Railroad
Site Location: 14134 Midland Rd, Poway CA 92074
Phone: 858-486-4063
Website: www.powaymidlandrr.org
E-Mail: pmrr-info@cox.net

Rail Journeys West
Site Location: 3770 Flora Vista Ave,
      Santa Clara CA 95051
Phone: 408-241-7807
Website: www.railjourneyswest.com
E-Mail: info@railjourneyswest.com

Railroad Park Resort
Site Location: 100 Railroad Park Rd,
      Dunsmuir CA 96025
Phone: 530-235-4440
Website: rrpark.com

Railway & Locomotive Historical Society,
      Southern California Chapter
Site Location: Fairplex, Pomona CA
Phone: 909-623-0190
Website: www.trainweb.org/rlhs
E-Mail: rlhs-pomona@rrmail.com

Redwood Valley Railway
Site Location: Grizzly Peak Blvd and Lomas
      Cantadas Rd, Tilden Regional Park,
      CA 94705
Phone: 510-548-6100
Website: redwoodvalleyrailway.com
E-Mail: rvry@redwoodvalleyrailway.com

Riverside Live Steamers
Site Location: 1496 Columbia Ave, Riverside CA
      94705
Phone: 951-779-9024
Website: www.steamonly.org

Sacramento Valley Live Steamers
Site Location: 2197 Chase Drive, Sacramento CA
      95670
Phone: 916-361-7140
Website: www.svlsrm.org

San Diego Model Railroad Museum
Site Location: 1649 El Prado, San Diego CA 92101
Phone: 619-696-0199
Website: www.sdmrm.org
E-Mail: info@sdmrm.org

South Coast Railroad Museum
Site Location: 300 N Los Carneros Rd,
Goleta CA 93117
Phone: 805-964-3540
Website: www.goletadepot.org

Travel Town Transportation Museum
5200 Zoo Dr, Los Angelos, CA 90027
323.662.5874
www.laparks.org/grifmet/tt/index.htm
traveltown@lacity.org

Waterfront Red Car Line
Site Location: 6th St at Harbor Blvd,
San Pedro CA 90731
Phone: 310-732-3473
Website: www.railwaypreservation.com/page8.html
E-Mail: jsmatlak@earthlink.net

Western America Railroad Museum
Site Location: 685 N First St, Barstow CA 92311
Phone: 760-256-WARM
Website: www.barstowrailmuseum.org
E-Mail: warm95@verizon.net

COLORADO
Boulder County Railway Historical Society
Site Location: Valmont and Indian Roads,
Boulder CO 80544
Phone: 303-809-6105
Website: www.bcrhs.org
E-Mail: bcrhs@bcrhs.org

Denver Rail Heritage Society – Platte Valley Trolley
Site Location: 23rd and Water St, Denver CO 80201
Phone: 303-458-6255
Website: www.denvertrolley.org
E-Mail: pvt@denvertrolley.org

Fort Collins Municipal Railway
Site Location: 1500 W Oak St, Fort Collins, CO 80521
Phone: 970-224-5372
Website: www.fortnet.org/trolley

Forney Museum of Transportation
Site Location: 4303 Brighton Blvd, Denver CO 80216
Phone: 303-297-1113
Website: www.forneymuseum.org
E-Mail: museum@forneymuseum.org

Limon Heritage Museum & Railroad Park
Site Location: 899 1st St, Limon CO 80828
Phone: 719-775-8605
Website: www.townoflimon.com

Museum of Northwest Colorado
Site Location: 590 Yampa Ave, Craig CO 81625
Phone: 970-824-6360
Website: www.museumnwco.org
E-Mail: musnwco@moffatcounty.net

Platte Valley Trolley
Site Location: 15th St and Platte St, Denver CO
Phone: 303-458-6255
Website: www.denvertrolley.org
E-Mail: pvt@denvertrolley.org

Ridgway Railroad Museum
Site Location: 150 Racecourse Rd, Ridgway CO 81432
Phone: 970-626-5181
Website: www.ridgwayrailroadmuseum.org
E-Mail: ridgwayrailroadmuseum@ouraynet.com

Tiny Town Railroad
Site Location: 6249 S Turkey Creek Rd, Tiny Town CO 80465
Phone: 303-697-6829
Website: www.tinytownrailroad.com

Windsor Museum
Site Location: 116 N 5th St, Windsor CO 80550
Phone: 970-674-2443
Website: www.ci.windsor.co.us

CONNECTICUT
SoNo Switch Tower Museum
Site Location: 77 Washington St,
South Norwalk CT 06854
Phone: 203-246-6958
Website: www.westctnrhs.org/tower.htm
E-Mail: info@westctnrhs.org

FLORIDA
Boca Express Train Museum
Site Location: FEC Railway Station 747 South Dixie Hwy, Boca Raton FL 33428
Phone: 561-395-6766
Website: www.bocahistory.org

Central Florida Railroad Museum
Site Location: 101 S Boyd St, Winter Garden FL 32803
Phone: 407-656-0559
Website: www.wghf.org/aboutrrm.htm
E-Mail: museum@WGHF.org

Mount Dora Trolley
Site Location: 100 North Alexander St, Mount Dora FL 3257
Phone: 352-385-1023

Naples Depot
Site Location: 1051 Fifth Ave S, Naples FL 34102
Phone: 239-262-1776
Website: www.colliermuseums.org/naples_depot.php

Railroad Museum of South Florida's Train Village
Site Location: 7330 Gladiolus Dr, Fort Meyers. FL 33911
Phone: 941-481-7565
Website: www.trainweb.org/lprr

TECO Line Streetcar System
Site Location: St. Pete Times Forum Dr, Tampa FL
Phone: 813-254-4278
Website: www.tecolinestreetcar.org
E-Mail: riverl@gohart.org

GEORGIA
Agrirama Musem of Culture & Historic Village
Site Location: 1392 Whiddon Mill Rd, Tifton GA 31793
Phone: 800-767-1875 or 229-386-3344
Website: www.agrirama.com
E-Mail: director@agrirama.com

Southern Museum of Civil War and Locomotive History
2829 Cherokee St, Kennesaw, GA 30144
770.427.2117
www.southernmuseum.org

Okefenokee Heritage Center
Site Location: 1460 N Augusta Ave, Waycross GA 31503
Phone: 912-285-4260
Website: www.okefenokeeheritagecenter.org

HAWAII
auai Plantation Railroad
3-2087 Kaumualii Hwy, Lihue, HI 96766
808.245.7245
www.kauaiplantationrailway.com

Laupahoehoe Train Museum
Site Location: 36-2377 Mamalahoa Hwy, Laupahoehoe HI 96764
Phone: 808-962-6300
Website: www.thetrainmuseum.com
E-Mail: laupahoehoetrainmuseum@yahoo.com

Pineapple Express
Site Location: Dole Plantation, 64-1550 Kamehameha Hwy, Wahiawa HI 96786
Phone: 808-621-8408
Website: www.pineappleexpress.com
E-Mail: info@pineappleexpress.com

IDAHO
Canyon County Historical Museum
Site Location: 1200 Front St, Nampa ID 83651
Phone: 208-467-7611
Website: www.canyoncountryhistory.com
E-Mail: info@canyoncountryhistory.com

ILLINOIS
Amboy Depot Museum
Site Location: Main St, 2 blocks west of US-52
Phone: 815-857-4700
Website: www.amboydepotmuseum.org
E-Mail: information@amboydepotmuseum.org

Historic Greenup Depot
Site Location: 204 W. Cumberland St, Greenup IL 62428
Phone: 217-923-9306
Website: www.greenupdepot.org

E-Mail: historic@rr1.net

Kankakee Railroaod Museum
Site Location: 197 S East Ave, Kankakee IL 60901
Phone: 85-929-9320
Website: www.kankakeerrmuseum.com

Rochelle Railroad Park
Site Location: 124 N 9th St, Rochelle IL 61068
Phone: 815-562-7031
Website: www.rochellerailroadpark.org

Union Depot Railroad Museum
Site Location: 683 Main St, Mendota IL 61342
Phone: 815-538-3800
Website: www.mendotamuseums.org/UDRR.htm
E-Mail: mmhs@mtco.com

Waterman & Western Railroad
Site Location: 435 S Birch St, Waterman IL 60556
Phone: 815-264-7753
Website: www.petestrain.com
E-Mail: events@petestrain.com

Wheels O' Time Museum
Site Location: 11923 N Knoxville Ave, Peoria IL 61612
Phone: 309-243-9020
Website: www.wheelsotime.org
E-Mail: wotmuseum@aol.com

INDIANA
Fort Wayne Railroad Historical Society
Site Location: 15808 Edgerton Rd, New Haven IN 46774
Phone: 260-493-0765
Website: www.765.org
E-Mail: contact@765.org

Hesston Steam Museum
Site Location: 1201 E 1000 N, La Porte IN 46350
Phone: 219-872-5055
Website: www.hesston.org

Linden Railroad Museum
Site Location: 520 N Main St, Linden IN 47955
Phone: 765-339-7245
Website: www.lindendepot.com

Louisville, New Albany, & Corydon Railroad
Site Location: 210 W Walnut St, Corydon IN 47112
Phone: 812-738-3171
Website: www.lnacrr.com
E-Mail: lnacrr@aol.com

Wabash Valley Railroaders Museum
Site Location: 1316 Plum St, Terre Haute IN 47804
Phone: 812-238-9958
Website: www.haleytower.org

IOWA
Trainland USA
Site Location: 3135 Hwy 117 N, Colfax IA 50054
Phone: 712-329-8307
Website: www.trainlandusa.com
E-Mail: red@trainland-usa.com

KANSAS
Ellis Railroad Museum
Site Location: 911 Washington, Ellis KS 67637
Phone: 785-726-4493
Website: www.ellis.ks.us/rrmuseum.htm
E-Mail: ellisrrm@triohomecenter.com

KENTUCKY
Paducah Railroad Museum
Site Location: 200 Washington St,
Paducah KY 40004
Phone: 270-519-7377
Website: www.paducahrr.com

Railway Museum of Greater Cincinnati
Site Location: 315 W Southern Ave,
Covington KY 41015
Phone: 859-491-7245
Website: cincirailmuseum.org
E-Mail: questions@cincirailmuseum.org

LOUISIANA
DeQuincy Railroad Museum
Site Location: 400 Lake Chares Ave, DeQuincy LA 70633
Phone: 337-78-2823
Website: http://www.louisianatravel.com/dequincy-railroad-museum

MAINE
Cole Land Transportation Museum
Site Location: 405 Perry Rd, Bangor ME 04401
Phone: 207-990-3600
Website: www.colemuseum.org
E-Mail: mail@colemuseum.org

Oakfield Railroad Museum
Site Location: Station St, Oakfied ME 04763
Phone: 207-757-8575
Website: www.oakfieldmuseum.org
E-Mail: oakfieldmuseum@pwless.net

MARYLAND
Baltimore Streetcar Museum
1901 Falls Rd, Baltimore, MD 21211
410.547.0264
www.baltimorestreetcar.org

owie Railroad Station Museum
Site Location: 8614 Chestnut Ave,
Old Bowie MD 20715
Phone: 303-809-3089

Website:
http://www.cityofbowie.org/LeisureActivities/Museum/Railroad_Museum.asp
E-Mail: pwilliams@cityofbowie.org

Brunswick Museum
Site Location: 40 West Potomac St, Brunswick MD 21716
Phone: 301-834-7100
Website: www.brrm.net
E-Mail: contact@brrm.net

Chesapeake Beach Railway Museum
Site Location: 4155 Mears Ave, Chesapeake Beach MD 20732
Phone: 410-257-3892
Website: www.cbrm.org
E-Mail: cbrailway@co.cal.md.us

Ellicott City Station
Site Location: 2711 Maryland Ave,
Ellicot City MD 21043
Phone: 410-461-1945
Website: www.ecborail.org

Gaithersburg Community Museum
Site Location: 9 Summit Ave,
Gaithersburg MD 20877
Phone: 301-258-6160
Website: www.gaithersburgmd.gov/museum

Hagerstown Roundhouse Museum
Site Location: 300 S Burhans Blvd,
Hagerstown MD 21741
Phone: 301-739-4665
Website: www.roundhouse.org

MASSACHUSETTS
Edaville USA
Site Location: 7 Eda Ave, South Carver MA 02336
Phone: 877-332-8455 or 508-866-8190
Website: www.edaville.com
E-Mail: info@edaville.com

Lowell National Historical Park
Site Location: 67 Kirk St, Lowell MA 01852
Phone: 978-970-5000
Website: www.nps.gov/lowe

Old Colony & Fall River Railroad Museum
Site Location: 2 Water St, Battle Ship Cove,
Fall River MA 02721
Phone: 508-674-9340
Website: www.ocandfrrailroadmuseum.com
E-Mail: info@ocandfrrailroadmuseum.com

Providence and Worcester Railroad Company
Site Location: 75 Hammond St,
Worcester MA 01610

Phone: 508-755-4000
Website: www.pwrr.com

Shelburne Falls Trolley Museum, Inc
Site Location: 14 Depot St, Shelburne Falls,
MA 01370
Phone: 413-625-9443
Website: www.sftm.org
E-Mail: trolley@sftm.org

**Walker Transportation Collection, Beverly
Historical Society & Museum**
Site Location: 117 Cabot St, Beverly MA 01915
Phone: 978-922-1186
Website: www.walkertrans.org
E-Mail: info@walkertrans.org

MICHIGAN
Adrian & Blissfield Rail Road
Site Location: 301 E Adrian St, Blissfield MI 49228
Phone: 800-594-5162 or 248-541-1000
Website: www.murdermysterytrain.com

Clinton Northern Railway
Site Location: 107 E Railroad St, St Johns MI 48879
Phone: 989-668-7246
Website: www.clintonnorthernrailway.org

Durand Union Station
Site Location: 200 Railroad St, Durand MI 48429
Phone: 989-288-3561
Website: www.durandstation.com
E-Mail: dusi@durandstation.com

Flushing Area Museum
Site Location: 431 W Main St, Flushing MI 48433
Phone: 810-487-0814
Website: www.flushinghistorical.org

Houghton County Historical Museum
Site Location: 5500 Hwy M-26,
Lake Linden MI 49945
Phone: 906-296-4121
Website: www.houghtonhistory.org
E-Mail: info@houghtonhistory.org

Iron Mountain Iron Mine
Site Location: US-2 Vulcan MI 49892
Phone: 906-563-8077
Website: ironmountainironmine.com
E-Mail: ironmine@uplogon.com

Junction Valley Railroad
Site Location: 7065 Dixie Hwy, Bridgeport MI 48722
Phone: 989-777-3480
Website: www.jvrailroad.com
E-Mail: jvrr@charter.net

Little River Railroad
29 W Park Ave, Coldwater, MI 49036
260.316.0529
www.littleriverrailroad.com
customerservice@littleriverrailroad.com

Michigan AuSable Valley Railroad
Site Location: 230 S Abbe Rd, Fairview MI 48621
Phone: 989-848-2229 or 989-848-2225
Website: www.michiganausablevalleyrailroad.com
E-Mail: support@railroadcatalog.com

Thomas Edison Depot Museum
Site Location: 510 Edison Pkwy Port Huron MI
48060
Phone: 810-982-0891
Website: www.phmuseum.org

Tri-Cities Historical Museum
Site Location: 1 North Harbor Dr, Grand Haven,
MI 49417
Phone: 616-842-0700
Website: www.tri-citiesmuseum.org
E-Mail: dswartout@tri-citiesmuseum.org

MINNESOTA
End-O-Line Railroad Park & Museum
Site Location: 440 N Mill St, Currie MN 56123
Phone: 507-763-3708
Website: www.endoline.com
E-Mail: endoline@co.murray.mn.us

Minnehaha Depot
Site Location: 4926 Minnehaha Ave,
Minneapolis MN 55130
Phone: 651-228-0263
Website: http://www.mnhs.org/places/sites/md
E-Mail: minnehahadepot@mnhs.org

Minnesota Discovery Center
Site Location: 801 SW Hwy 169 Ste 1,
Chisolm, MN 55719
Phone: 800-372-6437 or 218-254-7971
Website: www.mndiscoverycenter.com
E-Mail: info@mndiscoverycenter.com

Minnesota Zephyr
Site Location: 601 N Main St, Stillwater MN 55082
Phone: 800-992-6100 or 651-430-3000
Website: www.minnesotazephyr.com
E-Mail: info@minnesotazephyr.com

The Old Depot Railroad Museum
Site Location: 651 W Hwy 12, Dassel MN 55325
Phone: 320-275-3876
Website: www.theolddepot.com
E-Mail: dassoldepot@hotmail.com

MISSOURI

Railroad Historical Museum
Site Location: 1300 N Grant St, Springfield,
MO 63122
Phone: 417-882-9106
Website: www.rrhistoricalmuseum.zoomshare.com
E-Mail: rrhistoricalmuseum@zoomshare.com

Silver Dollar City
Site Location: 399 Indian Point Rd,
Branson,
MO 65616
Phone: 800-475-9370
Website: www.bransonsilverdollarcity.com

**Wabash Frisco & Pacific Steam Railway –
"The Uncommon Carrier"**
Site Location: 199 Grand Ave,
Wildwood Glencoe MO
Phone: 636-587-3538
Website: www.wfprr.com
E-Mail: wfprr1@gmail.com

Walt Disney Hometown Museum
Site Location: 120 E Santa Fe St,
Marceline MO 64658
Phone: 660-375-3343 or 660-375-2332
Website: www.waltdisneymuseum.org
E-Mail: waltdisneymuseum@att.net

MONTANA

Izaak Walton Inn
Site Location: 290 Izaak Walton Inn Rd, Essex MT
59916
Phone: 406-888-5700
Website: www.izaakwaltoninn.com

NEBRASKA

Golden Spike Tower
Site Location: 1249 N Homestead Road, North
Platte NE 69101
Phone: 308-532-9920
Website: www.goldenspiketower.com

Omaha's Henry Doorly Zoo
Site Location: 3701 S 10th St, Omaha NE 68107
Phone: 402-733-8400 or 402-733-8401
Website: www.omahazoo.com

Stuhr Museum of the Prairie Pioneer
Site Location: 3133 W Hwy 34, Grand Island NE
68801
Phone: 308-385-5316
Website: www.stuhrmuseum.org
E-Mail: info@stuhrmuseum.org

Trails & Rails Museum
Site Location: 710 W 11th St, Kearney NE 68845
Phone: 308-234-3041

Website: www.bchs.us/museum.html
E-Mail: bchs.us@hotmail.com

NEW HAMPSHIRE

Ashland Railroad Station Museum
Site Location: 69 Depot St, Ashland NH 03217
Phone: 603-968-3902
Website: http://www.aannh.org/heritage/grafton/ash-land.php
E-Mail: mwruell@worldpath.net

Gorham Rail Station Museum
Site Location: 25 Railroad St, Gorham NH 03581
Phone: 603-466-5338
Website: http://www.gorhamnewhampshire.com/rail-roadmuseum.html
E-Mail: gorhamhistoricalsociety@gmail.com

Hartmann Model Railroad Ltd.
Site Location: 15 Town Hall Rd, Intervale NH 03845
Phone: 603-356-9922 or 603-356-9933
Website: http://www.hartmannrr.com
E-Mail: info@hartmannrr.com

Raymond Historical Society
Site Location: 1 Depot Rd, Raymond NH 03077
Phone: 603-895-2866
Website: www.raymondhistoricalsociety.home.com-cast.net

Sandown Depot Museum
Site Location: 1 Depot Rd, Sandown NH 03873
Phone: 603-887-6688
Website:
www.sandown.us/historical_society/HistoricalHomePa
ge.htm
E-Mail: ahighbid@comcast.net

Winnepesaukee Scenic Railroad
Site Location: 154 Main St, Meredith NH 03254
Phone: 603-279-5253
Website: www.hoborr.com

NEW JERSEY

Delaware River Railroad
Site Location: 100 Elizabeth St, Phillipsburg NJ
08865
Phone: 877-872-7433
Website: www.nyswths.org
E-Mail: ccotty@fastwww.com

Mahwah Railroad Museum
Site Location: 201 Franklin Turnpike, Mahwah NJ
07430
Phone: 201-512-0099
Website: www.mahwahmuseum.org

Northlandz
Site Location: 495 US 202 Flemington NJ 08822
Phone: 908-782-4022
Website: www.northlandz.com

Phillipsburg Railroad Historians
Site Location: 10 Pine Alley, Phillipsburg NJ 08865
Phone: 908-859-1146
Website: www.prrh.org
E-Mail: contact@prrh.org

South Jersey Railroad Museum
Site Location: 1721 Mt. Pleasant Rd. Tuckahoe NJ 08250
Phone: 609-628-2850
Website: www.sjrails.net
E-Mail: info@sjrails.net

NEW MEXICO
Clovis Depot Model Train Museum
Site Location: 221 W First St, Clovis NM 88101
Phone: 888-762-0064
Website: www.clovisdepot.com
E-Mail: philipw@3lefties.com

Toy Train Depot Foundation
Site Location: 1991 North White Sands Blvd, Alamogordo NM 88310
Phone: 888-207-3564
Website: www.toytraindepot.homestead.com
E-Mail: railfanewmexico@hotmail.com

NEW YORK
Alco Brooks Railroad Display
Site Location: 1089 Central Ave, Dunkirk NY 14048
Phone: 716-366-3797
Website: www.wnyrails.org
E-Mail: wnyrails@wnyrails.org

Catskill Mountain Railroad
Site Location: 5408 Route 28, Mt Tremper NY 12457
Phone: 845-688-7400
Website: www.catskillmtrailroad.com
E-Mail: info@catskillmtrailroad.com

Central Square Station Museum
Site Location: 132 Railroad St, Central Square NY 13036
Phone: 315-676-7682
Website: www.cnynrhs.org/CentralSq.html
E-Mail: contact@cnynrhs.org

Empire State Railway Museum
Site Location: 70 Lower High St, Phoenicia NY 12464
Phone: 845-688-7501
Website: www.esrm.com

Hyde Park Station
Site Location: 34 River Rd, Hyde Park NY 12538
Phone: 845-229-2338
Website: www.hydeparkstation.com
E-Mail: milotsukroff@netscape.net

LeHigh Valley Railroad Historical Society
Site Location: 8 E High Street, Shortsville NY 14548
Phone: 585-289-9149
Website: www.lvrrhs.org
E-Mail: info@lvrrhs.org

Martisco Station Museum
Site Location: Martisco Rd, Marcellus NY 13108
Phone: 315-673-1749
Website: www.cnynrhs.org/Martisco.html
E-Mail: contact@cnynrhs.org

New York Museum of Transportation
Site Location: 6393 East River Rd, West Henrietta NY 14586
Phone: 585-533-1113
Website: www.nymtmuseum.org
E-Mail: info@nymtmuseum.org

New York Transit Museum
Site Location: 130 Livingston St 10th Floor, Brooklyn NY 11201
Phone: 718-694-1600
Website: www.mta.info/mta/museum

North Creek Railway Depot Museum
Site Location: 5 Railroad Pl, North Creek NY 12853
Phone: 518-251-5842
Website: www.northcreekdepotmuseum.com
E-Mail: director@northcreekdepotmuseum.com

Railroad Museum of Long Island, Greenport
Site Location: 440 Fourth St, Greenport NY 11944
Phone: 631-477-0439
Website: www.rmli.us/RMLI/Welcome.html
E-Mail: info@rmli.us

Railroad Museum of Long Island, Riverhead
Site Location: 416 Griffing Ave, Riverhead NY 11944
Phone: 631-727-7920
Website: www.rmli.us/RMLI/Welcome.html
E-Mail: info@rmli.us

Railroad Museum of the Niagara Frontier
Site Location: 111 Oliver St, North Tonawanda, NY 14120
Phone: 716-694-9588
Website: www.railroadniagara.com
E-Mail: rrrrmuseum@nfcnrhs.com

Roscoe O&W Railway Museum
Site Location: 7 Railroad Ave, Roscoe NY 12776
Phone: 607-498-4346
Website: www.nyow.org/museum.html
E-Mail: wilsil@frontiernet.net

Utica Union Station
Site Location: 321 Main St, Utica NY 13501
Phone: 315-724-0700
Website: www.adirondackrr.com/adkrr_utica.php

NORTH CAROLINA
Charlotte Trolley
Site Location: 1507 Camden Rd
Charlotte, NC 28203
Phone: 704-375-0850
Website: www.charlottetrolley.org
E-Mail: andrea@charlottetrolley.org

National Railroad Museum and Hall of Fame
Site Location: 120 Spring St, Hamlet NC 28345
Phone: 910-582-2383
Website: www.nationalmuseum.tripod.com
E-Mail: wwilliams11@carolina.rr.com

Piedmont & Western Railroad Club
Site Location: 400 W Main St, Valdese NC 28690
Phone: 874-612-2112
Website: www.pwrr.org

Smoky Mountain Trains
Site Location: 100 Greenlee St, Bryson City NC 28713
Phone: 866-914-5200
Website: www.smokymountaintrains.com
E-Mail: info@smokymountaintrains.com

Wilmington Railroad Museum
Site Location: 505 Nutt St, Wilmington NC 28401
Phone: 910-763-2634
Website: www.wilmingtonrailroadmuseum.org

NORTH DAKOTA
Western Minnesota Steam Threshers Reunion
Site Location: 2610 First Ave, Fargo ND 58102
Phone: 701-212-2034
Website: www.rollag.com
E-Mail: secretary@rollag.com

OHIO
Bradford Ohio Railroad Museum
Site Location: 200 N Miami Ave, Bradford OH 45308
Phone: 937-448-2185
Website: www.bradfordrrmuseum.org

Byesville Scenic Railway
Site Location: 100 Tolliver Trail, Byesville OH 43723
Phone: 800-933-5480

Website: www.bsrw.org
E-Mail: info@visitguernseycounty.com

Carillon Historical Park
Site Location: 1000 Carillon Blvd, Dayton OH 45409
Phone: 937-293-2841
Website: www.carillonpark.org

Cedar Point & Lake Erie Railroad
Site Location: 1 Cedar Point Dr, Sandusky OH 45250
Phone: 419-627-2350
Website: www.cedarpoint.com

Cincinnati Railroad Club
Site Location: 1301 Western Ave, Cincinnati OH 45250
Phone: 513-651-7245
Website: www.cincinnatirrclub.org
E-Mail: cincinnatirrclub@hotmail.com

Cincinnati Railway Company
Site Location: 11013 Kenwood Rd, Cincinnati OH 45242
Phone: 513-933-8022
Website: www.cincinnatirailway.com
E-Mail: info@cincinnatirailway.com

Conneaut Area Historical Society
Site Location: 363 Depot St, Conneaut OH 44030
Phone: 440-599-7878
Website: www.conneauthistorical.org

Dennison Railroad Depot Museum
400 Center St, Dennison. OH 44621
877.278.8020 or 740.922.6776
www.dennisondepot.org
depot@tusco.net

Lorain & West Virginia Railway
Site Location: Hwy 18, Wellington OH 44090
Phone: 440-647-6660
Website: www.lakeshorerailway.org

Ohio Railway Museum
Site Location: 990 Proprietors Road, Worthington, OH 43085
Phone: 740-383-3768
Website: www.ohiorailwaymuseum.org

Toledo, Lake Erie & Western Railway
Site Location: 49 North Sixth St, Waterville OH 43566
Phone: 866-638-7246
Website: www.tlew.org
E-Mail: info@tlew.org

Warther Carving Museum
Site Location: 331 Karl Ave, Dover OH 44622

Phone: 330-343-7513
Website: www.warthers.com
E-Mail: info@warthers.com

OKLAHOMA

Frisco Depot Museum
Site Location: 307 North B St, Hugo OK 74743
Phone: 580-326-6630
Website: www.friscodepot.org
E-Mail: friscodepot@live.com

Heritage Express Trolley
Site Location: 300 S Grand Ave, El Reno OK 73036
Phone: 888-535-7366
Website: www.elreno.org/tour/attractions.asp
E-Mail: info@elreno.org

Oklahoma Railway Museum
Site Location: 3400 NE Grand Blvd, Oklahoma City OK 73111
Phone: 405-424-8222
Website: www.oklahomarailwaymuseum.org

Omniplex Science Museum
Site Location: 2100 NE 52nd St, Oklahoma City OK 73111
Phone: 405-424-8222
Website: www.sciencemuseumok.org/trains
E-Mail: reservations@sciencemuseumok.org

Orr Family Farm & RR LLC
Site Location: 14400 S Western Ave, Oklahoma City OK 73170
Phone: 405-799-3276
Website: www.orrfamilyfarm.com

Waynoka History Museum
Site Location: 1383 Cleveland St, Waynoka OK 73860
Phone: 580-824-1886
Website: www.waynoka.org/harveyhouse.php

OREGON

Canby Depot Museum
Site Location: 888 NE 4th Ave, Canby OR 97103
Phone: 503-266-6712
Website: www.canbyhistoricalsociety.org

Medford Railroad Park
Site Location: 2222 Table Rock Rd, Medford OR 97501
Phone: 541-944-2230
Website: www.soc-nrhs.org
E-Mail: mail@soc-nrhs.org

Port of Tillamook Bay Railroad
Site Location: 4000 Blimp Blvd, Tillamook OR 97141
Phone: 503-842-2413

Website: www.potb.org
E-Mail: info@potb.org

Willamette Shore Trolley
Site Location: 311 N State St, Lake Oswego OR 97034
Phone: 503-697-7436
Website: www.oerhs.org/wst/index.htm

PENNSYLVANIA

Allegheny Portage Railroad
Site Location: 110 Federal Park Rd, Gallitzin PA 16641
Phone: 814-886-6150
Website: www.nps.gov/alpo

Altoona Railroaders Memorial Museum
Site Location: 1300 Ninth Ave, Altoona PA 16602
Phone: 888-425-8666
Website: www.railroadcity.com

Bellafonte Historical Railroad Society
Site Location: 320 W High St, Bellefonte PA 16823
Phone: 814-355-1053
Website: www.bellefontetrain.org

Choo Choo Barn, Traintown USA
Site Location: Route 741 East, Strasburg PA 16823
Phone: 800-450-2920 or 717-687-7911
Website: www.choochoobarn.com
E-Mail: info@choochoobarn.com

Dutch Wonderland Family Amusement Park
Site Location: 2249 Lincoln Hwy E, Lancaster PA 17602
Phone: 717-291-1888 or 866-FUN-ATDW
Website: www.dutchwonderland.com
E-Mail: infodw@dutchwonderland.com

Electric City Trolley Museum
Site Location: 300 Cliff St, Scranton PA 18503
Phone: 570-963-6447
Website: www.ectma.org

Franklin Institute Science Museum
Site Location: 222 N 20th St, Philadelphia PA 19103
Phone: 215-448-1200
Website: www.fi.edu

Friends of the East Broad Top Museum
Site Location: Main St, Robersdale PA 19103
Phone: 814-635-2388
Website: www.febt.org
E-Mail: FEBT@aol.com

Greenville Railroad Park & Museum
Site Location: 314 Main St, Greenville PA 16125
Phone: 724-588-4009
Website: www.greenvilletrainmseum.org

400

E-Mail: greenvillerailroadpark@gmail.com

Horseshoe Curve National Historic Landmark
Site Location: 1300 Ninth Ave, Altoona PA
Phone: 888-425-8666 or 814-946-0834
Website: www.railroadcity.com
E-Mail: info@railroadcity.com

Lake Shore Railway Museum
Site Location: 31 Wall St,North East PA
Phone: 814-725-1911
Website: www.velocity.net/~lsrhs
E-Mail: lsrhs@velocity.net

Lincoln Train Museum
Site Location: 425 Steinwehr Ave, Gettysburg PA
17325
Phone: 717-334-5678
Website: www.gettysburgbattlefieldtours.com/lincoln-train-museum.php
E-Mail: gbgtours@embarqmail.com

National Toy Train Museum
Site Location: 300 Paradise Ln, Strasburg PA 17579
Phone: 717-687-0742
Website: www.traincollectors.org
E-Mail: tca-office@traincollectors.org

Old Mauch Chunk Model Train Display
Site Location: 41 Susquehanna St, Jim Thorpe PA
18229
Phone: 570-325-4371
Website: www.ocmtraindisplay.com
E-Mail: info@ocmtraindisplay.com

Pennsylvania Trolley Museum
Site Location: 1 Museum Rd, Washington PA 15301
Phone: 724-228-9256
Website: www.pa—trolley.org
E-Mail: ptm@pa-trolley.org

Pioneer Tunnel Coal Mine and Steam Train
Site Location: 19th & Oak Sts, Ashland PA 17921
Phone: 570-875-3850 or 570-875-3301
Website: www.pioneertunnel.com

Portage Station Museum
Site Location: 400 Lee St, Portage PA 15946
Phone: 814-736-9223
Website: www.portagepa.us
E-Mail: mlcgeo@verizon.net

Reading Railroad Heritage Museum
Site Location: 500 S Third St, Hamburg PA 19526
Phone: 610-562-5513
Website: www.readingrailroad.org
E-Mail: info@readingrailroad.org

Red Run Park
Site Location: 12143 Buchanan Trail East,
Waynesboro PA 17268
Phone: 717-762-3128
Website: www.washtwp-franklin.org/content/view/104/132

Roadside America
Site Location: 109 Roadside Dr, Shartlesville,
PA 19554
Phone: 610-488-6241
Website: www.roadsideamericainc.com

The Station Inn
Site Location: 827 Front St, Cresson,
PA 16630
Phone: 814-886-4757
Website: www.stationinnpa.com

Stewartstown Railroad
Site Location: route 851, Stewartstown PA 17363
Phone: 717-654-7530
Website: www.stewartstownrailroad.com
E-Mail: friendsofstrt@hotmail.com

Stourbridge Line Rail Excursions
Site Location: 32 Commercial St, Honesdale, PA
18431
Phone: 570-253-1960
Website: www.waynecountycc.com

**Thomas T. Taber Museum of the Lycoming County
Historical Society**
Site Location: 858 W Fourth St, Williamsport, PA
17701
Phone: 570-326+3326
Website: www.tabermuseum.org
E-Mail: lchsmuseum@verizon.net

Tunnels Park & Museum
Site Location: 411 Convent St, Ste 20,
Gallitzin, PA 16641
Phone: 814-886-8871
Website: www.gallitzin.info
E-Mail: info@gallitzin.info

West Chester Railroad
Site Location: 250 E Market St,
West Chester, PA 19382
Phone: 610-430-2233
Website: www.westchesterr.com

SOUTH CAROLINA
Lancaster & Chester Railway and Museum
Site Location: 512 S Main St, Lancaster SC 29721
Phone: 803-286-4158
Website: www.landcrail.com

TENNESSEE

A.C. Kalmbach Memorial Library – National Model Railroad Association
Site Location: 4121 Cromwell Rd, Chattanooga TN 37421
Phone: 423-892-2846
Website: www.nmra.org/library

Cookeville Depot Museum
Site Location: 116 W Broad St, Cookeville TN 38501
Phone: 931-528+8570
Website: www.cookeville-tn.org/ls/historical-arts/cookeville-depot-museum
E-Mail: depot@cookeville-tn.org

Little River Railroad
Site Location: 7747 E Lamar Alexander Pkwy, Townsend TN 37882
Phone: 865-428-0099
Website: www.littleriverrailroad.org
E-Mail: president@littleriverrailroad.org

Lookout Mountain - Incline Railway
Site Location: 3917 St Elmo Ave, Chattanooga TN 37409
Phone: 423-821-4224
Website: www.lookoutmountain.com

Lynnville Railroad Preservation Society
Site Location: 162 Mill St, Lynnville TN 38472
Phone: 931-478-0880
Website: www.lynnvillerailroadmuseum.com
E-Mail: tim@lynnvillerailroadmuseum.com

Nashville, Chattanooga & St. Louis Depot and Railroad Museum
Site Location: 528 S Royal St, Jackson TN 38301
Phone: 731-425-8223
Website: www.cityofjackson.net
E-Mail: thedepot@cityofjackson.net

TEXAS

Flatonia Rail Park
Site Location: I-10 Exit #661, Flatonia TX 78941
Phone: 979-743-5366
Website: www.railcrossroadstx.com

Forest Park Miniature Train
Site Location: 2116 Morning Glory Ave, Fort Worth TX 76111
Phone: 817-336-3328
Website: www.fpmt.us
E-Mail: fpmt@fpmt.us

Galveston Railroad Museum
Site Location: 123 Rosenberg, Galveston TX 77550
Phone: 409-765-5700
Website: www.galvestonrrmuseum.com
E-Mail: galvrrmuseum@sbcglobal.net

Historic Jefferson Railway
Site Location: 400 E Austin St, Jefferson TX 75657
Phone: 866-398-2038
Website: www.jeffersonrailway.com

The History Center
Site Location: 102 N Temple, Diboll TX 75941
Phone: 936-829-3543
Website: www.thehistorycenteronline.com
E-Mail: info@TheHistoryCenterOnline.com

Houston Railroad Museum
Site Location: 7390 Mesa Rd, Houston TX 77028
Phone: 713-631-6612
Website: www.kingswayrc.com
E-Mail: info@houstonrrmusem.com

Interurban Railway Museum
Site Location: 901 E 15th St, Plano TX 75074
Phone: 972-941-2117
Website: www.interurbanplano.org

New Braunfels Railroad Museum
Site Location: 302 W San Antonio St, New Braunfels TX 78131
Phone: 830-627-2447
Website: www.newbraunfelsrailroadmuseum.org
E-Mail: info@newbraunfelsrailroadmuseum.org

Railway Museum of San Angelo
Site Location: 703 South Chadbourne, San Angelo TX 76903
Phone: 325-486-2140
Website: www.railwaymuseumsanangelo.home-stead.com

Square House Museum
Site Location: Fifth and Hwy 207, Panhandle TX 79068
Phone: 806-537-3527
Website: www.squarehousemuseum.org
E-Mail: shm@squarehousemuseum.org

Wichita Falls Railroad Museum
Site Location: 500 9th St, Wichita Falls TX 76308
Phone: 940-723-2661
Website: www.wfrrm.com

UTAH

S&S Shortline Railroad Park and Museum
Site Location: 575N 1525W, Farmington UT 84025
Phone: 801-451-0222
Website: www.sssrr.8m.com

Tooele Valley Railroad Musem
Site Location: 35 N Broadway, Tooele UT 84074
Phone: 435-882-2836 or 435-843-2110
Website: www.tooelecity.org/citydepartments/railroad-museum.asp

Western Mining & Railroad Museum
Site Location: 294 S Main, Helper UT 84526
Phone: 435-472-3009
Website: www.wmrrm.org
E-Mail: helpermuseum@helpercity.net

VERMONT
New England Transportation Institute and Museum
Site Location: 100 Railroad Row, White River Junction VT 05001
Phone: 802-921-9838
Website: www.newenglandtransportationmuseum.org
E-Mail: info@netransportation.org

VIRGINIA
Chesapeake & Ohio Historical Society
Site Location: 312 East Ridgeway St, Clifton Forge VA 24422
Phone: 540-862-2210
Website: www.cohs.org
E-Mail: cohs@cohs.org

City of Roanoke Rail walk
Site Location: Norfolk Ave & Jefferson St, Roanoke VA
Phone: 540-853-6428
Website: www.roanokeva.gov/railwalk

Fairfax Station Railroad Museum
Site Location: 11200 Fairfax Station Rd, Fairfax, Station VA 22039
Phone: 703-425-9225
Website: www.fairfax-station.org

The Lancaster Toy and Train Collection
Site Location: 420 High St, Portsmouth, VA 23704
Phone: 757-393-5258
Website: www.childrensmuseumva.com/trains.html

Old Dominion Railway Museum
Site Location: 2500 W Broadway St, Richmond, VA
Phone: 800-451-6318 or 804-231-4324
Website: www.odcnrhs.org

Suffolk Seaboard Station Railroad Museum
Site Location: 326 N Main St, Suffolk, VA 23434
Phone: 757-923-4750
Website: www.suffolktrainstation.org
E-Mail: info@suffolktrainstation.org

WASHINGTON

Camp Six Logging Museum & PDQ&K Railroad, Tacoma Chapter NRHS
Site Location: 5400 N Pearl St, Tacoma WA 98401
Phone: 253-752-0047
Website: www.camp-6-museum.org/c6.html

Northern Pacific Railway Museum
Site Location: 10 S Asotin Ave, Toppenish WA 98948
Phone: 509-865-1911
Website: www.nprymuseum.org

North Pend Oreille Valley Lions Club
Site Location: Main St, Lone WA 99139
Phone: 877-525-5226
Website: www.lionstrainrides.com
E-Mail: info@lionstrainride.com

Pioneer Village and Museum
Site Location: 600 Cotlets Way, Cashmere WA 98815
Phone: 509-782-3230
Website: www.cashmeremuseum.org
E-Mail: pioneer@cashmeremuseum.org

Remlinger Farms
Site Location: 32610 NE 32nd St, Carnation WA 98041
Phone: 425-333-4135
Website: www.remlingerfarms.com
E-Mail: info@remlingerfarms.com

Washington State Railroads Historical Society Museum
Site Location: 122 N Tacoma Ave, Pasco WA 99301
Phone: 800-465-5430 or 509-543-4159
Website: www.wsrhs.org
E-Mail: email@wsrhs.org

WEST VIRGINIA

Benedum Science Center
Site Location: Route 88 N, Oglebay Resort, Wheeling, WV 26003
Phone: 800-624-6988 or 304-243-4100
Website: www.oglebay-resort.com/goodzoo/train.htm

Huntington Railroad Museum
Site Location: Memorial Blvd & 14th St W, Huntington, WV
Phone: 304-523-0364
Website: www.newrivertrain.com

Kruger Street Toy & Train Museum
Site Location: 144 Kruger St, Wheelin,g WV 26003
Phone: 304-242-8133 or 877-242-8133\
Website: www.toyandtrain.com
E-Mail museum@toyandtrain.com

New River Gorge/Mystery Train
Site Location: Huntington, WV 25705
Phone: 866-529-6412
Website: www.themysterytrain.com
E-Mail: information@themysterytrain.com

WISCONSIN
Brodhead Historical Society Depot Museum
Site Location: 1108 1st Center Ave,
Brodhead WI 53520
Phone: 608-897-4150
Website: www.brodheadhistory.org/depot/html
E-Mail: info@brodheadhistory.org

Colfax Railroad Museum
Site Location: 500 Railroad Ave, Colfax WI 54730
Phone: 715-962-2076
Website: www.colfaxrrmuseum.org

East Troy Electric Railroad Museum
Site Location: 2002 Church St, East Troy WI 53120
Phone: 262-642-3263
Website: www.easttroyrr.org
E-Mail: info@easttroyrr.org

Heritage Historical Village
Site Location: 900 Montgomery St, New London WI 54961
Phone: 920-982-8557 or 920-982-5186
Website: www.historicalvillage.org

Mining Museum & Rollo Jamison Museum
Site Location: 405 E Main St, Platteville, WI 53818
Phone: 608-348-3301
Website: www.mining.jamison.museum
E-Mail: museums@platteville.org

Osceola & St. Croix Valley Railway
Site Location: 114 Depot Rd, Osceola, WI 54020
Phone: 715-755-3570
Website: www.mtmuseum.org

Ozaukee County Pioneer Village
Site Location: 4880 Cty Hwy I, Saukville, WI
Phone: 262-377-4510
Website:
www.co.ozaukee.wi.us/ochs/PioneerVillage.htm

Pinecrest Historical Village
Site Location: 924 Pine Crest Ln,
Manitowoc, WI 54220
Phone: 920-684-4445
Website: www.mchistsoc.org

Railroad Memories Museum
Site Location: 424 N Front St, Spooner, WI 54810
Phone: 715-635-3325 or 715-635-2752
Website: www.railroadmemoriesmuseum.org
E-Mail: info@railroadmemoriesmuseum.org

Riverside & Great Northern Railway
Site Location: N115 County Road N,
Wisconsin Dells, WI 53956
Phone: 608-254-6367
Website: www.randgn.com

Whiskey River Railway, Little Amerricka Amusement Park
Site Location: 700 E Main St, Marshall, WI 53559
Phone: 888-607-7735
Website: www.littleamericka.com

Zoofari Express Milwaukee County Zoo
Site Location: 10001 W Bluemound Rd,
Milwaukee, WI 53226
Phone: 414-771-3040
Website: www.milwaukeezoo.org

WYOMING
Douglas Railroad Interpretive Center
Site Location: 121 Brownfield Rd, Douglas, WY 82633
Phone: 307-358-2950
Website: www.douglaschamber.com

Union Pacific Railroad
Site Location: UP Steam Shop, Cheyenne, WY
Phone: 307-778-3214
Website: www.uprr.com/aboutup/excurs/index.shtml

ALBERTA
Alberta Railway Museum
Site Location: 24215 34th St, Edmonton, AB T5C 3R6
Phone: 780-472-6229
Website: www.railwaymuseum.ab.ca
E-Mail: hdixon@incentre.net

BRITISH COLUMBIA
Bear Creek Park Train
Site Location: 13750 88th Ave, Surrey BC V3W 3L1
Phone: 604-501-1232
Website: www.bctrains.com

Kamloops Heritage Railway
Site Location: #6-510 Lorne St, Kamloops BC V2C 1W3
Phone: 250-374-2141
Website: www.kamrail.com
E-Mail: info@kamrail.com

Kwinitsa Railway Station Museum
Site Location: 100 First Ave W, Prince Rupert BC V8J 3S1
Phone: 250-624-3207
Website: www.museumofnorthernbc.com
E-Mail: mnbc@citytel.net

Prince George Railway & Forestry Museum
Site Location: 850 River Rd, Prince George BC V2L 5S8
Phone: 250-563-7351
Website: www.pgrfm.bc.ca
E-Mail: trains@pgrfm.bc.ca

Revelstoke Railway Museum
Site Location: 719 Track St W, Revelstoke BC V0E 2S0
Phone: 250-837-6060 or 877-837-6060
Website: www.railwaymuseum.com
E-Mail: railway@telus.net

Rocky Mountaineer Vacations
Site Location: 1755 Cottrell St, Vancouver BC
Phone: 877-460-3200 or 604-606-7200
Website: www.rockymountaineer.com
E-Mail: reservations@rockymountaineer.com

NEW BRUNSWICK
Salem & Hillsborough Railroad
Site Location: 2847 Main St, Hillsborough NB E4H 2X7
Phone: 506-734-3195 or 506-734-3733
Website: www.nbrm.ca
E-Mail: info@nbrm.ca

NOVA SCOTIA
Sydney & Louisbourg Railway Museum
Site Location: 7330 Main St, Louisbourg Nova Scotia B1C 1P5

ONTARIO
Aberfoyle Junction Model Railway, Inc
Site Location: 128 Brock Rd, S Aberfoyle ON N1H 6H1
Phone: 905-527-5474
Website: www.aberfoylejunction.com

Chatham Railroad Museum
Site Location: Queen St, Chatham ON N7M 2H6
Phone: 519-352-3097
Website: www.chatham-kent.ca
E-Mail: Cktourism@chatham-kent.ca

CNR School Car
Site Location: 76 Victoria Terr, Clinton ON N0M 1L0
Phone: 519-482-3997
Website: www.schoolcar.ca
E-Mail: cnrschoolonwheels@gmail.com

Elgin County Railway Museum
Site Location: 225 Wellington St, St. Thomas ON N5P 4H4
Phone: 519-637-6284

Halton County Radial Railway
Site Location: 13629 Guelph Line, Milton ON 1L9T 5A2
Phone: 519-856-9802
Website: www.hcry.org
E-Mail: streetcar@hcry.org

Huntsville& Lake of Bays Railway Society
Site Location: 88 Brunel Rd, Huntsville ON P1H 1R1
Phone: 705-789-7576
Website: www.portageflyer.org

Komoka Railway Museum Inc
Site Location: 133 Queen St, Komoka ON N0L 1R0
Phone: 519657-1912
Website: www.komokarailmuseum.ca
E-Mail: station-master@komokarailmuseum.ca

Memory Junction Museum
Site Location: 60 Maplewood St, Brighton ON K0K 1H0
Phone: 613-475-0379
Website: www.memoryjunction.netfirms.com
E-Mail: re.bangay@sympatico.ca

Muskoka Heritage Place
Site Location: 88 Brunel Rd, Huntsville ON P1H 1R1
Phone: 705-789-7576
Website: www.muskokaheritageplace.org
E-Mail: ron.gostlin@huntsville.ca

Northern Ontario Railroad Museum & Heritage
Site Location: 26 Bloor St, Capreol ON P0M 1H0
Phone: 705-858-5050
Website: www.northernontariorailroadmuseum.nca
E-Mail: normhc@vianet.ca

Port Stanley Terminal Rail
Site Location: 309 Bridge St, Port Stanley ON N5L 1C5
Phone: 877-244-4478 or 519-782-3730
Website: www.pstr.on.ca

Smiths Falls Railway Museum of Eastern Ontario
Site Location: 90 William St West, Smiths Falls ON K7A 5A5
Phone: 613-283-5696
Website: www.sfrmeo.ca
E-Mail: sfrmchin@superaje.com

Waterloo Central Railway
Site Location: 10 Father David Bauer Dr, Waterloo ON N2J 4V1
Phone: 519-885-2297
Website: www.steam-train.org

PRINCE EDWARD ISLAND
Elmira Railway Museum
Site Location: 457 Elmira Rd, Elmira PE C0A 1K0
Phone: 902-357-7234
Website: www.elmirastation.com
E-Mail: Elmira@gov.pe.ca

SASKATCHEWAN
Saskatchewan Railway Museum
Site Location: Hwy 60, Saskatoon SK S7K 3J6
Phone: 306-382-9855
Website: www.saskrailmuseum.org
E-Mail: srha@saskrailmuseum.org

Western Development Museum
Site Location: 50 Defenbaker Dr, Moose Jaw SK S6J 1L9
Phone: 30-693-5989
Website: www.wdm.ca
E-Mail: moosejaw@wdm.ca

YUKON TERRITORY
Dawson City Museum & Historical Society
Site Location: PO Box 303, Dawson City, YT Y0B 1G0
Phone: 867-993-5291
Website: www.users.yknet.yk.ca/dcpages/Museum.html
E-Mail: dcmuseum@yknet.yk.ca

WEST INDIES
St. Kitts Scenic Railway Ltd.
Site Location: PO Box 191 Basseterre, St. Kitts WE
Phone: 869-465-7263
Website: www.stkittsscenicrailway.com
E-Mail: scenicreservations@sisterisles.kn

INDEX

Museum of the American Railroad 309
Museum of Science and Industry 103
Museum of Transportation 180
My Old Kentucky Dinner Train 129

N

Napa Valley Wine Train 30
National Capital Trolley Museum 145
National New York Central Railroad 112
National Railroad Museum 352
Naugatuck Railroad 72
Nevada County Traction Company LLC 31
Nevada Northern Railway Museum 196
Nevada State Railroad Museum 197
New Hope and Ivyland Railroad 273
New Hope Valley Railway 235
New Jersey Museum of Transportation 211
New River Train 345
Newport Dinner Train 287
Niles Canyon Railway 32
North Alabama Railroad Museum 7
North Carolina Transportation Museum 237
North Dakota State Railroad Museum 244
North Shore Scenic Railroad 170
Northern Pacific Railway Museum 337
Northwest Ohio Preservation, Inc. 252
Northwest Railway Museum 338

O

Ogden Union Station 320
Oil Creek & Titusville Railroad 274
Old Hickory Railroad 132
Old Road Dinner Train 158
Orange Empire Railway Museum 34
Oregon Coast Scenic Railroad 263
Orrville Railroad Heritage Society 253

P

Pacific Southwest Railway Museum at Campo 35
Patee House 181
Pikes Peak Historical Street Railway Foundation 61
Polar Bear Express 383
Potomac Eagle Scenic Railroad 346
Portola Railroad Museum 46
Prairie Dog Central Railway 374
Prairie Village, Herman & Milwaukee Railroad 293
Pueblo Railway Museum 62

R

Railroad and Heritage Museum 310
Railroaders Memorial Museum 276